The Marx Dictionary

For Jo,

In memory of our times together
at NTU.

Ian.

The Marx Dictionary

Ian Fraser and Lawrence Wilde

continuum

Continuum International Publishing Group
The Tower Building, 11 York Road, London SE1 7NX
80 Maiden Lane, Suite 704, New York NY 10038

British Library Cataloguing-in-Publication Data
A catalogue record for this book is available from the British Library.

ISBN: 978-1-4411-7832-9

Library of Congress Cataloging-in-Publication Data
Fraser, Ian, 1962-
   The Marx dictionary / Ian Fraser and Lawrence Wilde.
      p. cm.
   Includes bibliographical references (p.   ).
   ISBN 978-1-4411-7832-9 -- ISBN 978-1-4411-0011-5   1. Marx, Karl,
1818-1883--Dictionaries.   I. Wilde, Lawrence. II. Title.

   B3305.M73Z83 2011
   335.4092--dc22

                                        2011008375

Typeset by Fakenham Prepress Solutions, Fakenham, Norfolk NR21 8NN
Printed and bound in India

Contents

Acknowledgements

We would like to thank Marx scholars past and present for their contributions to the debates concerning the interpretation of Marx's thought that have informed this project. Thanks to Terrell Carver and Tony Smith for their initial advice and support for the dictionary, and to Tom Crick, editor at Continuum. We are grateful for the valuable feedback provided by participants at the Marxism Panel of the 2010 Workshops in Political Theory Conference at Manchester Metropolitan University, where we first presented the dictionary entries.

Introduction

Few philosophers have inspired such extremes of adulation and loathing as Karl Marx (1818–1883), but he was, of course, no ordinary philosopher. After starting his intellectual career by immersing himself in the philosophical ferment generated by Hegel and his critics, he came to be virulently opposed to this purely theoretical discourse. For example, in the eleventh of the *Theses on Feuerbach* (1845) he stated that 'the philosophers have only interpreted the world in various ways; the point is to change it'. Similarly, in *The German Ideology* (1845–1846) he declared that philosophy and the study of the natural world have the same relation to one another as masturbation and sexual love. However, as these statements indicate, Marx was not opposed to philosophy itself, but to philosophy that did not unite theory with practice. Consequently, he abandoned plans for an academic career in his mid-twenties in order to become a full-time theorist of a practical world revolution. This revolution was intended to abolish the private ownership of the means of production, bringing to an end the economic basis on which social classes and class antagonisms had developed over thousands of years. The possibility of such a transformation was grounded in his analysis of capitalism, through which he exposed its inherently contradictory nature and identified the socio-economic tendencies that could lead to its abolition. The revolutionary goal was the formation of classless societies throughout the world, free from exploitation and oppression, in which the majority of the people would take conscious control over their social systems for the first time in history. It was, in short, a vision of human emancipation. How is it, then, that in the eyes of many Marx's ideas are seen as a threat to human freedom? Liberalism, for example, maintains that the right to own property is a prerequisite for individual freedom, and so opposes the view that freedom is possible only when private ownership has been replaced by social control of the means of production. The liberal view suggests that collectivism leads to political despotism, something that Marx strenuously denies. The problem for the defence of Marx's position is not simply theoretical, but, crucially, historical. It centres on the practices of Marxism as a political doctrine, for it is the bleak experience of the communist dictatorships of the twentieth century that has been the decisive factor in the negative judgement on Marx. His ideas, as set down in this dictionary, leave no doubt that he would have been appalled by the tyrannies that have wielded power in his name. But if we are correct to claim that his theories were hideously distorted, how could such distortion arise?

Between Marx's death and 1917, major socialist parties across Europe harnessed the power of the growing working class and adopted his ideas as their guiding theoretical force. There was a consensus among these parties that their task was to fulfil Marx's challenge in *The Communist Manifesto* (1848) to 'win the battle for democracy', that is, to achieve universal franchise, win an electoral majority and begin to transform their societies as part of an international socialist movement. This was designed to build on the progress that Marx had readily identified in his description of the rise of bourgeois power in the *Manifesto*. The goal was to extend democracy from the political sphere to the socio-economic sphere, which is why most of the parties adopted the name of 'social democracy'. All this changed in November 1917 when the Bolshevik wing of the Russian Social Democratic Workers' Party seized power. Isolated in a country where the working class constituted a small minority, they quickly abandoned political democracy and reinterpreted Marx's political thought to justify their dictatorship. While implementing Marx's injunction to abolish private property, the dictatorship dispensed with his commitment to human freedom and radical democracy. The doctrinal orthodoxy of the official communist movement under the dictatorship of Stalin spread internationally, and when similar dictatorships were imposed in Eastern Europe in the aftermath of the Second World War and the Chinese communists seized power in 1949, one third of the world's populace lived under regimes that were a travesty of Marx's vision. In the nineteenth century Marx had reviled the dictatorships of the Czars in Russia and Napoleon III in France, yet in the twentieth century despotic regimes claimed to be enacting his 'science'. The worldwide communist movement not only distorted Marx's views on democracy, but claimed that their dictatorships constituted a superior, 'proletarian' form of democracy. The democratic Marxists, who stayed outside the communist camp, gradually lost their influence within social democratic parties, and to a great extent the reading of Marx as a theorist of human emancipation was kept alive by politically independent intellectuals. It is to be hoped that new generations of readers of Marx will not pre-judge his thought on the basis of its association with the discredited communist dictatorships and will judge his work on its merits, which are considerable. What we find in Marx is a compelling critique of capitalism, acute analyses of modern power structures and a rich philosophy of human potential.

In writing this dictionary, we have been acutely aware that many of the issues raised by Marx have been the subject of multiple differences of interpretation, passionately debated, often for high political stakes. It is beyond the remit of this dictionary to consider these debates, but we have pointed out the areas of his thought that have given rise to controversy, and readers are encouraged to read further and form their own conclusions. One such area of controversy is the intellectual relationship between Marx and his friend Friedrich Engels. In the past many commentators have equated the views of Engels with those of Marx, but we have not used the views of Engels to explicate Marx's position in any of the entries. It is a Marx dictionary, not a Marx and Engels dictionary. While we have striven to supply accurate accounts of Marx's views, we acknowledge that every description is also an interpretation. Marx's favourite motto was '*de omnibus dubitandum*', 'have doubts about everything', and this is sound advice for all critical readers.

How to Read This Dictionary

Marx's dialectical approach comprehends concepts relationally rather than in fixity or isolation, as is the case in most philosophical approaches. So for example, following Marx, we cannot fully understand labour without some understanding of labour power, and we cannot fully understand labour power without some understanding of value, and we cannot fully understand value without some understanding of surplus value, and so on. In this dictionary, therefore, perhaps more than any other there will be a good deal of cross-referencing where readers are encouraged to track back and forth over these concepts in a process of dialectical assimilation. Indeed, where there is cross-reference, to avoid duplication we may have focused on different aspects of the entry considered, so that cross-referencing gives a more comprehensive understanding of the concept, thinker or text under discussion. To aid readers in this activity all entries appearing anywhere in the text are highlighted in bold in the first instance. We do not claim to cover all the occasions on which Marx made reference to the entries identified, but we highlight the most important places where he did or where the definition is most evident. Readers are then encouraged to follow up the entries they read and engage with the core primary texts, written by Marx himself, to deepen and enrich their understanding of his work and ideas.

Life and Work

Marx was born in Trier, in the Rhineland area of Germany, on 5 May 1818. The Rhineland had been annexed by the authoritarian Kingdom of Prussia only four years earlier, after being administered by France during the Napoleonic regime. Many of Trier's educated middle classes had been inspired by the liberal ideals of the French enlightenment and the political goals of the French Revolution. Amongst them was Marx's father, Heinrich, son of the local Jewish rabbi, and his mother, Henrietta, daughter of a rabbi from Holland. Heinrich was not religious, but converted to Protestantism in order to be able to continue work as a lawyer under the Prussian regime. Karl was baptized as an evangelical Protestant and attended the local school, where most of the scholars were Catholic, from 1830 to 1835. In his youth he was deeply influenced by the humanism of his future father-in-law, Baron Ludwig von Westphalen, from whom he developed his lifelong love of the work of Homer and Shakespeare. Marx became engaged to the Baron's daughter, Jenny, in 1836, following a year of study at the nearby University of Bonn, before transferring to the University of Berlin. At Berlin he studied history and law but quickly developed his interest in philosophy. He became engrossed by the philosophy of Hegel, drawing inspiration from a group of lecturers and senior students who convened as 'the Doctors' Club'. Marx became part of the intellectual movement known as the Young Hegelians, sharing their criticism of religion and their commitment to the radical reform of the state along liberal and democratic lines. With the intention of pursuing an academic career, he undertook a PhD comparing the atomic theories of Democritus and Epicurus, obtaining his doctorate from the University of Jena in 1841. He returned to Bonn in the hope that his friend Bruno Bauer could find him a post at the University, but Bauer's dismissal on the grounds of his atheism made it clear that the Prussian authorities would no longer countenance the appointment of radicals to university posts.

In 1842 Marx moved the short distance to Cologne to become editor of the *Rheinische Zeitung*, a liberal weekly newspaper, gaining his first experience of dealing with social and political problems. Although its circulation doubled under Marx's editorship the paper fell foul of the authorities and was banned in March 1843. The daily confrontation with material concerns, following years of immersion in abstract philosophical argument, played a vitally important role in radicalizing Marx. His brief life as a full-time journalist involved not only looking at particular examples of class oppression, such as the debate on the law of theft from woods and the impoverishment of the Mosel wine-growers, but also dealing with the eager censors of the Prussian state. In the summer that followed the paper's closure, Marx married Jenny after an engagement of seven years. He wrote the unpublished *Critique of Hegel's Philosophy of Right*, rejecting Hegel's defence of the Prussian state and asserting the irreconcilable differences of class interest. His method of inverting Hegel's conceptual categories into real social relationships owed much to Ludwig Feuerbach, but it was already evident that Marx was moving towards a revolutionary political commitment far beyond the scope of Feuerbach's philosophy. He also wrote a brilliant critique of liberal rights theory, *On the Jewish Question*, in which he warned that the achievement of political democracy did not in itself deliver human emancipation. In the autumn of 1843, in the *Contribution to the Critique of Hegel's Philosophy of Right: Introduction*, Marx declared that it was the working class, or the proletariat, who in the course of winning their own emancipation would free all humanity by abolishing private property, the basis of all class oppression.

Marx departed for Paris in October 1843 to edit a magazine, the *Deutsch-Französische Jahrbücher*, in order to escape the Prussian censorship and develop links between German and French socialist theorists. One of the first contributions to the new publication was Engels' 'Outlines of a Critique of Political Economy', and it made an enormous impression on him. Marx was already determined to analyze the structural causes of oppression, and Engels' compelling criticisms of the apologetic nature of classical British political economy was an inspiration to him. This resulted in Marx's unpublished Paris notebooks of 1844, including the *Comments on*

James Mill and the *Economic and Philosophical Manuscripts*. The concept of alienation is the central motif of these manuscripts, and his account of human essence and potential, contrasted with its systematic perversion in the modern production process, constitutes an outstanding contribution to humanist philosophy. It is also Marx's first avowal of communism as the movement through which alienation can be overcome. Unfortunately, those in possession of the manuscripts did not see fit to publish them until 1932, and even then they were given little prominence within Marxist circles. It is a grisly irony that the man responsible for their publication in the Soviet Union, David Ryazanov, was executed by Stalin's regime in 1938. We can only speculate as to how the reception of Marx would have been altered if they had been available. Their significance as the philosophical basis of his later economic theories has been hailed by some commentators and denied by others, but the thematic continuity can be seen quite clearly in the notebooks of 1857–1858 known as the *Grundrisse* and in the passages on commodity fetishism in *Capital* 1 (1867). Unfortunately, the *Grundrisse* was not published until several years after the *Manuscripts*. These important philosophical works were not widely available until the 1960s and 1970s, when many readers were able to contrast Marx's commitment to human freedom with the absence of freedom and democracy in states claiming to be 'Marxist'.

In early 1845 Marx moved with his family to Brussels, where he was to remain for three years. Now committed to analyzing the material conditions that gave rise to social and political problems, he was scathing about the incapacity of his former associates in the Young Hegelian movement to move beyond abstract philosophical observations and 'spiritual' aspirations. This is evident in the tone and content of *The Holy Family*, published in 1845, and also in the unpublished *Theses on Feuerbach* and *The German Ideology*, written in 1845–1846. The first part of *The German Ideology* contained the first expression of his theory of historical development, later labelled by Engels 'the materialist conception of history' and 'historical materialism'. Here the emphasis is placed on the driving force of the production and reproduction of material life in shaping social, political and legal relations, and human history is seen as the development of successive modes of production. This general interpretation of the development of class struggle is accompanied by strong calls for more empirical investigation as well as a commitment to revolutionary action. Marx now saw no point in abstract philosophical or moral debate, and this was to remain his stance for the rest of his life. This is not say that the economic and political analyses that occupy Marx for the rest of his life are not without philosophical content or normative force, but the philosophy and the ethics now became immanent in his political economy and political analyses rather than explicit, as they had been in 1844.

Marx's main activities in the Brussels years consisted in continuing his research into political economy and in developing an international network of political contacts. His developing knowledge of political economy was brought to bear in *The Poverty of Philosophy* (1847), an attack on Pierre-Joseph Proudhon's attempts to apply a form of Hegelian dialectics to economic matters. He was particularly angry that Proudhon, although sympathetic to the working class, opposed strike action or trade union organization. At this time Marx considered it imperative to oppose those contributions to working-class politics that he considered to offer nothing constructive to the struggle against the status quo. As well as participating in the meetings of the Democratic Association, he worked with other German radicals in the Brussels Correspondence Committee, part of a wider European network of socialist or communist groups. At one of its meetings on political propaganda in 1846 he attacked the popular German communist Wilhelm Weitling for encouraging workers to conspire in the illusion that a communist revolution could be achieved instantly. Making use of contacts he had made with German communists in London, Marx joined the Communist League that was formed there in 1847. He travelled to London for its second Congress in December and outlined his political views for building an independent working class movement that would participate in the struggle for democracy. He wanted the League to reject popular alternatives that he considered futile, such as the communitarian experiments favoured by the utopian socialists or the reckless insurrectionism of Weitling and his followers. Marx and Engels were charged by the Communist League with the task of producing a programme. At the time Marx was busy delivering lectures outlining his economic theory, later published as *Wage Labour and Capital*, but when they were completed he quickly wrote *The Communist Manifesto*, which was published in February 1848. This incendiary text, a summary of the modern class struggle and a guide to the revolutionary creation of a classless society, coincided with the outbreak of democratic revolutions, first in France and then in other European states.

Marx's stay in Brussels ended in March 1848, when he went to Paris at the invitation of Ferdinand Flocon, a radical member of the provisional republican government that had seized power following the overthrow of King Louis Philippe. There followed one of the most intensive periods of political activity in his life. When the March uprisings in Berlin and Vienna forced major concessions from the autocratic regimes of Prussia and Austria, Marx and Engels travelled to Cologne to assist in the revolutionary movement. The situation in Germany was complex, primarily because there was no single unified German state, and the hopes of the radical democrats hinged on creating a united Germany centred on a parliament at Frankfurt. Marx assumed the editorship of a daily newspaper, the *Neue Rheinische Zeitung*, and this became the focus of his revolutionary work. From its first edition in June 1848 until its final closure in May 1849 Marx wrote something like 100 articles, travelling throughout Germany to raise funds and urge workers' leaders to support the movement for a united democratic republic. He wrote the 'Demands for the Communist Party in Germany', calling for the vote for all over 21, the arming of the people to counter the threat of the standing armies, measures to help the peasants, free education for all and a steeply progressive income tax.

For much of 1848 Marx operated entirely within the democratic camp, but when it became obvious that the German bourgeoisie was too irresolute to carry through a successful democratic revolution he argued that only a 'red' revolution led by the working class, with the support of the peasantry, could bring democracy to Germany. At the same time he was consistently critical of those who advocated insurrections that had no chance of success against vastly superior armed forces. The German situation exposed a major tension implicit in the prescriptions of *The Communist Manifesto*, namely that the working class should support the bourgeoisie in its immediate struggle against autocracy, while at the same time acknowledging that in the near future the bourgeoisie was the class enemy that eventually had to be defeated. Marx was tried for sedition in February 1849, but defended himself with great eloquence and was acquitted. By this time, however, the Prussian and Austrian monarchies had ridden the storm and the Frankfurt Parliament was dispersed in May. Marx was expelled from Germany the following month and travelled to Paris, but within weeks was told by the French government that he was not welcome there.

In August 1849 Marx began his lifelong exile in London, where he was joined by his wife and three children and the family helper, Helene Demuth.

In 1850 he summarized the lessons of the German experience in the March Address to the Central Committee of the Communist League, proposing that the communists adopt a strategy of 'permanent revolution', constantly pushing a timid bourgeoisie towards more radical action that would break the power of the old ruling class. While stating that communist demands would not be possible to realize at this stage, he urged support for measures such as more state control of the economy and a more progressive system of taxation. Marx repeated his call for permanent revolution in *The Class Struggles in France*. When the French Second Republic was overthrown by the *coup d'état* that brought Napoleon III to power as Emperor, Marx wrote a scintillating account of its rise and fall in *The Eighteenth Brumaire of Louis Bonaparte* (1852). The *Brumaire* is a brilliant example of class analysis as a means of unlocking complex political manoeuvrings, but it also showed the difficulty of identifying the most effective strategy for the working class. On the one hand, Marx was totally sympathetic to the workers in the abortive June uprising of 1848, but on the other, he considered insurrectionary tactics to be premature. He wanted the working class to play a leading role in alliances with other classes and try to make democracy work for them, but he found the reality of the parliamentary-based politics to be a dismal failure. Marx's response to these dilemmas was to support the growth of independent working-class political and industrial movements, urging them to reassert their revolutionary socialist goals in preparation for struggles in more auspicious circumstances.

The long years of English exile saw Marx engaged in three quite distinct forms of activity. The first, his priority, was to perfect his grasp of political economy in order to publish a detailed analysis of the contradictory nature of the capitalist system. For this purpose, in June 1850 he obtained a ticket for the old Reading Room of the British Museum and spent many years there and in its 1857 successor, the great domed room, studying a vast range of sources in at least eight languages. Getting the results into press was a slow process, despite repeated promises of imminent completion. *A Contribution to the Critique of Political Economy* was published in 1859, but this was really only preparatory to his planned systemic analysis: it was most notable for its Preface, which contained a succinct account of his theory of historical development. It was not until 1867 that the first edition of *Capital* 1 appeared, and the manuscripts for the other volumes (*Capital* 2, *Capital* 3 and *Theories of Surplus Value*) were all left for Engels and others to edit and prepare for publication. Whatever the difficulties posed by his philosophical approach to commodity fetishism in chapter one, *Capital* 1 is Marx's masterpiece. Its use of government statistics, surveys and reports as well as historical sources are testimony to the scrupulous research that went into it, and the tightness of the argument is matched by the shocking vividness of the details of working life in Britain. It was both a philosopher's analysis of the systemic development of the exploitation of working people and a sociological dissection of the experience of that exploitation. Even though the form of capitalism has changed markedly since Marx's day, his analysis of the 'laws of motion' of the system, conducted through all the volumes, retains a compelling relevance.

Marx's second activity, from 1852 until 1863, was his journalism, his chief source of regular income besides the help he received from Engels. In a letter to a former Communist League comrade Adolf Cluss in 1854, Marx complained that the journalism bored him, took a great deal of his time, dissipated his energy and was 'worthless' compared with his 'scientific' work. This is, however, too harsh a judgement, for he was a gifted journalist and the articles provide important insights not only into the application of his broader historical principles but also into his profound anger at the abuses of power he reported on. He produced over 300 pieces for the *New York Daily Tribune*, including some damning indictments of British colonial rule in India and Ireland and the imposition of the opium trade on China. He wrote at length and with passion in favour of the fight against slavery in the American Civil War for the Vienna-based liberal newspaper *Die Presse*. He also wrote for English radical newspapers such as the Chartist *People's Paper* and the *Free Press*, and this enabled him to keep in contact with British socialist and trade union leaders. He may have been a reluctant journalist, but this work was far from worthless.

Just as the need to turn out newspaper articles receded, another area of activity arose to divert him from his political economy, but this was much more welcome to Marx. As co-founder and member of the General Council of the First International, he plunged into his second bout of intensive political activity between 1864 and 1872. The energy he poured into this task reflected his consistent commitment to the need for international action to challenge an economic system that had been international from its inception. Although the concrete achievements of the International were limited, its symbolic power was enormous, as an inspiration for workers and as a mortal threat to the ruling classes. Marx used his good contacts with British trade unionists and impressed on socialists throughout Europe the importance of careful analysis of the conditions and circumstances that confronted them, and the imperative of organizing the growing strength of the working class. In the end he effectively closed down the organization for fear of it slipping into the control of the anarchists, but his work in the International played a vital role in encouraging the development of socialist parties committed to struggle within mainstream national politics. His most famous political publication of this period, *The Civil War in France* (1871), written on behalf of the General Council, extolled the virtues of the radical democracy adopted by the workers of the Paris Commune before its bloody suppression. However, it should not be taken as an endorsement of insurrectionary politics, for Marx later made it clear that the Communards could not have succeeded and should have negotiated a compromise. He also made it clear, in a speech in Amsterdam in 1872, that it was entirely possible for the working class to achieve its goals by peaceful means in those countries that were moving towards political democracy. Peaceful means, however, did not mean erosion of the central message of the workers' struggle against capital. As the 1875 *Critique of the Gotha Programme* makes clear, he considered it imperative that the socialist parties should always declare their unswerving commitment to the abolition of private property, and with it to the end of the class rule of the bourgeoisie.

Although we have identified some of the activities that prevented Marx completing his projected four volumes of *Capital*, plus other promised items such as a volume on the state, we also have to take into account his difficult personal circumstances. When he came to London in August 1850, he moved his family into a flat in Chelsea with the support of the German émigré community. In November Jenny gave birth to their second son, Guido (named after Guy Fawkes), but he died ten months later. By this time the family had been evicted from their flat and forced to take poor accommodation in Dean Street, Soho. Their third daughter, Franziska, was born in March 1851, but she lived for only thirteen months. In 1855 his other son, Edgar, died aged nine. In all the Marxes had six children, three of whom died in childhood, and another child was stillborn. In 1860 Marx's wife, Jenny, almost died of smallpox. Their lives in London were desperately poor for many years before legacies enabled them to move to more spacious accommodation in the more salubrious district of Maitland Park. The Marx family were not free from major financial concerns until Engels made an annual settlement to them on his retirement from work in 1869. On one occasion Marx confided in a letter to Engels that he regretted bringing such hardship on his wife and family, but the family bond was immensely strong, and Jenny and their daughters bestowed great affection on old 'Moor', as they nicknamed him.

In addition to the economic hardships, Marx suffered from poor health throughout his life. He had been declared unfit for military service in 1838 because of a weak chest, and he was later regularly plagued by boils and carbuncles. In his final years he was forced to abandon serious writing, concentrating on moving around places with drier climates to stave off the results of bronchitis and other illnesses. Even so, during these years he taught himself to read Russian and took voluminous notes on books of anthropology and history. Marx was grief-stricken by the death of his wife in December 1881 and then the death of their eldest daughter, Jenny, early in 1883. He died on 14 March 1883 and was buried in London's Highgate Cemetery three days later. Engels gave the funeral oration, declaring that 'his name will live on through the centuries and so will his work'.

Chronology: Marx's Life and Works

1818   Born in Trier in the Rhineland area of Germany on 5 May 1818, eldest son of Heinrich Marx, a lawyer, and Henrietta Marx. Both parents converted from Judaism to Protestantism. His name is registered as 'Carl', as it appears in his University leaving certificates.

1824   Baptized as a Protestant.

1830   Begins studies at the Frederick William III High School in Trier.

1835   Enrols at the University of Bonn. Studies law, classics and the history of modern art.

1836   Becomes engaged to Jenny von Westphalen. Enrols at the University of Berlin; studies mainly law and philosophy. Immerses himself in Hegel's philosophy and associates with radical Young Hegelians.

1838   Father dies. Declared unfit for military service in the Prussian Army due to weak chest.

1841   Obtains doctorate from the University of Jena for his dissertation comparing the atomic theories of Democritus and Epicurus. Moves to Bonn; associates with Bruno Bauer in the criticism of religious thought.

1842   Writes articles for the *Rheinische Zeitung* and becomes its editor (October). First meeting with Friedrich Engels (November).

1843   Closure of *Rheinische Zeitung* (March). Marries Jenny von Westphalen (June). Writes *On the Jewish Question*, which is published the following year, and the *Critique of Hegel's Philosophy of Right*, which is unpublished. Leaves for Paris (October). Declares commitment to the proletariat as the class whose struggle for freedom will emancipate the world.

1844   Publication of *On the Jewish Question* and *Contribution to the Critique of Hegel's Philosophy of Right: Introduction*. Studies British and French political economy and writes the unpublished *Comments on James Mill* and the *Economic and Philosophical Manuscripts*. Begins work, with Engels, on *The Holy Family*, exposing the short-comings of some of their former associates in the Young Hegelian movement. Birth of first daughter, Jenny.

1845   Publication of *The Holy Family*. Moves to Brussels (February). Birth of second daughter, Laura. Writes the unpublished *Theses on Feuerbach*.

1846   Works with Engels on the unpublished manuscripts of *The German Ideology*, establishing his distinctive theory of historical development. Birth of first son, Edgar.

1847   Joins the Communist League (January). Publishes *The Poverty of Philosophy*, attacking Proudhon.

1848   Publishes *The Communist Manifesto*, co-written with Engels. Moves to Paris following the February revolution in France, then to Cologne (April) as editor of the *Neue Rheinische Zeitung*. Writes many articles supporting the democrats in their unsuccessful struggles throughout Europe. Travels widely in Germany and Austria.

1849   On trial in Cologne for plotting to overthrow the Prussian regime; he is acquitted. Publishes more articles for the *Neue Rheinische Zeitung*, including the text of *Wage Labour and Capital*, before it is forced to close in May. Marx leaves for Paris (June) but is expelled from France and begins his lifelong exile in London (August). Birth of second son, Guido (November).

1850   Death of Guido (September). Writes *Address of the Central Committee to the Communist League* and *The Class Struggles in France*. Settles with his family and family helper Helene Demuth in Dean Street, Soho (December). Lacking resources or income, relies on Engels' financial support. Begins his intensive study of economics in the reading room of the British Museum.

1851   Birth of third daughter, Franziska (March).

1852   Death of Franziska (April). Marx engineers the dissolution of the Communist League following protracted disputes with revolutionary German refugees (November). Publishes *The Eighteenth Brumaire of Louis Bonaparte* to explain the reasons behind the demise of the French Second Republic. Writes articles for the *New York Daily Tribune*, mainly on British politics.

1853   Continues to write articles for the *New York Daily Tribune*, including articles on 'the Eastern question' concerning Russia and Turkey, as well as the British rule in India. Publishes *Revelations Concerning the Communist Trial in Cologne*. Publishes eight articles attacking Lord Palmerston, the British Foreign Secretary, in the *People's Paper*, some of which are reprinted as a widely read pamphlet.

1854   Writes numerous articles for the *New York Daily Tribune*, including many on the Crimean War.

1855   Birth of fourth daughter, Eleanor (January). Death of Edgar (April). Writes numerous articles for the *Neue Oder-Zeitung* as well as the *New York Daily Tribune*.

1856   Moves to Grafton Terrace near Maitland Park in London. Writes articles for the *People's Paper*. His wife Jenny has a stillborn child.

1857   Begins work on the General Outlines of a Critique of Political Economy, the unpublished manuscripts known as the *Grundrisse*. Writes articles for the *New American Cyclopaedia*.

1858   Completes the *Grundrisse* notebooks.

1859   Publishes *A Contribution to the Critique of Political Economy* in Germany. It has little impact but its Preface contains an important summary of his theory of historical development.

1860   Jenny, Marx's wife, contracts smallpox; she survives but her health is impaired.

1861   Begins to write articles on the American Civil War for the liberal Austrian newspaper *Die Presse*. Visits Berlin.

1862   Works on criticisms of bourgeois political economy, later published as *Theories of Surplus Value*.

1863   Continues work on *Theories of Surplus Value*. Begins work on the circulation of capital, later published as *Capital* 2. Death of his mother; visits Trier and relatives in Holland.

1864   Participates in the founding of the First International in London (September). Writes the *Inaugural Address* and *Provisional Rules* of the International. Works on material later published as *Capital* 3. Inheritances from his mother and his friend Wilhelm Wolff enable the family to move to a more spacious house, Modena Villas, in Maitland Park, London.

1865   Serves on the General Council of the International. Delivers two lectures outlining his political economy, published posthumously as *Value, Price and Profit*.

1866   Writes the Programme for the First Congress of the First International in Geneva. Works on the final draft of *Capital* 1. Suffers continuous poor health, manifested in boils and carbuncles.

1867   Publication of *Capital* 1 in Germany (September), subtitled *A Critique of Political Economy*. Continues political work within the International.

1868   Persistent indebtedness and poor health. Writes the General Council's Report for the Brussels Congress of the International.

1869   Continues political work within the International, including active support for Irish independence. Writes the General Council's Report for the Basle Congress of the International. Engels retires and provides an allowance for Marx that settles his financial worries.

1870   Writes two *Addresses on the Franco-Prussian War* on behalf of the General Council of the International.

1871   Publishes *The Civil War in France* on behalf of the General Council, giving total support to the Paris Commune and condemning its bloody suppression. The London Conference of the International reveals a major split between Marx and the anarchists led by Bakunin. Marx denounces the anti-political doctrines of the anarchists in *The Alleged Splits in the International*.

1872 At the Hague Congress of the International, Marx, afraid of the growing influence of the anarchists, engineers moving the headquarters of the International to New York. In a speech in Amsterdam he argues that the working class can achieve its goals by peaceful means in countries moving towards democracy.

1873 Writes Postface to the second German edition of *Capital* 1.

1874 Spends two months in the spa town of Karlsbad to receive treatment for a liver complaint.

1875 Re-visits Karlsbad in late summer. Moves with family to Maitland Park Road, London. Strongly criticizes the proposed programme of the newly united German Social Democratic Workers' Party in the *Critique of the Gotha Programme*.

1876 Repeats health treatment in Karlsbad.

1878 Does final work on the manuscripts later published as *Capital* 2.

1879 Writes the *Circular Letter* to German socialist leaders warning them to resist firmly any deviation from the class struggle. Begins extensive notebooks on pre-industrial and non-Western societies.

1880 Publication of the *Workers' Questionnaire* (*L'Inqûete Ouvrière*) in France. Publishes *Introduction to the French Workers' Programme*.

1881 Writes *Notes on Adolph Wagner*, his final comments on political economy. Letter to Vera Zasulich advising flexibility in applying his historical theory to Russian conditions. Spends two months in France. Death of his wife Jenny (December).

1882 Suffering from acute bronchitis, spends most of the year in drier climates of Algiers, Monte Carlo, Argenteuil in France and Vevey in Switzerland.

1883 Death of his daughter Jenny (January). Death of Karl Marx (14 March) in London; buried in Highgate Cemetery (17 March), the eulogy provided by Engels.

The Marx Dictionary

—**A**—

abstract labour The substance of **value**, which itself is the socially necessary **labour** time required to produce a **commodity**. Marx wanted to understand how value lies behind **exchange** value in **capitalism**. In *Capital* **1** (1867) he argues that when two commodities exchange, e.g. a coat and linen, the **individual** labour time expended on one is being brought into relation with the labour time expended on another: the labour on a coat is being brought into relation with the labour expended on making the linen. The concrete or determinate **form** of labour is different for the different use values, though, because individuals differ in the skills, effort and labour time that they expend on making such commodities. When these two commodities are quantitatively related to each other in exchange, as, say, twenty yards of linen for one coat, there must be a common element between them that equates them in this way. This cannot be their use values, as they are qualitatively different: a coat to wear to keep warm and the linen for sheets for a bed, for example. It also cannot be the concrete labour that has been expended, as they differ in the **production** of the linen and the coat. Marx deduces that the only way we can equate these two different use values and the concrete labour specific to their production is to abstract from them. The common element is therefore abstract labour, labour abstracted both from the use values and human labour expended on the commodities. So we have then a general **abstraction** of labour, or abstract labour as Marx calls it, and this finds expression in the form of exchange value. Abstract labour is therefore at the basis of the exchange value of a commodity. Capitalism, as a system based on the production of commodities for exchange in order to realize **surplus value**, reduces all labour to abstract labour.

Marx's analysis shows that abstract labour as the substance of value regulates commodity production and exchange because it operates as a measure of value by determining the socially necessary labour time required to produce a commodity. For example, a number of producers may have created coats through their specific and concrete labour, but they only know if they have expended their time as socially necessary when they try to exchange their goods on the **market**. The market itself tends to reduce the specific labours expended to make them measurable with each other, and a socially necessary labour time for making a coat will be revealed. So if it takes on average eight hours to make a coat, then that is its socially necessary labour time and represents the abstract labour of society that has been expended on making the coat. Abstract labour will therefore determine the level around which the coat's **price** will fluctuate on the market. This is subject to change because all capitalists are attempting to produce below the existing socially necessary labour time, say through increases in technology and/or intensification of the **exploitation** of the workers, and this will change the exchange value of the commodity, which in this case is the coat. So a rise in productivity can reduce the value at which things exchange.

Additionally, abstract labour is also important for exposing how capital engages in the real process of making labour the same through the division of labour, as Marx states clearly in the Introduction to the ***Grundrisse*** (1857–1858). This homogenization of labour and its reduction to tasks that are so simple that workers can be moved from one to the other quite easily in a production line is typical of advanced **capitalist** forms of organization. Consequently, labour as an abstraction becomes true in practice in a system of advanced commodity production. However, the fact that abstract labour represents what is common to labour across many different occupations is, ironically, the way to understand the workers as a **working class**, and as such a threat to capitalism.

abstraction   Takes two main forms: general and determinate, as Marx explains in the ***Grundrisse*** (1857–1858). General abstraction refers to the abstraction from concrete social circumstances that allows a common element amongst phenomena to be focused on. An example of this is **production** in general, which is an abstraction from the differences that arise in production in particular social periods. Determinate abstraction is a movement from the general to the particular or concrete. For Marx the scientifically correct **method** is the ascent from the simple relations, such as **labour**, division of labour, need, **exchange value**, to the level of the **state**, exchange between nations and the **world market**. Hence determinate abstraction involves understanding the concrete as a concentration of many determinations. The world market is thus a concentration of determinate abstractions that go all the way back to labour. Indeed, Marx mentions how the abstraction of the category labour itself becomes true in practice. In **capitalist** society labour as an abstraction in thought becomes determinate, i.e. manifests itself in concrete reality and so takes a determinate **form**.

On the basis of these two aspects of abstraction, Marx argues that bourgeois political economists share a common weakness, confusing determinate with general abstractions. They posit what is particular to capitalist society as true for all societies. Inevitably, then, they are unaware that their categories are ahistorical and have grown in the soil of capitalist society. This implies that they have become imprisoned in the modes of thought created by **capitalism**. They see the form labour or production takes in capitalism as always being this way, an everlasting truth. They fail to realize that labour and production take the form that they do specific to the historical **mode of production** that they are in. In this sense, **political economy** stopped being a scientific inquiry and simply became an apology for capital itself. **Smith** and **Ricardo**, for instance, make the mistake of conceiving the **individual** as a general abstraction, the isolated hunter and fisherman, which they then project into the past as a natural individual. The general abstraction of the individual is made into the determinate abstraction, not as an individual necessarily was in that particular historical circumstance, but as Ricardo and Smith suppose the individual to be based on their own notion of **human nature**. Only by recognizing these abstractions as distinct, but also in a unity, can this type of problem be overcome.

The importance of understanding abstraction in its general and determinate form becomes readily evident when considering how Marx begins his analysis of *Capital* **1** (1867). Marx's first point in presenting his argument here is not the **commodity**, but the general abstraction of **wealth**. As Marx states, the wealth of societies in which the capitalist mode of production prevails appears as an immense collection of commodities, and the individual commodity appears as its elementary form. Investigation should begin, therefore, with the commodity. So wealth, the general abstraction, takes the form of the commodity. The commodity is itself a determinate abstraction with further determinate abstractions in terms of use value and exchange value. The commodity has to be analyzed because that is the elementary form wealth takes in society. This seemingly innocuous starting point is therefore steeped in the basically antagonistic nature of the capitalist system itself. It is through the commodity-form that capital forces people to labour to survive and thereby receive part of the social wealth they have created. This process develops through further determinate abstractions as value manifests itself in the circulatory sphere in the form of prices, interests etc. Eventually we reach the contradictory unity of the concrete itself with all the different forms wealth can take. So Marx is moving from the abstract to the concrete, the simple to the complex, when presenting his argument in *Capital* 1. However, in terms of investigation, Marx begins with the concrete, from which he makes general abstractions.

accumulation   Takes two main forms: primitive and **capital**. Marx discusses primitive accumulation extensively in part eight of ***Capital* 1** (1867), referring to the historical process of divorcing the producer from the means of **production**. It is primitive because it forms the pre-history of capital and the **capitalist mode of production**, and is the way in which the majority of the agricultural **population** are forcefully thrown off the land to be turned into wage-labourers who have nothing to sell but their **labour power**. Under **feudalism**, the serfs or peasants were tied to the lord who allowed them to work the land for themselves in **exchange** for creating produce for him. With the lands enclosed, these serfs were now 'free' to leave for the towns to become factory **labour** for capital. Without access to the means of production, which is the land in feudalism, wage-labour is the only way they can ensure their means of subsistence. However, many peasants became vagabonds rather than submit to the oppression and low **wages** that typified capitalist factories. Legislation was therefore used to punish these individuals by whipping, branding and torturing them in order to make them enter these workplaces and submit to factory discipline. Marx concludes that the process of primitive accumulation, one that is written in the annals of humankind in 'letters of blood and fire', means that capital comes into the world 'dripping from head to toe, from every pore, with blood and dirt'.

Marx also defines capital accumulation as the employment of **surplus value** as, or re-conversion into, capital. Capitalists engaging in **exploitation** amass a certain sum of surplus value and are forced through **competition** to invest part of that surplus into further production to gain further increases in surplus value. The other part of the surplus will go into capitalists' own **consumption** and enjoyment, and they must decide how they divide these two conflicting aspects of their **wealth**. Consequently, capitalists can only preserve their capital by extending it, and they can only extend it by means of progressive accumulation. Capitalists that fail to re-invest surplus value in improving their methods of production run the risk of falling behind their competitors and going out of business. Their competitors will produce their commodities more cheaply and offer a lower **price** on the **market** than the non-investing capitalist. So they are all subject to the external and coercive laws of capitalist production, and all must engage in capital accumulation to survive. Accumulation therefore seems to take place for the sake of accumulation and production seems to take place for the sake of production.

alienation   The central philosophical theme of the 1844 *Economic and Philosophical Manuscripts*, alienation refers to a process through which human beings suffer a loss of control over their interactions with **nature** and their fellow human beings. Marx identifies four forms of alienation (*Entaüsserung* or *Entfremdung*) experienced in the modern **labour** process. First, the worker is alienated from the product of labour, for although the worker is the creator, it is the employer who owns the product and has the power to sell it. Second, the worker is alienated from the act of **production** within the labour process, since the work is forced labour and is experienced as suffering and weakness. In illustrating the first and second aspects of alienation, Marx bemoans the fact that work is experienced as deadening compulsion, with the worker feeling free only in functions such as eating, drinking and making love, which, taken abstractly, are animal functions. Third, the worker experiences alienation from **species-being** (*Gattungswesen*), a term taken from **Feuerbach** to denote the qualities that make us distinctively human. Marx refers frequently to the dehumanization of the workers, with the clear implication that they are being denied something which is their due as human beings. He uses the metaphor of a worker's reduction to a machine three times in as many pages in the *Manuscripts*, and it recurs in both *The Communist Manifesto* (1848) and also in *Capital* **1** (1867). The fourth aspect of alienation, a consequence of the other three, is the alienation of human beings from their fellow humans. Marx argues that we are estranged from each other in every relationship and the alienated situation of the worker is generalized through society at large.

In discussing alienation from species-being, Marx enlarges on the difference between humans and **animals**. Conscious life activity distinguishes humans from animals, according to Marx, for whereas animals are at one with their life activity, humans make their life activity the object of their will and **consciousness**. This emphasis on activity is followed by a sharper focus on production, the ability of humans to create products for each other in a consciously planned way, not simply for their immediate **needs** but for their long-term sustainability. Truly human production, then, transcends the instinctive response to immediate physical needs, and we are able to create things in accordance with the standards of other species and imbue our products with aesthetic qualities. However, truly human production is denied to the producers under **capitalism**, and alienated labour transforms our human **essence** into nothing more than a means to our existence. Marx comments that the workers lose their **freedom** in the service of greed, becoming depressed spiritually and physically to the condition of a machine. This perversion of human potential is brought about through the medium of **money**, which, when raised to an all-powerful position, confounds and confuses all natural human qualities. Marx concludes that private **property** has made us so 'stupid and one-sided' that we think of an object as ours only when we possess it, rather than appreciating it as a social, *human* object.

Marx develops his concept of alienation through a critical engagement with the idealist **dialectic** of **Hegel** and the **materialism** of Feuerbach. Marx credits the latter with exposing alienation in **religion**, in which humans consider themselves worthless and powerless before an omnipotent God who is in fact a creation of the human imagination. In this way human power is imputed to God and needs to be reclaimed if humanity is to achieve real freedom. This example of the alienated relationship between the human being and God is seized on by Marx in the early writings and in *Capital* 1 as analogous to the way in which power relations between labour and capital become inverted in the modern production process. However, in applying the concept of alienation to modern economic and social issues, Marx recognizes the **value** of Hegel's dialectic. In the final part of the *Manuscripts*, following some critical remarks concerning Hegel's **idealism**, he praises Hegel for conceiving labour as humanity's act of 'self-genesis'. By grasping the centrality of labour as the driving force in human history, Hegel sees the development of human power through alienation and the supersession of that alienation. Although Marx does not accept Hegel's purely abstract resolutions of alienation within pure thought, he accepts the positive significance given to the supersession of alienation (*Die Aufhebung des Entaüsserung*) and offers an alternative materialist reading of 'the **negation** of the negation' as the confirmation of true being.

In the *Manuscripts*, Marx recognized that the system of production that reproduced alienation could be replaced only through a social **revolution** of the **working class** against the **bourgeoisie**, and he illustrates this by referring to French socialist workers coming together politically to make a reality of the idea of the 'brotherhood of man'. In *The Holy Family* (1845) he confidently asserts that a large part of the English and French working class was already conscious of its historic task and was constantly working to develop that consciousness into complete clarity. He was anxious to distance himself from the way his former acquaintances among the **Young Hegelians** treated alienation as a problem of consciousness that could be overcome within consciousness itself. This rejection of the purely philosophical use of alienation recurs in the isolated references to alienation in *The German Ideology* (1845–1846) and in the criticisms of the German 'true socialists' in *The Communist Manifesto*. The philosophical discourse of human essence and alienation then recedes into the background, but the alienation theme recurs throughout his later economic writings.

The issue of whether or not Marx's conception of alienation is retained in his mature **political economy** has been the subject of protracted debate among interpreters of Marx's thought. Some have argued that it is present only as a rhetorical device, but the discussions in the *Grundrisse* (1857–1858) and the analysis of **commodity fetishism** in the first chapter of *Capital* 1 (1867) suggest otherwise. In his analysis of **capitalist accumulation**, Marx consistently points out that although the worker produces objective **wealth** as capital, it appears as an alien power that dominates and exploits the worker. In the chapter on money in the *Grundrisse*, he comments that not only is the **individual** alienated from him or herself and from others, but that all relations and capacities are alienated universally and comprehensively. In the discussion of commodity fetishism in *Capital* 1,

Marx returns to the analogy between religious alienation and alienation in production that he had first used in the **Comments on James Mill** (1844). The fetishism described by Marx can be overcome when the practical relations of everyday life become transparent and rational, with production conducted by freely associated workers under their conscious control. In part seven of *Capital* 1, Marx refers to the alienation of the workers occurring as they are deprived of the physical and intellectual benefits of the wealth they have created, and he returns again to the image of the reduction of the worker to an appendage of the machine. In these later writings there is more emphasis on how workers and owners experience this alienation as something natural, and also how it was accepted as such by some bourgeois political economists. For example, in **Theories of Surplus Value** (1861–1863), he comments that some apologists for capitalism feel completely at home with the alienated **form** in which different parts of value confront one another in the same way that theologians are at home with the idea of three persons in one God.

anarchism A political doctrine defined by its total opposition to the **state**. It was considered by Marx to be a dangerous alternative to socialist attempts to build mass industrial and political organizations within the **working class**. Inspired in France by Pierre-Joseph **Proudhon** and throughout Europe by Mikhail **Bakunin**, anarchists developed effective revolutionary movements in the 1860s and participated in the **First International** (1864–1872) alongside followers of Marx, Louis Auguste Blanqui, Giuseppe Mazzini and the leaders of British **trade unions**. In the early years of the International, the Proudhonists opposed Marx's calls for the organization of the working class in trade unions and political parties. They demanded the abolition of the state and its replacement by spontaneously developed forms of self-government linked by loose federal structures. Marx considered that this stance deprived the working class of all political power and instead urged the workers to organize themselves in order to seize state power. Recognizing that new forms of socialist government would take time to develop, he argued that the modern bourgeois state needed to be replaced by the revolutionary **dictatorship of the proletariat**, taking as his model the democratic forms adopted by the **Paris Commune** of 1871. Marx believed that only when the working class seized state power could it bring about the end of class society and replace the state with a more open system of self-government. Mikhail Bakunin and his followers saw this as a smokescreen for replacing an oppressive bourgeois state with an oppressive state staffed by the followers of Marx. The anarchists also disagreed with Marx that the urban working class was the privileged agent for successful revolutionary change, arguing that all dependent peoples, including peasants, independent urban workers and the **lumpenproletariat**, constituted potential revolutionary forces. Although they recruited widely among these groups, their efforts were of limited success due to their continued unwillingness to participate in legal trade unions and political parties. This became a major source of tension between Marx and the anarchists in the International. He opposed Bakunin's support for secret insurrectionary organizations and denounced the involvement of some of his supporters in terrorism. In Marx's view this threatened to undo all the good work of the International by provoking state repression. His opposition to the anarchists was the decisive factor in his decision to move the International's headquarters to New York in 1872, effectively bringing its active life to a close.

animals   In the *Economic and Philosophical Manuscripts* (1844) Marx discusses the differences between humans and animals in order to establish what constitutes distinctively human **needs** and potentials. According to Marx, conscious life activity distinguishes humans from animals, for whereas animals are immediately one with their life activity, humans make their life activity the object of their will and **consciousness**. By creating a world of objects, humans prove themselves to be conscious species-beings, or, in other words, they demonstrate their **essence**. Although animals also produce, they do so only for what they or their young immediately need. Marx accepts that animals are able to develop their productive capabilities, as he makes clear in chapter seven of **Capital 1** (1867) when stating that tool-using and even tool-making is present 'in germ' amongst certain species of animals. However, he argues that this limited animal capability cannot be compared with the complexity characteristic of the human **labour** process. The key distinction is between intuition and rational intention. In the chapter on the labour process he comments that the work of bees and spiders is often more impressive than the efforts of architects and weavers, but concludes that what distinguishes the worst architect from the best of bees is that the architect 'builds the cell in his mind before he constructs it in wax'. Marx's discussion of the human–animal distinction is carefully worded so as not to imply disrespect to animals, although this is not always apparent in English translations. In the passages dealing with the distinction between humans and other animals in both the *Manuscripts* and *Capital* 1, most of the English translations have insisted on describing animal life as primitive or low-level, implying deficiency by using the word 'mere', but Marx is careful to avoid this.

Although Marx's intention in discussing the distinction between humans and other animals is primarily to elucidate what it is to be human, he nevertheless argues that there are animal needs, with the clear implication that they should be respected by humans. When discussing the plight of the impoverished native Irish in the *Manuscripts*, he comments that not only have they been deprived of their human needs but that even their animal needs are not met. He goes on to say that animals have the need to hunt, to roam and to have companionship. His sympathies towards animals are revealed in a passage in **On the Jewish Question** (1844) in which he cites approvingly the view of the sixteenth-century German revolutionary Thomas Müntzer that 'all creatures have been turned into **property**, the fishes in the water, the birds in the air, the plants on the earth; the creatures, too, must become free'.

appearance   Forms of phenomena that must be penetrated to expose the underlying **essence** of social reality. Marx's dialectical approach suggests that when we begin to examine phenomena we do so as they appear in reality, and at the level of appearance. **Capitalism**, for example, seems to be a free, equal and open society. However, in essence it is really exploitative and based on the appropriation of **surplus value**. Consequently, its inner logic and real relations remain hidden from sight. Marx argues that as bourgeois theorists take the appearances of capitalism for granted, they therefore cannot grasp the true **nature** and workings of the system.

Aristotle (384–322 BC)   Greek philosopher described by Marx in *Capital* **1** (1867) as a genius and the 'greatest thinker of antiquity'. Marx read Aristotle deeply for the first time in 1839 while working on his *Doctoral Dissertation* (1841) and there are numerous references to his work in both the dissertation and the preparatory notes. Shortly before writing the *Economic and Philosophical Manuscripts* (1844) Marx translated

Aristotle's *De Anima* ('On the Soul') into German, and this influence can be seen in Marx's discussion of what it is to be truly human. Marx agrees with Aristotle that humans are by **nature** social and rational beings and that it is necessary to develop all the senses in order to lead a fully developed life. The Aristotelian emphasis on humans as quintessentially social beings is used by Marx to attack liberal assumptions about the autonomous **individual**. More generally, Marx adopts Aristotle's **method** of identifying the **essence** of things and the expression or distortion of that essence in its social development or **appearance**. In *A Contribution to the Critique of Political Economy* (1859) and later in *Capital* 1 Marx praises Aristotle for being the first thinker to analyze the value-form in economics. He notes Aristotle's 'genius' in discovering a relation of **equality** in the value-expression of commodities. For Aristotle, **money** enables the fair **exchange** of goods by making them commensurable. However, Marx comments that Aristotle did not go further by establishing what explains commensurability, i.e. the amount of **abstract labour** involved in the creation of the goods. In his view, Aristotle failed to understand that labour was the common ingredient because he lived in a slave society that lacked a conception of human equality. It was only when the idea of equality had taken root that the basis of exchange **value** could be established. Marx also appreciated Aristotle's denunciation of money-lending as a distortion of the essential function of money as a means of exchange.

Many scholars have argued that Aristotle's ethics exerted a significant influence on Marx. Certainly the passages on what it is to be human in the *Manuscripts* are consistent with Aristotle's views of humans as social and rational beings. Marx's commitment to human **freedom** is also similar to Aristotle's commitment to *eudaemonia*, or human flourishing.

art References to art in its many forms are scattered throughout Marx's writings and this infuses his understanding of the creative powers of human beings. He was introduced to the great works of literature from a very early age, most notably Homer, **Shakespeare** and Goethe. Whilst at the University of Bonn, where he took a course in the history of modern art, and later at Berlin between 1835–1841, he accompanied his study of philosophy, history and **law** with that of literature, composed his own poetry and attempted to write novels. He also studied the aesthetic works of Kant, Fichte, Lessing, Schelling, Schiller and **Hegel** and read extensively on the history of art. He was meant to contribute to a study of Hegel's aesthetics and philosophy of **religion** in a book to be edited by Bruno Bauer, but this was never published. The only explicit engagement he had with art later was an 1857 encyclopedia article he was commissioned to write but failed to finish.

One crucial way art informs his work is in the way that Marx sees human beings as artists themselves when they engage in an affirmation of their creative and productive powers. In the *Economic and Philosophical Manuscripts* (1844) Marx captures this through the way humans assert their **species-being**. He argues that non-human **animals** remain tied to their instincts and produce only for what they materially need. Humans, on the other hand, produce beyond such basic **needs**, in the **form** of intellectual and spiritual endeavours that manifest themselves in **culture**. Such an understanding of humans as artists is, of course, negated in **capitalism** through **alienation**, but it is Marx's hope that in a non-alienated world the true artistic and productive powers of humans would predominate.

This theme continues in *The German Ideology* (1845–1846), where Marx argues that the **mode of production** in any given society should not simply be considered as the means to reproduce ourselves physically. Rather, it should also cover our activity in terms of collective expression, imagination and **consciousness** in which we affirm ourselves: what we would call art. All art is therefore shaped by the productive practices prevailing at the time, but as active subjects humans relate in a complex and vibrant manner to these often alienating situations, which arise in particular from the division of **labour** in society. Marx argues that a society based on the division of labour severely limits spontaneous and diverse creative activity, and instead forces people into a single activity that they must perfect in order to maintain their livelihood. The negative effects of the division of labour even extend to artistic talent itself, which becomes concentrated in particular individuals whilst being generally suppressed in the masses. Even within these artistic individuals, the division of labour forces their creative activity into one aspect of artistic endeavour – as a painter or a sculptor, for example. Similarly, the demand for their work and the conditions of human culture of the society they are in also determine the extent to which they will successfully develop their talents. So even the great classical artists such as Raphael, Leonardo de Vinci and Titian, Marx maintains, all produced under these constraints. In contrast, in a communist society, the artist breaks free from these restrictions because there are now no painters as such, but only people who engage in painting among other activities, once the division of labour has been overcome. Marx contends, then, that individuals could become creatively multifaceted in communist society.

The role of the division of labour also forces Marx to consider how art is related to the technology pertaining to past and future societies. In the *Grundrisse* (1857–1858) he poses the question of how the technologically advanced society that had emerged from the industrial **revolution** could still be charmed by Greek art, given the social conditions that created it had now ceased to exist. Marx's response is that Greek art as all art, from whatever epoch, teaches us about the material **production** and development of our societies. Art gives us an insight into the **nature** of production in societies in general and also shows us how artistic and economic production develops, albeit unevenly rather than in parallel with each other. Greek art itself was, for Marx, an expression of the highest of human values.

—B—

Bakunin, Mikhail (1814–1876) A Russian aristocrat by birth, Bakunin was one of the leading exponents of **anarchism**, a doctrine that rivaled Marxism in its appeal to revolutionary workers. Marx and Bakunin first met in Paris in the autumn of 1844 during discussions with **Proudhon**. Later on they became bitterly opposed, theoretically and politically, about the nature of revolutionary political activity in bourgeois society and the nature of the post-revolutionary **state**. In *Statism and Anarchy* (1873) Bakunin accused Marx of planning an authoritarian state. Marx responded in his *Conspectus on Bakunin's Statism and Anarchy* (1874–1875) by charging Bakunin with having no understanding of the realities of the **politics** of **class struggle**. Bakunin wanted the immediate revolutionary abolition of the state whereas Marx advocated its replacement by a revolutionary **dictatorship of the proletariat** that would initiate the move towards communist society. For

Bakunin this amounted to replacing one **form** of repressive state with another staffed by followers of Marx. In turn, Marx accused Bakunin of operating within a hierarchical conspiratorial organization that had ambitions to take power into its own hands after the **revolution**. Politically, Marx opposed Bakunin and his followers in the **First International** (1864–1872) for their uncompromising opposition to participation in **trade unions** or legal political parties. He judged that Bakunin and his followers obstructed constructive political work by the **working class**, leaving it only to 'wait for the day of universal liquidation – the last judgement'.

base and superstructure   Marx uses this architectural metaphor in the **Preface to *A Contribution to the Critique of Political Economy*** (1859) to summarize his conception of historical development. The real base (*die reale Basis*) of society is the economic structure of society, the 'totality' of the social relations of **production**. This base shapes the legal and social superstructure (*Überbau*) along with appropriate forms of social **consciousness**. Marx contends that the **mode of production** conditions the general process of social, political and intellectual life. Whereas idealist conceptions of historical development had emphasized the importance of ideas developing independently and giving rise to social change, Marx argues that the ideas themselves have to be explained by looking at how economic power struggles have developed. He reiterates the point first made in ***The German Ideology*** (1845–1846) that it is not consciousness that determines existence, but social existence that determines consciousness. The problem with the metaphor is that it suggests a static condition, but Marx gives it a developmental dynamic. He suggests that at a certain point the productive forces of society come into **contradiction** (*Widerspruch*) with the relations of production, which means that the old **property** relations are no longer compatible with efficient economic development. For example, a legal and political system developed under **feudalism** provides major obstacles to the emergence of **capitalist** relations of production, and if the latter are to develop more freely a social **revolution** must take place. In other words, there is a constantly changing relationship within the base between the forces of production and the relations of production. When the contradiction between them explodes the old mode of production, changes in the economic base lead to 'the transformation of the whole immense superstructure'. Marx describes **law**, **politics**, **religion**, **art** and **philosophy** as elements of the superstructure and argues that in these areas the underlying causes of the struggles for power are not always obvious to those engaged in these struggles. He comments that just as it would be a mistake to judge people by what they think about themselves, so too it would be wrong to judge social change by the rhetoric of the activists. Importantly, Marx insists that no social order is ever destroyed while it is still successfully developing the productive forces, and any new social order must already have proved its superiority within the old society. If a successful revolution is to occur, **capitalism** should be evidently dysfunctional and superior socialist forms should already be available. In terms of the metaphor, this means that the superstructure not only reflects the dominant power relations in the base, but also reflects the struggles against that dominance.

The base–superstructure metaphor is used to offer a methodological guide to investigate how politics, law and **culture** develop in relation to the constantly changing economic structure. However, it has given rise to conflicting and controversial interpretations. One alleges that the metaphor implies a crudely deterministic relationship between the economic structure and the elements of the superstructure. Where Marx writes that the base conditions the superstructure, the word 'conditions' (*bestimmen*) has often been translated or understood as 'determines', meaning that there is a direct causal relationship and that it is possible to read off all developments in the superstructure as simple reflections of the economic structure. Marx's own political and economic writings make it clear that the relationship is much more complex. Another problem is the implication that historical change occurs as a result of structural factors in which human agency plays only a pre-determined role. Unlike *The Communist Manifesto* (1848) there is no emphasis on **class struggle**, so that the verdict that capitalism is the last antagonistic **form** of the social process of production has a teleological flavour. This is perhaps a consequence of presenting a general 'guiding principle' to understanding socio-historical change in little more than a single page. 'Politics' is explained as a reflection of the economic structure, but the economic structure is dynamic, and the political struggles will reflect that dynamism. This is made clear when Marx applies his historical **method** in a complex and nuanced way in *The Eighteenth Brumaire of Louis Bonaparte* (1852). Here he argues that a whole superstructure of feelings, illusions and views of life arises on the basis of different forms of property, and provides an analysis of how these property interests invariably assert themselves at the expense of political principles in times of crisis. (See also **historical materialism**.)

bourgeoisie   The French name given by Marx to describe the owners of capital. In *The German Ideology* (1845–1846) he describes the development of the bourgeoisie in the towns of the early modern period as a **class** of independent traders and manufacturers who had emerged from the collapse of the old guild system. They engaged in struggles with the landed aristocracy to create a political and legal system that would promote their economic interests, a **class struggle** that was still going on during Marx's lifetime. The bourgeoisie, through its economic power, was able to transform the relations of **production** in Europe so that production for **profit**, or 'production for the sake of production', became the hallmark of the bourgeois **mode of production**, as opposed to production for use. All previous indicators of **wealth** and power became secondary to capital ownership, and even the landed aristocracy became the owners of landed capital and were therefore 'bourgeoisified', as Marx put it in *The Eighteenth Brumaire of Louis Bonaparte* (1852).

The rise of the bourgeoisie is summarized in exhilarated fashion in *The Communist Manifesto* (1848). The bourgeoisie is credited with putting an end to all feudal and patriarchal relations and with developing more productive forces in 100 years than all preceding generations put together. It had done so vigorously, with 'everlasting uncertainty and agitation', and through its **exploitation** of the **world market** it had given a 'cosmopolitan character' to production and **consumption** in every country. In so doing, it had helped to overcome 'national narrow-mindedness' as the whole world is brought into its mode of production. Marx concludes that the bourgeoisie had created a world after its own image. However, there are also problems facing the bourgeoisie. The market-based economic system it had created expands in impressive surges, but its inherent instability is demonstrated by recurring **economic crises**. The bourgeoisie is likened to a sorcerer 'who is no longer able to control the powers of the nether world whom he has called up by his spells'. Above all, the bourgeoisie produces its own 'gravediggers', the **working class** or **proletariat**, on whose exploitation its power depends. The working class is at first impoverished and abject, but it grows, organizes and begins its class struggle with the bourgeoisie. Marx predicts that at a certain time in this struggle a small section of the **ruling class** will cut itself adrift and join the revolutionary class. In the course of its struggles with the aristocracy, the bourgeoisie attacks autocratic political systems and demands a democratic republic. However, the increasingly powerful working class can take advantage of the more open political system and 'win the battle for **democracy**', seizing power from the bourgeoisie and ushering in the classless society.

When Marx looks in greater detail at how the bourgeoisie operates politically we see a much more complex picture emerge. In the *Brumaire* he describes a situation in which the interests of the landed, financial and industrial sections of the bourgeoisie are represented by separate factions who find it hard to reconcile their differences. They are only able to cooperate effectively when faced with the threat of the revolutionary workers. At other times the fragmented bourgeoisie is unable to control **state** power, and when Bonaparte abolishes the National Assembly and declares himself Emperor the state power appears to have attained 'a completely autonomous position'. However, Bonaparte is still obliged to promote economic development to the benefit of the bourgeoisie, and in this sense the state is used to force the different factions to work together for their own collective good. The simple model of direct class rule, as described in *The Communist Manifesto*, is not reflected in the intricate relationship between the bourgeoisie and the state described in the *Brumaire*. In the French Second Republic the bourgeoisie was unable to manipulate collectively the state, but the state was still obliged to operate in its interests. One of the things that Marx points out in the *Brumaire* is that the members of the republican opposition that loosely represented the interests of the industrial bourgeoisie were not for the most part factory owners, but rather writers, lawyers and officials motivated initially by political rather than economic interests. Although they discarded their political principles when the class struggle became violent, Marx's analysis makes it clear that political representation did not necessarily directly reflect economic interest.

bureaucracy Marx consistently denounced the bureaucracy of the modern **state**, the public bodies staffed by large numbers of salaried administrators. Politically, he associates the bureaucracy with the dominant economic interests within society and views it as one part of its repressive apparatus. He first felt the oppressive power of the Prussian bureaucracy when the paper he edited, the *Rheinische Zeitung*, was banned by the

Prussian censorship in April 1842. He had already denounced the Prussian Censorship Instruction but was unable to publish his opposition in Germany itself. The following year he rejected all justifications of the existing state system in the then-unpublished **Critique of Hegel's Philosophy of Right** (1843). In Hegel's work, the bureaucracy or executive provides an effective **mediation** between the monarchy on the one hand and the corporations, or organizations of **civil society**, on the other. The members of the bureaucracy in the Prussian state were selected from the Junker **class**, the class of self-sufficient landowners who were deemed to be incorruptible and dedicated to the public good. In Hegel's terms they were the 'universal' class, able to manage the many conflicting 'particular' interests of civil society. Marx rejects this 'fiction of harmony', arguing instead that the civil servants, like the state itself, represent the interests of the owners of private **property**.

In his political writings on France, Marx argues that the **bourgeoisie** have a major interest in maintaining an extensive state machine, a 'parasitic' body of some half a million officials that provides jobs and salaries to those who were not making **money** by other means. Marx argues that the bourgeoisie was compelled by its class position to support the power of the executive, even at the expense of its own parliamentary power. The Second Empire further expanded the state power to the extent that in **The Civil War in France** (1871) Marx comments that it apparently soared high above society, beset by rottenness and corruption. He contrasts this with the **Paris Commune** (1871), which, he claims, made 'cheap government' a reality by replacing expensive state functionaries with officials who worked for a fraction of their salaries. However, despite his consistent denunciation of bureaucracy, Marx was faced with a problem he did not confront directly, namely, how the regulation of national **production** according to a 'common plan', as called for in The Civil War in France, could be achieved without a large bureaucracy, and indeed one with immense strategic power. In the first edition of **The Eighteenth Brumaire of Louis Bonaparte** (1852) he argued that the demolition of the state machine would not endanger centralization, describing bureaucracy as 'only the low and brutal **form** of a centralization that is still afflicted with its opposite, with **feudalism**'. However, Marx did not explain how the central control of a common plan could be implemented without a bureaucracy. The passage endorsing centralization was cut from the second edition of 1869, probably to avoid drawing criticism from the anarchists and their sympathizers in the **First International** (1864–1872).

capital   A mobile **form** of **property** based on **commodity production** and **exchange**. In *Capital* **1** (1867) Marx introduces the term capital in relation to the circulation of commodities to show that the first **form** it takes is **money** (M), which is transformed into capital (C) and back into money (M): M-C-M. However, a **capitalist** only uses money to buy commodities to make more money, **surplus value** (M'), what Marx refers to as buying in order to sell. This is in contrast to selling in order to buy, where commodities are turned into money and then the money is turned into commodities (C-M-C) and equivalent is exchanged for equivalent. In the circulation of capital in the form of money there is no such equivalence, because a capitalist invests with the sole purpose of getting more back than he or she put in, which is surplus value. Marx refers to this process as the valorization of **value**, where the circulation of money as capital is an end in itself and the movement of capital is therefore limitless. He indicates that capital exists only as part of this valorization process, so if a sum of money is hoarded and not put into circulation as part of this procedure, then it is no longer capital.

When money-capital is invested within the valorization process it also takes two other important forms: constant and variable capital. Constant capital refers to capital that has been used to acquire such things as raw materials and machinery, what Marx also calls dead **labour**, and variable capital refers to capital that has been turned into **labour power**, what Marx also calls living labour. Constant capital, as its name implies, adds no value to the creation of a commodity, whereas variable capital, again as its name implies, does so by creating its own value, the wage, and an excess, which is surplus value. Through variable capital in the form of labour power, the **working class** is integrated into the process of valorization, not just in a subservient manner, but in a dialectical process of **class struggle**. Marx's dynamic understanding of capital as a social relation is therefore in stark contrast to bourgeois theorists who see it only fetishistically in things such as the means of production or investment funds. To counter this further, Marx uses the striking imagery of capital as 'dead labour, that vampire-like, only lives by sucking living labour, and lives the more, the more labour it sucks'. Consequently, by incorporating living labour power in this way, capital itself becomes an 'animated monster'. (See also **commodity fetishism**, **fictitious capital** and **mode of production**.)

Capital 1 (1867)   The first volume of Marx's analysis of the **capitalist mode of production**, subtitled *A Critique of Political Economy*. Only Volume 1, which was completed and edited by Marx, was published during his lifetime. It was not translated from the German into English until 1887. The others, *Capital 2* (1863–1878) and *Capital 3* (1864–1865), were unfinished and published under the editorship of **Engels** after Marx's death. A further volume, ***Theories of Surplus Value*** (1861–1863), was also unfinished and again published posthumously. *Capital* 1, as Marx informs us in the Preface to the first edition of that volume, was also a continuation of his 1859 work ***A Contribution to the Critique of Political Economy***, which he says is here explained and developed more extensively.

In 1857, when Marx was making his first plan of the whole enterprise, he envisaged a six-volume study comprising the following topics: **Capital**, Landed **Property**, Wage **Labour**, the **State**, International Trade, and the **World Market** and Crises. By 1865–1856, he had decided on the four volumes, with Volume 1 focusing on the process of **production** of capital. Volume 2 was to focus on the process of circulation of capital; Volume 3 was to look at the various forms of the process of capital as a totality; and Volume 4 would deal with the history of the theory. It is important to remember that Volume 1 is but one part, albeit a major one, of a greater project in the schema that constitutes *Capital*.

In the first Preface, and in anticipation perhaps of what was to come, Marx states that the first chapter of Volume 1 would prove the most difficult for the reader to understand. However, he then adds that beginnings are always difficult in all sciences, and claims that, with the exception of the section on the **form** of value, difficulty was not an accusation to be levelled at Volume 1 overall.

The work is divided into eight parts comprising the following headings: Part 1: Commodities and **Money**; Part 2: The Transformation of Money into Capital: Part 3: The Production of Absolute **Surplus Value**; Part 4: The Production of Relative Surplus Value; Part 5: The Production of Absolute and Relative Surplus Value; Part 6; **Wages**; Part 7: The Process of **Accumulation** of Capital; Part 8: So-Called Primitive Accumulation.

Part 1 begins with an analysis of the **commodity** because it is the most elementary form in which the **wealth** of capitalist society appears. Immediately, then, Marx is making the point that capital is a world of appearances, and it is through his dialectical **method** that he will penetrate these appearances to reveal the inner **essence** of capital and expose its laws of motion. By beginning his analysis with the commodity it allows Marx to show that it has both a use value and an exchange value, and capital is the rule of exchange value over use value. This enables him to develop his analysis from the commodity to money, which acts as universal form of exchange in a society based on commodity production and exists as the money-form of **value**. The whole of this process is shrouded in **commodity fetishism**, as the labour producing these commodities becomes almost hidden from sight and the commodities themselves take on a life of their own that seem devoid of any social content.

Such mystification of the real relations of production deepens even further when Marx considers the transformation of money into capital in Part 2 and begins his examination of the sale and purchase of **labour power**. Marx states that in the sphere of circulation labour and capital appear to confront each other on a fair and equal basis, but to discover the real relations that govern the operations of the system means entering the 'hidden abode of production'. Hence, he makes his major discovery of the secret of the source for profit-making and the production of surplus value. That commodity is labour power, which is not only a source of value, but a commodity that produces more value than it has itself.

In Part 3 he first considers surplus value production in its absolute form and shows how capitalists attempt to increase it by lengthening the **working day**. Indeed, chapter ten on the working day is a particularly important historical document because Marx uses government records on the conditions in factories to expose the brutal **exploitation** that was suffered by the **working class** at this time. He also shows the working day to be a site of continuing **class struggle** between capital and labour around the issue of the extraction of surplus value. In Part 4 he considers surplus value in its relative form, where the unpaid surplus labour of the workers is extracted through intensifying work to make the workers work harder during a shorter period of time, which takes in issues of the division of labour and the use of machinery. In Part 5 he considers both of these latter processes together through various examinations of the relation between variable capital, living labour power, and constant capital, dead labour, or machinery. Part 6 is concerned with the role of wages within capitalist production and Part 7 considers the process of accumulation, which capitalists must constantly engage in if they are to survive the incessant pressure of **competition** that they inflict on each other in the search for surplus value. Part 8 considers the expulsion of the agricultural **population** from the land, what Marx calls primitive accumulation, which he describes as being bloody and violent. This process resulted in the move away from feudal relations of production to the new social relations of capitalist and worker, which was to typify the new capitalist mode of production.

Marx's analysis of capital in Volume 1 is without doubt one of the most original and daring ever written. It is infused with a dialectical under-standing of conceptual reality, displays an erudite knowledge of political economy across a wide range of thinkers and grasps the historical devel-opment of humanity over centuries, all supported by evidence developed from the thinkers he was critiquing himself. Using **state** sources that he showed to be condemning the very system they were meant to support, combined with his use of literary and artistic works to enhance and illustrate his own arguments, the book is unsurpassed in its scope and style and still remains as an affront to all those who perpetuate and act as apologists for capitalist **ideology** today.

Capital **2 (1863–1878, posthumously published 1885)** The second volume of Marx's analysis of the **capitalist mode of production**, which focuses on the process of circulation through a critique of **political economy**. Volume 2 was unfinished and published after Marx's death under the editorship of **Engels**. Often referred to as the 'forgotten volume', its importance stems from Marx's attempt to extend the analysis of the process of **production** in Volume 1 to consider the social intertwining of the different capitals, or the different parts of **capital**, and of revenue. For example, he says that in Volume 1 he assumed that in the circuit of capital a certain amount of **money** (M) invested in production (C) would, through the **exploitation** of **labour power**, result in the production of **surplus value**, and hence more money (M'), which would find in the **market** the possibility for further expansion. What he wants to investigate here is what happens to this extra money in its different forms on the market through its own movement, and through the movement of commodities, in this process of further expansion. The focus, then, is on how value and surplus value is realized in its various forms on the market through what Marx refers to as the capitalization of surplus value and expanded reproduction. Marx argues that this process of reproduction of capital is linked to a general movement of circulation that involves the sum total of capital in society. For example, part of the surplus value created by **labour** and taken by capitalists must be re-invested again, that is capitalized on, through the purchase of the means of production and labour power to create further surplus value in a process of capital **accumulation** and expanded reproduction. For Marx, expanded reproduction therefore implies bigger and bigger units of production involving more workers, more machinery and the production of more commodities, constituting a greater value than the previous process of production and hence more profits so the process can begin again. However, given that capital is a system where production is private and not consciously planned, this process is fraught with problems such as under- and over-production and the disequilibrium that can occur between supply and demand. Recognizing this allows Marx to offer an initial outline of the operations of the trade cycle and also to show how growth in capital will always be uneven.

Capital **3 (1864–1865, posthumously published 1894)** Edited and published by **Engels** after Marx's death and based on manuscripts written by Marx in 1864–1865. In a letter to Louis Kugelmann in October 1866 Marx had promised a separate volume dealing with the 'structure of the process as a whole' and for the most part this is what Volume 3 delivers, in 7 parts, with 52 chapters in all. In contrast to the prevalent **political economy** of the day, Marx reveals a system riddled with **contradiction,** inherently unstable and crisis-ridden. The first part deals with the **transformation problem**, the technically complex problem of transforming Marx's category of **value** into **profit**. The second part deals with how variations in the rate of profit occur and how they are equalized in the average rate of profit. The third part deals with the **tendency of the rate of profit to fall** and is Marx's clearest exposition of the contradictions that beset **capitalism** and make it unsustainable in the long term. It provides the underlying reasons for the recurrent systemic breakdowns in the **form** of **economic crises**.

The fourth part deals with commercial and financial **capital**. At the end of part two Marx had already commented on the vulnerability of business to 'paroxysms of speculation'. In part four he analyzes commercial capital and its turnover, as well as devoting separate chapters to money-dealing capital and the history of merchants' capital. Part five is the least reliable section, for Engels reveals that he was left without a complete draft or even a plan. It deals with the division of profit into interest and the profit of the enterprise. It includes detailed discussion of the specialized role of supervision in the **labour** process in which he contrasts the coercive **nature** of work under capitalism and **slavery** with the non-antagonistic experience of the cooperative factory. He also comments that the credit system will serve as a 'powerful lever' in the course of transition from capitalism to the **mode of production** of associated labour. Part six deals with the transformation of surplus profit into ground rent, in the course of which he critiques the work of **Ricardo**. Part seven deals with revenues and their sources and continues the work undertaken in *Capital* **2** (1863–1878). Also found here is Marx's picture of communist society as the 'realm of **freedom**'.

Marx also supplies an alternative summary of his theory of historical development (**historical materialism**). In chapter forty-seven he argues that the specific form in which unpaid surplus labour is pumped out of the direct producers 'determines the relationship of domination and servitude, as this grows out of **production** itself and reacts back on it in turn as a determinant'. In this version there is an element of reciprocity that is absent from the 1859 **Preface**. He also adds an important warning against oversimplified application of this perspective, arguing that the economic basis will display endless variations and gradations in its **appearance** as a result of different historical, natural and cultural conditions, and that these can be understood only through empirical analysis.

capitalism   An economic system where investment in and ownership of the means of **production**, distribution and **exchange** of **wealth** is made and maintained on the basis of private **property** by individuals or corporations in a process of profit-maximization. The term was first used in 1854 by William Makepeace Thackeray in his novel *The Newcomes* to refer to someone who has ownership of **capital**. Ironically, Marx did not use the term capitalism (*Kapitalismus*) in any of his main writings, preferring instead to use terms such as the **capitalist mode of production** (*kapitalistische Produktionsform*), bourgeois mode of production (*bürgerlichen Produktionsform*), capitalist system (*kapitalistischen System)* or capitalist period (*kapitalistischen Periode*). He only used it in the late 1870s in his correspondence with Russian writers regarding the issue of Russia's transition to capitalism.

capitalist   Defined by Marx in *Capital* 1 (1867) as the conscious bearer of the movement of profit-making and an owner of the means of production. A capitalist is concerned with the limitless process of buying commodities in order to sell, through the circulation of money as capital with the aim of making a profit. Marx denotes this process as the spending of money (M) on commodities (C) such as labour power and machinery, which are then put to work to create commodities for exchange in the pursuit of surplus value, and hence more money (M') than was first invested. It is what Marx calls a process of the valorization of value, which is an objective end in itself, and a reflection of the subjective driving force of the capitalist to accumulate more and more wealth. The capitalist is therefore the personification of capital and is its bodily form endowed with a consciousness and a will that is initially driven by greed in the pursuit of self-enrichment and power. By focusing on a capitalist as a bearer of the social relation of capital, Marx makes the point that as an individual a capitalist may be a model citizen and even a member of a charity such as the RSPCA. However, the fact that a capitalist engages in exploitation shows that he or she is a representative of something that 'has no heart in its breast'. This inhuman aspect is captured further by Marx's contention that in this process the capitalist devours and appropriates the living labour power of the worker as the life-blood of capital.

To illustrate the role of the capitalist further, Marx contrasts the capitalist with the miser. Whereas the miser is a capitalist gone mad, the capitalist is a rational miser, because unlike the miser who seeks to increase the value of his or her money by saving, the capitalist attempts to increase the value of his or her money by throwing it again and again into circulation in the pursuit of surplus value. The capitalist then uses this surplus value to satisfy two conflicting tendencies: his or her own **consumption** and the need to re-invest in the process of **accumulation**. The self-valorization of **capital** – the creation of surplus value – is therefore the determining, dominating and overriding purpose of the capitalist; it is the absolute motive and content of his or her activity. It is the rationalized motive and aim of the hoarder, which makes it plain that the capitalist is as much a cog in the machine of capitalist production as the worker, although in a quite different manner. Due to the external force of laws of capitalist **competition** and the need to accumulate, anyone assuming the role of capitalist will be forced to act in this way, irrespective of whether his or her intentions are good or bad. It is this need to accrue surplus value and accumulate that binds the behaviour of all capitalists together, whilst at the same time forcing them to oppose each other through the ruthless force of competition.

citizen   Marx thought of citizenship as denoting the communal ideal of politically emancipated society. However, in ***On the Jewish Question*** (1844) he makes it clear that political **emancipation** did not amount to **human** emancipation. Political emancipation, in the shape of a **democratic** republic, produces, on the one hand, an egoistic **individual** competing in **civil society**, and on the other, the citizen, or 'moral person'. Only with the abolition of **class** society can human emancipation be achieved, when individuals turn 'abstract' citizenship into real communal relations.

civil society   The term given by Marx to the realm of social relations outside the immediate operations of the **state**. He develops his early ideas on civil society in the ***Critique of Hegel's Philosophy of Right*** (1843), accepting Hegel's conceptualization of civil society (*bürgerliche Gesellschaft*) as the free **market** in which individuals pursued their private interests. Unlike **Hegel**, Marx does not consider that the state offers an ethical communal counterpart to the egoism of market society, considering it rather to be a protective force ruling on behalf of the propertied classes. Whereas Hegel identifies a **contradiction** between the state and civil society that is capable of resolution through institutional **mediation**, Marx considers the relationship to be an essential contradiction. In ***On the Jewish Question***, written in 1843, he refers to civil society as the sphere of egoism, using Hobbes' phrase of the **war** of each against all. In the

Economic and Philosophical Manuscripts (1844) he talks of a prosperous society as an ideal of bourgeois civil society that brings only 'misery for the worker'. However, while this negative view of civil society was empirically grounded, he did not see civil society itself as static or without potential. In **The Holy Family** (1845) he rejects the view that civil society is atomized, for even egoistic human beings need society, and even though human properties are alienated it is still 'natural necessity' as well as interest that hold the members of civil society together. We learn from Marx's reflections in the **Preface to A Contribution to the Critique of Political Economy** (1859) that it was around 1845–1846 that he began to understand that legal relations and political forms could be understood only by examining their origins in civil society, conceived of as the totality of the material conditions of life. The 'anatomy' of this civil society was to be discovered through the study of political economy. In this view, civil society constantly changes until its basis in private **property** is challenged by the **working class**. Only with the abolition of private property can the working class abolish both civil society and the state, replacing them with the association of free producers.

Civil War in France **(1871)** This pamphlet analyzed the short-lived existence of the **Paris Commune** and appeared shortly after its suppression by the army of the new French Third Republic on 28 May 1871. Commissioned by the General Council of the **First International** (1864–1872) and written in English, it is a wholly sympathetic account of the Commune and is significant for our understanding of Marx's political philosophy in three major respects. The first is his enthusiasm for the direct democratic measures taken by the Commune, which he considered far superior to the representative **democracy** of the French Second Republic (1848–1851) that he had analyzed in *The Eighteenth Brumaire of Louis Bonaparte* (1852). The measures endorsed by Marx were designed to destroy the entrenched power of unelected military, legal and bureaucratic elites in the **state**, and to ensure that the members of the Commune were truly representative. They included the election of all delegates by universal male franchise with the right to recall those who did not fulfil their mandates, as well as their payment at the level of workers' **wages**. The Commune abolished the standing army and replaced it with a militia and introduced the election of judges and magistrates. It was a working body as well as a legislature, with delegates responsible for enacting policies, bringing them closer to the people who would be affected by them. Marx's enthusiasm for this radical democracy indicates that the **dictatorship of the proletariat** that he envisaged entailed vigorous democratic life combined with a determination to protect its power.

A second theoretical issue is the justification for supporting the Commune, which was portrayed by its enemies as a revolt against a government legally elected by universal male franchise. From the text itself we learn that Marx did not consider the Commune to be **socialist**, and from his correspondence we know that he considered it had little chance of success. However, Marx not only defended it as a **working-class** government that introduced participatory democracy, but justified its right to defy the national government because the latter could claim no legitimacy. He goes to great lengths to argue that the new government was essentially a betrayal of those who were unwilling to surrender to Prussia, including those in Paris who had withstood the Prussian siege for four months. Following the replacement of the Emperor Napoleon after his capture by the Prussians, a Government of National Defence was set up under General Trochu. Marx states that the decision of some of its key members to surrender involved an agreement with the Prussians that an election be called within eight days, even though one third of the country was occupied and no electioneering was permitted there. Paris was deliberately under-represented and only the government leaders were able to appeal for support. The election returned a right-wing, rural majority, but it could not be regarded as a legitimate mandate by any standards. In the *Brumaire* Marx had not made an issue of the legitimacy of the elections of April 1848, or indeed of the justification of the workers' uprising in June 1848, but in his account of the Commune he clearly sees the need to make it clear that the Commune was not acting in defiance of democracy.

The third point concerns the implications of the Commune for future socialist political strategy. Marx's conclusion that the Commune was 'the glorious harbinger of a new society' indicates the importance he attached to its radical democratic practices, and in particular the measures taken to ensure that real power was in the hands of delegates rather than military or bureaucratic elites. The proposed national model of Communes indicated that both urban and rural Communes would send deputies to the national Commune in Paris, and that the 'few but important functions' remaining for central government would be controlled by the national Commune. Marx envisages these functions eventually including the regulation of national **production** by a common plan. He comments that the workers had no preconceived utopian scheme to be introduced by decree, but rather knew that they had to work out their own **emancipation** through long struggles, transforming both themselves and their circumstances. He argues that the only ideal that the workers had to realize was to set free the elements of the new society with which the 'collapsing bourgeois society itself was pregnant'. In defeat, he writes, the martyrs will be part of the collective memory of the working class, while for their exterminators, history has already nailed them 'to that eternal pillory from which all the prayers of their priests will not avail to redeem them'.

The implications for future strategy are ambiguous. On the one hand, the assertion that the working class cannot simply lay hold of the ready-made state machinery and 'wield it for its own purposes' appears to point in the direction of revolutionary root and branch change which is unlikely to be peaceful. On the other hand, the horrendous cost of such a risky endeavour cautioned against insurrectionary tactics. The following year, in a speech in Amsterdam, Marx declared that the workers could achieve their goals peacefully in democratic states. When the Third Republic itself was threatened with a right-wing *coup d'état* in 1877, Marx wrote to his friend Friedrich Adolph Sorge that he hoped the bourgeois republic would be victorious so that France would not again be returned to dictatorship. In a letter to Ferdinand Domela Nieuwenhuis in 1881, he confided that the Commune could not have succeeded, but 'with a modicum of common sense' could have reached a compromise with the government to the benefit of the whole people.

class   Despite class being at the forefront of Marx's critique of **capital**, he never gave a detailed and systematic account of the term during his lifetime. Hence there is much controversy over what constitutes class for Marx. All that can be done is to highlight those areas where he discusses the notion of class and draw some inferences of what the term means in his analysis of **capitalist** society.

In *Capital 3* (1864–1865) there is an unfinished fragment of a chapter in which Marx starts to discuss class. He states that the question to be asked is: What makes a class? However, he then says that this arises from another question: What makes wage-labourers, capitalists and landowners the formative elements of the three great social classes? Initially, it seems that the answer appears to relate to their revenues in terms of **wages**, **profit** and ground-rent, which they accrue from the valorization of **labour power**, capital and landed **property** respectively. However, he rejects this because it would follow that other social groups, such as doctors and government officials, for example, would also constitute classes as their revenue flows from a different source. Revenue, therefore, cannot be the way to understand class as it means that there would be an infinite division of classes, which are then fragmented further due to the different interests that arise amongst different workers, capitalists and landowners. The fragment breaks off here, but Marx has asserted, contrary to the assumptions of most modern theorists on class, that it is not related to income. What, then, constitutes class?

In his early writings in the ***Critique of Hegel's Philosophy of Right*** (1843) Marx has a brief discussion of class in relation to the way the estates, constituted bodies of various kinds that existed in feudal and early absolutist societies, transformed into social classes through the advent of the French **Revolution** and the creation of **civil society** separate from the **state**. Class distinctions in civil society were merely social differences between people and therefore had no significance in political life. Marx argues that civil society exists as the class of private citizens in a fluid division of a mass of people that are arbitrary and without organization. Indeed, he notes that one particular feature of civil society is the absence of property and the class of immediate **labour**, which in this form only provides the initial ground of becoming a class. It is only with the coming together of people through organization, based on their **needs** and their work, that a class can be formed, and he next discusses this possibility in his ***Contribution to the Critique of Hegel's Philosophy of Right: Introduction*** (1844).

Marx's focus is on Germany at this time, and he observes that the country is like a theory that is separate from practice, implying that political **emancipation** is at a lower level than in other nations. He argues that a revolution can only occur if a passive element or material basis is present, namely, the people's needs. Marx asks whether the enormous gap that exists between the demands of German thought and the responses of German reality now corresponds to the same gap between both civil society and the state and civil society and itself. Will the theoretical needs be directly practical needs? It is not enough that thought should strive to realize itself; reality must itself strive towards thought. So Marx is positing a gap between **theory and practice** that exists in Germany at his time of writing. This gap resembles the separation between civil society and the state, which arises because Germany is behind other modern nations in terms of political emancipation and industrialization. No bourgeois class has come forward in civil society in Germany to enact a political revolution. What we have instead is opposing classes causing civil society to be in conflict within itself. Such is the backward **nature** of German society that partial emancipation of a bourgeois form is no longer possible except with a class that is under the compulsion of its immediate situation, of material necessity and of its chains themselves. That class is the **proletariat**: a class of civil society that is, at the same time, not a class of civil society, and even though the low level of industrial development in Germany means that the proletariat is only beginning to appear, it is still only this class that can achieve the emancipation of Germany itself. For Marx, this is the only type of liberation that is practically possible for Germany if it is to cast off its feudal ties completely. The discord within civil society, along with its separation from the state, will then disappear. So Marx again understands class as a transformative and active aspect of human activity, and he identifies the proletariat as *the* class to enact revolutionary change.

In **The Communist Manifesto** (1848) Marx's emphasis on the active process involved in understanding class is further emphasized and explicitly linked with **class struggle**. He notes how throughout history there have been two main contending class relationships that exist antagonistically with each other. These class oppositions encompass freeman and slave, patrician and plebeian, lord and serf, and, finally, the **bourgeoisie** and proletariat of capitalism. Again, Marx emphasizes the transformative and active side of class composition. He notes how the bourgeoisie and the proletariat, the modern **working class**, were formed as opposing and antagonistic classes through a long course of historical development that was steeped in class struggle. Indeed, for Marx, the proletariat alone is really the revolutionary class, and although he recognizes that other classes exist, such as the lower middle class, the small manufacturer, the shopkeeper, the artisan and the peasant, he sees all these as being basically conservative and in the last instance reactionary. Even where these groups are revolutionary, they will only remain so, Marx contends, under the guidance of, and their impending transfer into, the proletariat. This will make them defend not their own present interests against the onslaught of capital, but the future interests of society as a whole. Marx even thinks this might be possible for the lowest strata of society, the **lumpenproletariat**, but cautions that given their conditions of life they are more likely to play the part of a bribed tool of reactionary intrigue. However, what is interesting in terms of Marx's understanding of class as an active process is that he does recognize the possibility of class formation across different strata of society and across different occupations, albeit under the tutelage of the proletariat.

In the later Marx of **Capital** **1** (1867) class mainly appears as an antagonistic relationship between capital and labour, which is personified in the form of the class struggle between workers and capitalists. Again, the understanding of class is mainly implicit and unfolds as Marx's argument develops throughout the work. It is with his initial starting point of the **commodity**, through to his examination of **exchange**, and the need to see the real relations of capitalist society in the hidden abode of **production** that allows Marx to identify these class relationships. On the one side is the owner of capital, the capitalist, and on the other side is the owner of labour power, the worker. Capital stands as the exploiter of labour in the thirst for **surplus value** and labour stands against capital for that very reason. Both are involved in a process of class struggle.

class consciousness   Although Marx famously remarked that human history had been the history of **class** struggles, he understood that these struggles were not always fought consciously by class actors fully aware of the priority of their material interests. In Marx's view, it is imperative for workers to achieve class consciousness in order to organize into political movements capable of achieving social **revolution**. Class consciousness involves recognition by workers that they share a common class position as exploited and oppressed, and an understanding that true **freedom** would be achieved only by replacing **capitalist** society with a classless society. In 1844 in the **Contribution to the Critique of Hegel's Philosophy of Right: Introduction** Marx first identifies the **working class** as the class that can achieve its own **emancipation** only by liberating all spheres of society and achieving 'the total redemption of humanity'. As Marx admitted, in Germany at that time the **working class** was only in its infancy, and it was to France and Britain that he looked for evidence that the class was developing a **consciousness** of its position. In **The Holy Family** (1845) there is a confident assertion that a large part of the English and French **proletariat** 'is already conscious of its historic task and is constantly working to develop that consciousness into complete clarity'. In **The German Ideology** (1845–1846) Marx argues that communist consciousness must become international or 'world historical' in response to the expansion of **capitalism**. He consistently stressed the need for **internationalism** in class consciousness, and in the **Critique of the Gotha Programme** (1875) he angrily criticizes the authors of the programme for neglecting this factor.

In **The Poverty of Philosophy** (1847) Marx draws an important distinction between a class characterized by a common situation but not yet united, and a class that is organized and is able to act as a 'class for itself'. Only through organizing in **trade unions** and political movements is it able to defend its class interests. This class in itself/for itself distinction is later developed in **The Eighteenth Brumaire of Louis Bonaparte** (1852), but this time in his discussion of the French **peasantry**. Although the peasants constituted the vast majority of the French **population**, their isolation and lack of organization effectively meant that they did not **form** a class, but simply shared a common objective position, much as 'potatoes in a sack form a sack of potatoes'. Marx argues that the peasants are unable to represent themselves and therefore need to be represented, in this case by Bonaparte. The *Brumaire* also reveals that class consciousness can be obstructed by competing material interests within a class, in this case the **bourgeoisie**, which was split into factions based on industry, finance and land, each reflected in rival political groupings. This resulted in a political paralysis that enabled Bonaparte to seize power.

One of the chief problems obstructing the development of working-class consciousness is the problem of '**competition** among the workers', first mentioned in *The German Ideology* and then in **The Communist Manifesto** (1848). Marx witnessed the hostility of English workers to Irish immigrants as well as the persistence of national rivalries. He was aware of the difficulties faced by the working class in achieving class consciousness, and in 1863 he remarked in a letter to **Engels** that the English workers were apparently suffering from a 'bourgeois infection'. Ultimately, he hoped that working-class consciousness would develop, and saw evidence of it in the expansion of **labour** and socialist organizations towards the end of his life. In his notes for delegates to the Geneva Congress of the **First International** (1864–1872) Marx comments that the trade unions are vital as 'organizing centres' of the working class in the broad interest of its complete emancipation, but he also criticizes them for concentrating on local and immediate struggles without understanding the need to act against 'the system of wage **slavery**' itself.

The vast amount of empirical material detailing the experience of the working class in **Capital** 1 (1867) suggests that Marx was well aware of the enormous difficulties faced by the workers in developing the level of class consciousness that he considered necessary to overthrow capitalism. In 1880 he wrote a questionnaire, L'Inquête Ouvrière, designed to find out the views of working people about their domestic and working conditions. It was published in 20,000 copies in France and later translated into other languages.

class struggle   Refers to the struggle over **exploitation** and thereby the extraction of **surplus value**. In *The Communist Manifesto* (1848) Marx declares that the history of all society up to now is the history of **class** struggles. In each major historical epoch there have been two main forces opposing one another – freeman and slave, patrician and plebeian, lord and serf, guild-master and journeyman – and all have struggled against each other in a sometimes hidden, sometimes open fight, which in each era has resulted either in a revolutionary re-constitution of society or in the ruination of these contending classes. Marx argues that modern bourgeois society that has emerged from the struggles between lord and serf in **feudalism** has not ended class antagonisms, but instead established new forms of struggle in place of these old ones. However, the contending classes that are in struggle with each other now are the **bourgeoisie** and the modern **working class** or **proletariat**.

However, whereas previously the exploitation that gives rise to this class struggle was hidden behind religious and political illusions, now such exploitation is naked, shameless, direct and brutal, as all relations are reduced to the power of **money**. The proletariat itself therefore engages in class struggle with the bourgeoisie in various stages. Initially, it is by **individual** labourers, then by factory **labour**, then by the operatives in one trade in a local area who direct their attacks on machinery and the factories themselves. As industry develops, the proletariat increases in number and density, grows in strength and begins to form **trade unions** to improve their **wages**. Such struggles often break out into riots, which may not always be victorious, but do bring together more and more workers to assert their own interests against the interests of **capital**. Every class struggle is therefore a political struggle and its initial form is always national because the proletariat of each country must always first settle accounts with its own bourgeoisie. However, in the final instance, the class struggle must be settled on a global scale as the workers of the world unite to overcome the common enemy of capitalism.

Marx has not yet developed his theory of surplus value at the time of writing the *Manifesto*, but when he does, he links it directly to the issue of class struggle. In **Capital 3** (1864–1865), for example, he argues that the 'specific economic form, in which unpaid surplus labour', surplus value, 'is pumped out of direct producers, determines the relationship of rulers and ruled, as it grows directly out of **production** itself and, in turn, reacts upon it as a determining element. Upon this, however, is founded the entire formation of the economic community which grows up out of the production relations themselves, thereby simultaneously its specific political form.' A basic antagonism therefore exists at the heart of society that involves the exploitation of one group by another. Class struggle, the struggle over the extraction of this surplus, is the basis of this conflict. It follows, then, that the class struggle will go on as long as these exploitative relationships persist, and one minority class oppresses the majority.

The Class Struggles in France (1850)   Marx wrote three long articles for a journal, the *Neue Rheinische Zeitung Politisch-ökonomische Revue*, on political events in the French Second Republic between 1848 and early 1850. **Engels** added a fourth chapter and included it when it appeared as a separate pamphlet in 1895. The first chapter covered the defeat of the workers' **revolution** of June 1848, the second examined events between June 1848 and June 1849, including the election of Louis Bonaparte as President in December 1849, and the third looked at events between June 1849 and March 1850. In *Class Struggles* Marx describes a much more complicated array of political forces than the simplified two-class struggle forecast in **The Communist Manifesto** (1848). He portrays a **bourgeoisie** divided into three factions, with its industrial wing enjoying far less political clout than its counterpart in England. He argues that the **peasantry** is a potential ally of the **working class** because they both suffer **exploitation** by capital, albeit in different ways. However, most peasants had illusions that Louis Bonaparte could restore the glory days of the prosperous small-holding. Marx shows total sympathy for the Paris workers, provoked into rebellion by the imminent closure of the National Workshops, but he also acknowledges that members of the working class were involved in the bloody suppression of the uprising.

Marx displays an ambivalent attitude towards representative **democracy** in the *Class Struggles*. He argues that universal male franchise, first used in the national elections in April 1848, was not a 'miracle-working magic wand', but it had the greater merit of openly unleashing the class struggles. He regarded the greatest **contradiction** of the 1848 constitution the fact that it gave political power to the classes 'whose social **slavery** it intends to perpetuate': the working class, the peasantry and the petty-bourgeoisie. However, this power was checked by the creation of an elected President and finally destroyed when the National Assembly voted to limit the franchise. Marx is scathing in his criticism of the various socialist elements operating within the National Assembly, accusing them of dispensing with the **class struggle** and posturing with their 'doctrinaire **socialism**'. Against this he lauds the 'revolutionary **socialism**' then associated with the name of the insurrectionary leader Auguste Blanqui and calls for the 'permanence of the **revolution**'. For the first time Marx endorses the '**dictatorship of the proletariat**' as a necessary intermediate stage on the path towards a classless society.

colonies   Marx wrote extensively about the British rule in India and Ireland and about foreign intervention in China, chiefly in his capacity as correspondent for the *New York Daily Tribune*. He condemned the brutality of colonial rule, but he also rejected what he thought of as misplaced respect for the traditional social and political practices that preceded it. Until the mid-1850s Marx was largely of the opinion that the colonized countries would achieve their **freedom** only when the **working class** seized power in the European countries. Later, however, he decided that the colonies needed to achieve their independence as a condition for the triumph of the working class in Europe. He characterized British rule in India as an example of 'the inherent barbarism of bourgeois civilizations', accusing the British of atrocious extortion and confiscation. In the mid-1860s he became convinced that Ireland needed to win independence, both to put an end to its economic and political oppression and to overcome the divisive effects that the Irish struggle for freedom was having within Britain. He noted the 'profound antagonism' between Irish and British workers caused by the national conflict. Marx did his best to persuade the English **trade unions** to support Irish independence, with limited success, and he also urged the International to support the Irish cause. In a letter to Engels in 1867 he wrote that in the past he had thought Irish independence was impossible, but now he considered it to be inevitable. In 1869 he commented that the English working class will 'never accomplish anything' until rule over Ireland is ended. In the same year Marx participated in a mass demonstration in London for the release of Irish political prisoners, members of the Fenian organization. He commented to the General Council of the International that the main feature of the demonstration was that at least a part of the English working class had lost their prejudice against the Irish. In a confidential communication in 1870 to German socialist leaders, defending the International's support for Irish independence, Marx declared that 'any **nation** that oppresses another forges its own chains'.

Comments on James Mill's Elements of Political Economy **(1844, posthumously published 1932)**   Written during Marx's time in Paris and part of his numerous notebooks that he kept whilst writing the ***Economic and Philosophical Manuscripts*** (1844). Through a critique of James Mill, Marx shows how, by an investigation of **money**, wage labour, credit and banking under the auspices of private **property**, **alienation** pervades human existence. Marx exposes how the system of **exchange** forces people to treat each other not as human beings but as a means to an end in pursuit of their egoistic interests. Even labouring activity is not an end in itself because it is reduced to nothing more than the maintenance of **individual** existence and a means to the end of ensuring a person's own physical survival. However, the manuscript also acts as a sort of antidote to the seemingly all-encompassing aspects of alienation depicted briefly here, but more extensively in the *Manuscripts*. Marx argues that communist society or the true community, which is the **essence** of humanity, actually arises out of the need and the egoism of individuals within these alienated forms. He argues that the true community contains the real, conscious and authentic existence of human's species-activity and species spirit through social activity and social enjoyment. As the realm of private property does not allow humans to recognize themselves as humans or give the world a human organization, this community appears in the **form** of estrangement. So even in the alienated form of a system of private property, elements of the true community are present.

commodity   An object or thing of some sort that is bought and sold on the **market** and not for immediate **consumption**. Whilst commodities have existed in pre-capitalist societies, it is only in **capitalism** as a highly developed system of **exchange** that they predominate and become the main basis on which people are forced to **labour** to survive, and through which capitalists generate **surplus value**. The commodity is therefore the precondition and the immediate result of the process of **capitalist production**. Consequently, Marx begins the opening chapter of *Capital* **1** (1867) with the commodity because it is the elementary **form** in which **wealth** appears in capitalism, whilst also being a way to satisfy human **needs**. The commodity represents an antagonism between those who sell their **labour power** in order to secure a wage to buy the goods they need, the **working class**, and those who put these people to work to create such commodities for sale on the market to realize surplus value in the form of **profit**, the capitalist class.

Marx argues that a commodity has a use value and an exchange value. The use value of the commodity has a use, e.g. linen to use as sheets on a bed, or a coat to wear to keep you warm. This is a qualitative under-standing that cannot be quantified. Exchange value refers to the fact that the commodity can be exchanged for something else, e.g. twenty sheets of linen for one coat. The exchange value of the twenty sheets of linen would be the coat, and the exchange value of the coat would be the twenty sheets of linen. This is a quantitative relation. It is the form in which use values exchange with each other. Capitalists are mainly concerned with the exchange value of a commodity (what it can realize in exchange) rather than its use value (what it can be used for). So in the example of the coat it is immaterial to a capitalist that its use value is something to wear to keep warm: its only real importance is what it can exchange for in the market and in capitalism that exchange is based on **money**. Capitalism, then, is the rule of exchange value over use value, and capitalists attempt to turn everything into a commodity. Even human beings undergo this process because they have nothing to sell but their labour power, and are treated as commodities by capitalists who put them to work to create other commodities on the

path to realizing surplus value. For Marx, the overall effect of this commodi-
fication process on society is quite devastating because it results in different
forms of **alienation** and **commodity fetishism**.

commodity fetishism A definite social relation between people that
assumes the fantastic **form** of a relation between things that mystifies the
true **nature** of **capitalism**. Marx discusses fetishism particularly in section
four of chapter one in **Capital** 1 (1867), and it must be read in conjunction
with, and as part of, his **value** theory as a whole. He also uses the term
fetishism synonymously with the lesser-used term **reification**.

Marx argues that in a **commodity**-producing society producers engage
in private **production** independently from each other. The sum total of
their private **labour** is the aggregate social labour of society. As the private
producers do not come into social contact with each other until they
exchange the products of their labour, the social basis of their private
labour only appears when they exchange their labour for that of others by
exchanging commodities. The social basis of production is therefore hidden
within the interchange of commodities that take on fetishized forms and
appear to be devoid of any social content, thus obscuring the antagonistic
basis of production between workers and the owners of **capital**. It is
through dissolving these forms that the social relation they deny can be
unearthed. Only by going behind the **appearance** of exchange can we
discover the social basis to production in **capitalism** and expose the **class
struggle** at the heart of the system. Then a relation that appears to be
between things can actually be seen as a social relation between people.

Marx says that for the producers themselves 'the social relations between
their private labours appear as what they are, that is, as material relations
between persons and social relations between things' rather than appearing
as direct social relations between persons in their work. The appearance is
not an illusion but perfectly real, because it is only through the exchange of
commodities that the social relations between producers exist. The fetishism
present here means that the producers do not consciously exchange their
labour with each other; instead they do so without realizing it by selling
their products as commodities. The real social relation to production is
therefore hidden. Additionally, commodities take an even more mystified
and fetishized form through the introduction of **money** as their common
expression. When commodities are exchanged for money then money must

also be understood as a social relation and not a thing. Money therefore also hides the social basis to production even further. The critique of the all-pervasive fetishization of social relations in capitalist society is fundamental in making us see the hidden reality of capitalism, and making us active in trying to overcome it. (See also **alienation**.)

communism   Marx declared his support for modern communism early in 1844, describing it as the movement that opposes private **property** and restores power to humanity. He consistently referred to communist society as the goal to strive for and communism as the movement to achieve it. In the *Economic_and Philosophical Manuscripts* (1844) he distinguishes between modern communism and forms of crude communism practiced by some revolutionary utopian movements such as the Anabaptists in Germany at the time of the Reformation. He denounces this 'crude' communism as a 'levelling down' that negates the world of **culture** and civilization and reproduces oppressive power in a different, collective, **form**. It is based on a form of 'general envy' that negates the human personality in every sphere, disregarding all talent and knowledge. He particularly abhors the way in which it reduces **women** to the status of sexual objects. Modern communism, in contrast, seeks to build on all the achievements of modern society, but aims to remove the considerable impediments to human progress. He describes this communism as the liberation of the social, human being, accomplished consciously and 'embracing the entire **wealth** of previous development'. He conceives it as a real phase in 'the **emancipation** and recovery of humankind'.

Marx was reluctant to prescribe precisely how communism was to achieve its goals, being wary of utopian formulations that were not based on clear analysis of existing conditions. In *The German Ideology* (1845–1846) he argued that only in the process of overthrowing the **ruling class** can the **working class** rid itself of 'all the muck of ages and become fitted to found society anew'. The general principle of communist society is announced in *The Communist Manifesto* (1848) when he declares that 'in place of the old bourgeois society, with its classes and class antagonisms, we shall have an association, in which the free development of each is the condition for the free development of all'. In this formula the free development of each **individual** is primary, but this presupposes a reciprocal harmony with all other individuals in a liberated society, possible only through processes of radical **democracy**. He calls for the **proletariat** to 'win the battle for democracy' and outlines a number of immediate measures, many of which were to be adopted by social democratic governments in Europe in the twentieth century.

Marx makes some interesting comments on the social relations of future communist society in chapter forty-eight of **Capital 3** (1864–1865). **Freedom** comes only when the associated producers collectively control **production** instead of being dominated by it. However, even social control of production remains confined to the realm of necessity, whereas the 'true realm of freedom', involving the development of human powers as an end in itself, only begins beyond it. He adds that the realm of freedom can flourish only with the realm of necessity as its basis, and that this would require the shortening of the **working day** as its basic prerequisite. Although work performed to meet basic **needs** could be satisfying and attractive once **exploitation** has been removed, the realm of freedom is really to be found in what we as individuals choose to do freely, regardless of obligation. He had hinted that this was the true expression of human powers when stating in the 1844 *Manuscripts* that we 'only truly produce' when free from physical need.

In the **Critique of the Gotha Programme** (1875) Marx distinguishes between the lower and higher phases of communist society, focusing on the principles of economic distribution. In the lower phase it is still emerging from **capitalism** and carries with it the expectation that the rewards for work should be proportionate to the amount of **labour** time expended. The principle is fundamentally the same as in capitalism, but now only labour counts as contributing to wealth and the means of production cannot pass into private ownership. The distribution is therefore fairer because, unlike capitalism, the principle of equal right is no longer 'at loggerheads' with its practice. Workers would be rewarded according to the amount of work put in without the huge differentials in income common in capitalist societies. However, this proportionality applies only to the first phase of communist society and suffers from 'a bourgeois limitation'. It will continue to reproduce inequalities, perhaps giving excessive rewards to those with scarce skills and failing to take into account the extra cost of special needs for those with lots of children, or disabilities.

In the higher phase of communist society, the oppressive aspects of the social division of labour would be overcome, as would the antithesis between mental and physical labour. Labour itself would no longer be drudgery but rather life's primary need and the productive forces would be so well developed that overall abundance was guaranteed. Only then can society operate according to its guiding principle, from each according to ability, to each according to need. Here the assumption is that people have overcome egoism and now view their self-actualization as being possible only in a society which is fair to everyone. In a developed communist society, democratic decisions are reached about such things as remuneration, supplementary pay, training and **education** without the need for some sort of calculable reward system. Common misinterpretations of these passages have suggested that Marx called the first phase of communist society '**socialism**', which he did not, and used as its distributive principle the slogan 'from each according to ability, to each according to work', which again he did not.

The Communist Manifesto (**1848**)   A short and dramatic account of Marx's revolutionary ideas, the *Manifesto* appeals for human **emancipation** through the abolition of private **property**, putting an end to the **class** rule of the **bourgeoisie** and replacing it with a classless society. Co-written with Friedrich **Engels**, it appeared as a pamphlet in German entitled *The Manifesto of the Communist Party* in February 1848, but was re-titled *The Communist Manifesto* in the second German edition in 1872. It was produced at the request of the Communist League, an organization of German refugees based in London. Engels had written earlier drafts in 1847, *Draft of a Communist Confession of Faith* and *Principles of Communism*, but the narrative of the *Manifesto* was put together by Marx.

The first of the four parts depicts the rise of the bourgeoisie and its inevitable struggle with the **working class**, opening with the bold explanatory framework that 'the history of all hitherto existing societies is the history of class struggles'. Marx gives a brief history of the dazzling rise of the bourgeoisie, ignited by the discovery of America and the rounding of the Cape. From being originally an oppressed class under the power of the feudal nobility, the bourgeoisie had risen to become the **ruling class**, in control of **state** power. He emphasizes the revolutionary **nature** of the bourgeoisie, destroying old myths and superstitions and transforming all social conditions, so 'all that is solid melts into air, all that is holy is profaned'. He also describes, with remarkable foresight, the global reach of the bourgeois **exploitation** of the **world market**, with cheap commodities acting as the heavy artillery to 'batter down all Chinese walls', compelling the whole world to adopt the bourgeois **mode of production**. However, for all its dizzying success, modern bourgeois society is not fully in control of the system it has produced. Marx likens it to a sorcerer who is no longer able to control the powers unleashed by his spells. Here he refers to the **economic crises** that regularly beset the system, giving rise to more intense **competition** and at the same time paving the way for even more destructive crises in the future.

The rise of the bourgeoisie also sees the rise of its nemesis, the modern working class or **proletariat**. Marx outlines its development from the early days of **capitalism** when the workers **form** an 'incoherent mass' divided by their mutual competition to the modern period when it becomes more concentrated and aware of its potential strength. The workers form **trade unions** and later political parties, since 'every **class struggle** is a political struggle'. Despite the appalling conditions faced by the workers, who are reduced to the status of 'an appendage of the machine' in the factory and crushed by **poverty**, the victory of the working class is declared to be as 'inevitable' as the fall of the bourgeoisie.

The second section concentrates on the relationship between the working class and the communists. The two things that distinguish the communists from other working-class parties are their commitment to the interests of all workers, irrespective of nationality, and their unwavering commitment to the interests of the movement as a whole. The theory of the communists is summarized as the 'abolition of private property', although Marx makes it clear that this refers to productive property rather than personal possessions. This section also contains an optimistic commitment to **internationalism**, stating that national antagonisms were visibly vanishing with the development of the world market. The workers, owning no property, are declared therefore to have no country. An important theoretical point in this section is that human **consciousness** changes with every change in the conditions of material existence, and that 'the ruling ideas of each age have ever been the ideas of its ruling class'. These ideas will be challenged by the communists in a most radical rupture with traditional thought. Previous struggles between classes have reproduced in different forms the exploitation of one class by another, but the communist **revolution** will put an end to classes altogether. To do so, however, the working class has to win the battle for **democracy** and become the new ruling class. Marx lists ten measures which could be introduced into most advanced countries, including the nationalization of land, banks, communication, transport and other major industries, the introduction of a heavily progressive or graduated income tax and the introduction of free **education**.

The third section discusses rival socialist ideas and movements. 'Socialist' is used broadly to refer to any form of opposition to the bourgeois mode of production, including the romantic harking back to feudal society. Other forms of **socialism** are criticized for failing to understand that the social and economic changes introduced by the bourgeoisie have created the conditions for the social revolution necessary to introduce a classless society. Marx is particularly scornful towards the 'true' German socialism of his old left-Hegelian acquaintances and the 'conservative' socialism associated with **Proudhon**. He is more appreciative of the utopian socialists for their fundamental opposition to existing society, but considers that their commitment to 'fantastic' alternative communities is an unrealistic diversion from the class struggle. The final section concerns the relationship of the communists to existing opposition parties. Marx argues that the communists will work everywhere 'for the union and agreement of the democratic parties of all countries', but insists that the communists always insist on the class struggle against the bourgeoisie – the 'property question' must always be the basic question for the movement. Controversially, he argues that the predicted bourgeois revolution in Germany will be followed immediately by a proletarian revolution, despite the tiny size of its working class. Finally, he declares that the proletarians have nothing to lose but their chains and have a world to win, issuing a resounding appeal for proletarians of all countries to unite.

competition   Referred to by Marx in *Capital* **1** (1867) as exposing the inherent laws of **capitalist production** in the shape of external coercive laws, which have power over every **individual** capitalist. Marx says that a scientific analysis of competition is not possible until we have a conception of the inner **nature** of **capitalism**, just as the apparent motions of the heavenly bodies can only be grasped by those acquainted with their real motions, which are not perceptible to the senses. However, the production of **surplus value** does give an insight into this process, which he will develop even further when he introduces competition proper in *Capital* **3** (1864–1865).

For now, Marx notes how competition arises between capitalists because, in a society based on **commodity** production, they are all attempting to gain as much surplus value as possible. If they do not, then they will go out of business. If they do, then they become part of the **accumulation** process that acts as a coercive **law**, and so demands them to re-invest in the further pursuit of even more **surplus value**. So these laws of competition have power over individual capitalists, who are competing with each other to sell their commodities, and realize the surplus value created in the production process by **labour**. They then try and reduce the socially necessary labour time required to produce their commodities to cheapen their products and so undercut their competitors. The capitalist that is successful in doing this will thus dominate the **market**, but other capitalists then respond by, for example, increasing the level of **exploitation** of **labour** in the production process in the hope of increasing their share of the surplus value created, and so the process goes on all over again. Competition thus imposes accumulation for accumulation's sake, and production for production's sake on to capitalists. On one side, this forces capitalists against each other, but on the other side, it means that all capitalists have a collective interest in promoting the right conditions for accumulation to take place.

In *Capital* 3 Marx considers competition proper as he analyzes capitalist production as a whole, which itself is a unity of the process of production and circulation. Now, capitals confront one another in certain concrete forms in their actual movement and Marx's concern is to analyze the **form** in which these capitals appear on the surface of society in competition with each other, and in the everyday **consciousness** of the agents of production. Marx then develops his understanding of competition by making a distinction between the cost **price**, **value** and sale price of a commodity. He argues that the cost price of a commodity refers to the cost of the means of production consumed, machinery, raw materials etc., and the **labour power** employed, and so simply replaces what the commodity cost the capitalist in his or her initial outlay. The value of the commodity refers to all of these factors plus the surplus value created in production, which is determined by the socially necessary labour time required to produce the product. The sale price of the commodity is the price the commodity achieves when it is actually sold on the market.

Marx contends that an indefinite series of sale prices are possible between the value of a commodity and its cost price. Moreover, the greater the amount of surplus value there is in the commodity, then the greater is the possibility for variation in these sale prices. Consequently, such fluctuations explain the everyday phenomena of competition that manifests itself in instances of under-selling, low levels in commodity prices in certain branches of industry and so on. Hence the basic law of capitalist competition, which **political economy** has failed to grasp, the law that governs the general rate of profit and the prices of production determined by it, depends on the difference between the value and the cost price of commodities and the possibility deriving from this of selling commodities below their value at a profit.

consciousness   Marx considers consciousness to be self-awareness and awareness of the world that is always a product of the actual process of social life. In **The German Ideology** (1845–1846) he attacks the Young Hegelian philosophers for treating consciousness (*Bewusstsein*) as though it has an independent existence. For Marx, consciousness can never be anything else than 'conscious being' (*bewusste Sein*), produced by our social interaction. In opposition to idealist conceptions, which view the world changing as a result of the development of ideas, Marx sees ideas developing as a result of changes in the way in which human beings organize the **production** and reproduction of material life. He summarizes this in the shorthand formulation 'it is not consciousness that determines life but life that determines consciousness'. Although this involves a move away from thinking about consciousness as an independent force, and therefore away from self-sufficient philosophy (*selbständige Philosophie*), the consciousness of individuals continues to be significant for Marx, for ideas themselves are considered to be a 'material force'. In the **Preface to A Contribution to the Critique of Political Economy** (1859) the idea that consciousness reflects real social processes is reiterated: 'it is not the consciousness of men that determines their existence, but their social existence that determines their consciousness'. It follows that the focus for inquiry should be human life activity itself as an empirically perceptible process of development under definite conditions. When this inquiry begins, speculation ends, and 'empty phrases' about consciousness are replaced by 'real, positive **science**'. Much of this science consists in engaging in critiques of the work of the political economists whose work underpins the **ideology** that supports **capitalism**. Exposing those ideas as reflections of the interests of the **bourgeoisie** would help to arm the **working class** with a clear **class consciousness** of its position so that it could fulfil its 'historic mission' to create the classless society.

consumption   Takes three main forms: productive, individual and unproductive, as Marx explains in *Capital* **1** (1867). Marx sees consumption as being inextricably tied to **production** because both are needed for societies to reproduce themselves. To this end, he denotes productive consumption as those products that replenish the means of production, instruments of **labour**, raw materials and so on, to allow society to maintain its existing **wealth** and renew itself. For the **working class**, productive consumption relates to how they consume the means of production and create new commodities that have a higher value than the **capital** advanced to make them. Capitalists are also consuming the **labour power** of the workers in this process of productive consumption, so the workers act as the 'motive power of capital'. In contrast, individual consumption refers to the ways in which workers use the **money** they have received for selling their labour power to buy their means of subsistence. Here the workers now belong to themselves rather than to capitalists as they engage in the 'vital functions' that allow them to survive outside the process of production. However, even in their individual consumption workers are replenishing themselves to go back into the production process where they can be exploited anew, and as such their individual consumption becomes productive consumption. So while it is possible for workers to engage in individual consumption to pursue their own interests rather than interests of capitalists, this is still accomplished within the production and reproduction of capital. As Marx states, 'the consumption of food by a beast of burden does not become any less a necessary aspect of the production process because the beast enjoys what he eats'. Capitalists and their ideological apologists therefore only consider that aspect of the workers' individual consumption that is productive. While the production and maintenance of the workers is therefore essential for the reproduction of capital, it is largely irrelevant to capitalists how workers do this, and they assume the workers will do so out of the drive for survival and self-propagation. All that interests capitalists is having labour power to consume and thereby exploit. What the workers consume over and above the minimum needed for their own pleasure is seen by capitalists as unproductive consumption. Nevertheless, Marx argues that in reality the individual consumption of the workers is also unproductive from their perspective, because it simply produces 'needy' individuals who are then, through their own consumption, productive both to capitalists and the **state**. The workers in their own consumption therefore act as a force that produces wealth for other people, and binds them further to the reproduction of **capitalism**. (See also **exchange** and **needs**.)

contradiction   A key term in Marx's dialectical **method**, referring to the existence of opposing tendencies within a developing phenomenon. Within formal logic, a contradiction is established when something is claimed to have mutually opposing qualities (both A and not A) at the same time and in the same sense. In this way we establish whether arguments are internally consistent or whether evidence is verified. Marx uses contradiction in this sense, but often qualifies the term by referring to 'formal' or 'flat' contradictions. However, he also uses contradiction (*Widerspruch*) in a specifically dialectical sense, to refer to opposed tendencies internal to a developing system or to oppositions within economic categories. In these cases contradictions are mediated to enable the system to progress, but ultimately the contradictory **nature** of the system reasserts itself in the **form** of **economic crises**.

There can be no doubt that Marx's dialectical use of contradiction owes much to his respect for the philosophy of **Hegel**, acknowledged by Marx as the first to present the general forms of motion of the **dialectic** in a 'comprehensive and conscious manner'. For Marx, Hegelian contradiction is the basis of all dialectics. However, his early analysis of Hegel, in the *Critique of Hegel's Philosophy of Right* (1843), shows his dissatisfaction with the way that Hegel produced conciliatory mediations within contradictions between the 'particularity' embodied by the monarchy and 'generality' in the form of **civil society**. Marx considers that Hegel had simply masked the real opposition of interests between the different classes of society in order to legitimate the autocratic Prussian **state**. For example, although Hegel identifies the contradiction between the state and civil society, he creates conceptual mediations through which the contradiction could be resolved. For Marx, the contradiction could not be resolved in a society based on private **property**.

When Marx analyses the 'laws of motion' of the **capitalist mode of production** he identifies contradictions and mediations as the driving force of a developing system. The totality within which contradictions occur is the capitalist mode of production, and the ultimate contradiction is the contradiction between the relations of **production** and the forces of production. Both categories are dependent on one another, for forces of production become forces only when people organize to activate them, while relations of production are conceivable only when there are forces to develop. At times within a mode of production the categories are in harmony, and the relations efficiently develop the forces, but eventually the relations of production enter into contradiction with the forces of production. Faced with alternative relations of production that would develop the forces more efficiently, a social **revolution** occurs and a new mode of production emerges. Although this central contradiction was first set down in **The German Ideology** (1845–1846), it took a lifetime's work by Marx to analyze the capitalist mode of production in sufficient detail to be able to show the contradictory nature of key categories of the economic structure.

In the chapter on **money** in the **Grundrisse** (1857–1858), when examining the relationship between money and commodities, Marx specifies four contradictions that are present. He begins with the contradiction within the **commodity** between the particular nature of the commodity as a product, or its use value, and its general nature as **exchange** value, expressed in money. The other contradictions involve the separation of purchase and sale by space and time, the splitting of exchange into mutually independent acts and the twofold nature of money as a general commodity to facilitate exchange and a particular commodity subject to its own particular conditions of exchange. These distinctions are treated as oppositional because as the system develops they give rise to real antagonisms, particularly between the producers, who have to sell their labour, and the money holders who purchase it, with money appearing to stand above the producers as an independent power. The oppositions are conceived as dialectical contradictions because they are mediated through the exchange process to allow production to develop, but only in such a way that the antagonisms reassert themselves at a systemic level.

In the **Contribution to the Critique of Political Economy** (1859) Marx introduces the concept of **labour power** as the commodity that can be exchanged at its value and at the same time gives rise to **surplus value**. This **exploitation** of the producers is the surface reflection of the contradiction between money and commodities. In **Capital 1** (1867) he identifies the source of monetary crises in a contradiction immanent in the function of money as a means of payment, between its purely nominal form, money on account, and the hard cash demanded at times of 'general disturbance'. The separation of functions leads to a contradiction between money as an abstract figure and its cash form. When discussing the circulation of commodities, Marx notes that the contradictions occur in the exchange of commodities, but this provides the room for the contradictions to develop and become systemic. Only when no further resolutions are possible will the system be replaced.

Marx's exposure of the contradictions of **capitalism** is completed in *Capital* **3** (1864–1865), particularly in his discussion of **the tendency of the rate of profit to fall** and its implications. For Marx, the desperate race for **profit** drives the system to more volatile and precarious **competition**, but it is always running against the problem of finding effective demand. Capitalists need low **labour** costs to make their profits, but they need consumers with money to buy their goods. This can lead to situations in which over-capacity of production goes hand in hand with unemployment. This is not something that can ultimately be resolved within the system, for it is the logical outcome of the contradictory premises of capitalist production. Marx concludes that the contradiction of this mode of production consists precisely in its 'tendency towards the absolute development of productive forces that come into continuous conflict with the specific conditions of production in which **capital** moves, and can alone move'.

Commentators have argued that Marx's dialectical contradictions could be expressed in terms compatible with the formal laws of logic, without invoking 'contradiction' at all. In this way analytical philosophy could make sense of Marx's analyses without recourse to dialectics. This is quite possible, for dialectics does not oppose the formal laws of thought, including the principle of non-contradiction. However, an analytic approach that insists on sharp either/or distinctions is less likely to grasp the internal tensions of a system in movement with the coherence achieved by Marx through his dialectical contradictions. (See also **mediation**.)

Contribution to the Critique of Hegel's Philosophy of Right: Introduction (1844)   Published in the *Deutsch-Französische Jahrbücher* and intended as the Introduction to Marx's unpublished *Critique of Hegel's Philosophy of Right* (1843). It was written in 1844 while Marx was in Paris, where he had come into contact with **working-class** revolutionaries. It is in this work that he first establishes his support for the proletarian struggle. Marx begins his discussion by considering **religion**, which he refers to as the 'opium of the people'. However, he argues that the task of philosophy is not simply to offer a critique of religion as the **Young Hegelians** had, but instead to offer a critique of the real world in order to transform it. Marx focuses on the situation in Germany at that time, depicting it as advanced in its philosophical thought but backward in terms of its political and industrial development, especially when compared to France and England. He argues that what was needed was something to unite the philosophical with the practical to enact a German **revolution**. That something was a **class** with 'radical chains' – the **proletariat**. Marx is therefore fusing theory with practice in order to change the world, and although he realizes that the proletariat is not fully formed in Germany yet, he maintains that it can eventually serve as an emancipatory force that will liberate both itself and the whole of society.

A Contribution to the Critique of Political Economy (1859)   Now best known for its **Preface**, where Marx outlines what has become known as his **materialist conception of history** or **historical materialism**. The work overall is an amalgamated version of the first part of the *Grundrisse* (1857–1858) and replicates some themes that appeared in the *Economic and Philosophical Manuscripts* (1844). It does offer one of the first expositions of his theories of **value** and **money**, and refutes Say's law that contends that supply creates its own demand. However, the work has receded in interest because most of the ideas in it are replicated in the first few chapters of *Capital* 1 (1867).

cooperation   Marx viewed cooperation as a natural element of social life through which human civilization had been created. In chapter thirteen of *Capital* 1, Marx comments that the productive power of social **labour** arose from cooperation itself. However, he draws a sharp distinction between imposed cooperation, as witnessed in each **mode of production** based on private **property**, from free cooperation. In **capitalism**, large numbers of workers are brought together to take advantage of the division of labour, but although this is a necessary condition for the transformation of the labour process into a social process, its social **form** is based on the 'more profitable **exploitation** of labour'. In **The Communist Manifesto** Marx argues that the enforced cooperation of the workers creates a **working class** capable of overcoming its internal divisions to challenge the economic and political power of the **bourgeoisie**. The free cooperation of the workers in **trade unions** and parties facilitates their collective struggle against the servitude imposed on them. There had been a number of experiments in free cooperative enterprises in France and England in the 1830s and 1840s, and in **Capital 3** (1864–1865) Marx comments that these factories, run by the workers themselves within a **capitalist** system, offered the 'first examples' of a new form of **production**, even though they were unable to escape from the defects of the old form. In the free cooperative factory the antithetical character of supervisory work disappears, since the manager is paid by the workers instead of representing **capital** in opposition to them. Marx viewed the cooperative factory as a transitional form, an indicator of a new mode of production arising from the old.

Critique of Hegel's Philosophy of Right (1843, posthumously published 1927)   An unfinished manuscript in which Marx, still under the influence of **Feuerbach**, attempts to offer his first critique of Hegel's political philosophy. Marx structures his analysis by focusing on paragraphs 261–313 of Hegel's *Philosophy of Right* that considers the constitution, the crown, the executive and the legislature. In this work Marx criticizes **Hegel** for what he sees as a recurring theme in his writings, the tendency to posit reality as a manifestation of abstract thought through his notion of the Idea, and in doing so to slip into mystification. He also shows how Hegel's understanding of the **state** as rational is prone to **contradiction** and rejects the contention that the state can be above classes. This allows Marx to offer his own critique of political institutions and examine the relationship between political and economic forces in society through the state, **civil society** and private **property**. Marx examines Hegel's attempts to solve the problem of the split between the egoism and self-interest present in people in civil society with the people as citizens of the state. Hegel does so through the institutions of the monarch, the **bureaucracy**, which he sees as a universal **class**, and the estates, which are made up of trades and professions. Hegel contends that these institutions overcome the dichotomy between the state and civil society in the following ways. The monarch does so by standing above and beyond all political groupings in society and as such cannot be affected by them. As the bureaucracy is paid by the state, its interests are at one with it. Finally, the estates act as a forum within which the different interests of civil society can be brought together and reconciled. However, Marx rejects Hegel's solution here because, following his general criticism of Hegel for dealing in abstract thought rather than reality, such reconciliations take place only at the level of **appearance**. Instead, the deep divisions that exist between state and civil society are still present and have not been overcome, not least through the way the bureaucracy itself forms a state within a state. Marx argues therefore that the only solution possible for the contradiction that exists between the state and civil society is universal suffrage. With this enacted, the reform of voting that allows all to participate in legislation will result therefore in both the dissolution of the state itself and the dissolution of civil society.

***Critique of the Gotha Programme* (1875, posthumously published 1927)**   Marx wrote these critical notes on the draft programme of the German Social Democratic Workers' Party shortly before its unification Congress in May 1875. The critique contains important objections to a document considered by Marx to reflect the theoretically sloppy and politically reformist position of the General Association of German Workers, founded by Ferdinand Lassalle in 1863. Marx supported the rival Social-Democratic Workers Party of Germany (SDAP), known as the *Eisenachers*, and sent the critique to one of their leaders, Wilhelm Bracke, with instructions to pass it on to other leading SDAP figures. It was too late to secure a revision of the programme, which was adopted by the new party. In 1891 **Engels** published an edited version of the critique, but he deleted some of the harsher comments in order to placate the leadership of the party (now the SPD). The SPD adopted a new party programme at Erfurt in 1891, in line with Marx's views.

The *Critique* offers valuable insight into Marx's views on how theory should be translated into programmatic **form** to act as a guide for political action. He regarded the programme as 'reprehensible and demoralizing for the party' and promised to fight against it. He saw the 'stamp' of Lassalle throughout the document, for although the latter had died in 1864, his ideas were still a major influence in German **socialism**. Four things in particular irked Marx. The first was the commitment for all members of society to have 'an equal **right** to the undiminished proceeds of **labour**', followed by the demand for the 'just distribution' of those proceeds. Marx pointed out that if the workers were given back everything they produced there would be nothing left for investment, administration and social goods, but his real concern was the failure of the programme to think beyond the narrow confines of getting 'just rewards'. Marx conceded that in the lower phase of communist society there would have to be some sort of reward by calculation of the worker's contribution, but in a more advanced phase such calculations would be unnecessary and the society would operate according to the slogan of from each according to ability, to each according to need. The second issue seized on by Marx was the description of all classes other than the **working class** as 'a single reactionary mass'. Marx argued that while the working class was the only really revolutionary **class**, it could attract support from those elements of the **petty bourgeoisie** and the **peasantry** who felt themselves marginalized and exploited by the bourgeoisie. The third aspect of the programme that angered Marx was its neglect of the international role of the German working class. He concurred with the view of a right-wing newspaper that the new party had effectively renounced internationalism. Finally, Marx was concerned that the new programme failed to identify the class nature of the existing **state**. He considered that the whole programme was 'thoroughly infected with the Lasallean sect's servile belief in the state' and instead insisted that the present state should be replaced by the 'revolutionary **dictatorship of the proletariat**'. Marx pointed out that the programme was making demands from a state which at that time did not even have the political freedoms of a democratic republic.

culture   In **The Communist Manifesto** (1848) Marx envisaged a cultural **revolution** to accompany the communist revolution, anticipating 'the most radical rupture with traditional ideas'. However, he comments that for the vast majority of people in bourgeois society culture is 'a mere training to act as a machine'. He dismisses bourgeois objections to **communism** by accusing the **bourgeoisie** of mistaking the attack on **class** culture as an attack on all culture. Like all ruling classes before them, they share the selfish misconception that the social forms they have developed are 'eternal laws of **nature** and **reason**'. In fact they are the products of a will whose essential character and direction are determined by the economic conditions of existence of that class. Marx believed that the working class would have to undergo a cultural revolution in the struggle against capitalism. In *The German Ideology* (1845–1846) he writes that for the success of communism 'the alteration of men on a mass scale is necessary'. In *The Eighteenth Brumaire of Louis Bonaparte* (1852) he comments that the social revolution of the nineteenth century 'can only create its poetry from the future, not from the past', and that it cannot begin its own work until it has sloughed off all its 'superstitious regard' for previous times.

—D—

Darwin, Charles (1809–1882)   Marx was greatly impressed when he first read Darwin's *Origin of Species* (1859). In a letter to **Engels** in December 1860 he commented that Darwin's breakthrough in natural history 'provides the basis for our views' and in a letter to Lassalle the following month he stated that the book dealt a 'mortal blow' to the idea of **teleology** in natural **science**. By this he meant that Darwin's idea of the development of species by means of natural selection effectively discredited old ideas of an immanent purpose to **nature**. What evidently attracted Marx was the idea that the natural order was not static or predetermined but rather the outcome of protracted struggle, a view he had held since his *Doctoral Dissertation* (1841). However, Marx became much more critical of Darwin on re-reading the *Origin* in 1862, commenting in a letter to Engels that he was depicting struggles in the natural world as though they were equivalent to the turmoil in bourgeois **civil society**. Marx was anxious not to conflate natural history with human history, as Darwin had, for human history was consciously contested with progressive goals that had to be struggled for. However, many socialist Darwinists, with some encouragement from Engels, insisted on implying scientific certitude to human history. In 1931 a Soviet journal claimed that it had a letter from Darwin rejecting a request by Marx to dedicate *Capital* 2 to him. In fact, the Darwin letter was written to Edward Aveling, partner of Marx's daughter Eleanor, who wanted to dedicate his own book, *The Student's Darwin*, to the great scientist. Darwin refused because he did not wish to be associated with open attacks on **religion**. It was almost fifty years before the myth that Marx had asked Darwin's permission to dedicate *Capital* 2 to him was disproved.

dehumanization   Refers to the alienating effect of the **capitalist** process of **production** on the workers. Marx first introduced the notion of dehumanization in a letter to his associate Arnold Ruge in 1843, condemning the Prussian monarchy as being based on the principle of the dehumanization of the world. In the *Economic and Philosophical Manuscripts* (1844) he uses it to describe the most extreme effects of the capitalist **mode of production**. Marx argues that humans are by **nature** social and productive beings, but in a condition of **alienation** workers are unable to exercise these truly human functions. Instead they are only able to enjoy such things as eating, drinking and procreation, functions that we have in common with all other **animals**. When workers sell their **labour** to capitalists, they must sell themselves and their humanity. Marx argues that workers are depressed spiritually and physically to the condition of a machine, an image he uses three times in as many pages in the *Manuscripts*, and which he repeats in *The Communist Manifesto* (1848) and in *Capital* **1**. While it is clearly a rhetorical device to draw attention to the cruelty of the system, it is firmly grounded in a view of what is distinctive about being human, and, implicitly at least, on what is entailed in a truly human existence. However, as with many rhetorical weapons, it exaggerates, for if the workers were completely dehumanized they would lack the potential to emancipate themselves. Marx, though, was convinced that the workers would achieve **class consciousness** of their own position and affirm their own humanity.

democracy   Marx consistently supported the principle of self-government, finding an ideal model in the radical democracy practised by the Paris Commune of 1871. He called for the establishment of democratic republics that would eventually enable the working class to seize power and constitute a classless society. He was critical, however, of those who saw the simple achievement of universal franchise as the answer to all social problems.

In his student days Marx was an ardent supporter of the idea of the democratic republic. In his *Critique of Hegel's Philosophy of Right,* written in 1843 but unpublished at the time, he rejected Hegel's defence of monarchy and instead favoured democracy as the only constitution that is 'the people's own creation'. Marx argued that democracy confers a rational **form** on the **state** as a whole. In an 1843 letter to Arnold Ruge he contended that only in a democratic state can society become a community that can fulfil the highest **needs** of human beings. However, although Marx considered that a democratic republic offered political **emancipation**, it fell short of delivering human emancipation. This is elegantly argued in *On the Jewish Question* (1844) when he states that democracy in itself does not provide the answer to social oppression but merely offers the ideal form through which opposing social forces can thrash out their differences.

Although Marx viewed representative democracy as progressive because it offered a forum in which **class** antagonisms could be fought out, he expressed major reservations about how it worked in practice. *The Communist Manifesto*, written immediately prior to the revolutions of 1848, tasks the **working class** and its political representatives with the duty to win the battle for democracy, both in terms of securing universal franchise and in winning political power. However, in the period of revolutionary turmoil that followed, Marx was critical of the impotence of parliamentary **politics**, particularly in *The Class Struggles in France* (1850) and *The Eighteenth Brumaire of Louis Bonaparte* (1852). The election of April 1848 was the first ever to take place on the basis of universal male franchise, but the predominantly rural and socially conservative electorate produced a National Assembly in which most of the Deputies were royalists. In the *Class Struggles* Marx commented that 'universal suffrage did not possess the magical power attributed to it by republicans of the old school'. In June the new government decided to close the national workshops that had been set up in March and provided a livelihood for more than 100,000 workers. This provoked the workers' uprising of June 1848, suppressed with great brutality by the conservative government. Marx's sympathies were entirely with the defeated workers and he was angered by the unwillingness of most of the radical leaders to support the uprising. He did not go so far as to say that the workers were right to revolt, but argued that they were left with no choice. As far as Marx was concerned, the defeat of the insurgent workers revealed that the 'bourgeois republic means the unlimited despotism of one class over the others'.

Marx was scathing in his treatment of the socialist leaders who tried to work within the National Assembly and was particularly critical of their failure to prevent the abolition of universal male franchise in 1850. In the *Brumaire*, Marx reveals his frustration at the vacuity of parliamentary politics by complaining of a 'sickness' that spread across Europe after 1848, namely 'parliamentary cretinism'. So disillusioned was Marx by the experience of the Second Republic that he argued that Louis Bonaparte's seizure of power could conceivably benefit the prospects of the proletarian **revolution** by perfecting the executive power so it might be overthrown more easily. However, the experience of Bonaparte's regime had a sobering effect on Marx, for when, in 1877, the French Third Republic was in danger of being replaced by a right-wing dictatorship, he wrote to his friend Adolf Sorge that he hoped the 'bourgeois republic is victorious', adding that 'a **nation** can repeat the same stupidities once too often'.

Marx enthused over the political system adopted by the **Paris Commune** in 1871 because it subordinated the armed forces and the **bureaucracy** and provided strong accountability and 'really democratic institutions'. However, unlike the situation in June 1848, Marx felt obliged to deal directly with the question of the legitimacy of the Commune itself. He takes great care to point out that the Commune was not opposing a legitimate government. In **The Civil War in France** (1871) he preceded his account of the Commune by rejecting the legitimacy of the national government, led by Adolphe Thiers, which assumed power following an election that was clearly neither free nor fair. For Marx, the Commune had more legitimate democratic credentials than the official government. He enthusiastically endorsed the radical democratic procedures of the Commune such as universal male franchise, the right to recall delegates, the abolition of the standing army and its replacement by a militia, and the payment of all officials at the rate of pay of the ordinary working man. He also admired the fact that it was not just a legislature but a working body directly responsible for administering its own decisions. Marx's enthusiasm for these radical democratic forms is an important indication of what he thought the 'self-government of the producers' might look like in a fully emancipated society. In a speech in Amsterdam in 1872 he stated that it was possible for the working class to achieve its goals by peaceful means in countries that were adopting democratic processes.

dialectic   The basis of Marx's materialist **method** that exposes contradictions in society to reveal its inner **essence** as distinct from its mystical **form**

of **appearance**. Marx inherited the dialectic from **Hegel** via **Feuerbach** and much controversy surrounds the way he is meant to have modified its usage in his own thought. Marx's intention, as he said in a letter of January 1858 to **Engels**, was to write down in two or three sheets what is rational in the method Hegel discovered but shrouded in mysticism. However, Marx did not complete this task, and instead we are left with only a limited number of places where he explicitly discusses the difference between his dialectic and that of Hegel's.

Marx makes his first critical analysis of Hegel's dialectic in the *Economic and Philosophical Manuscripts* (1844) through the work of Feuerbach. Marx praises Feuerbach's critique of Hegel's dialectic and its idealistic basis in three main ways: first, for showing how philosophy is nothing more than **religion** brought into and imprisoned within thought as another form of **alienation**; second, for founding true **materialism** by making the relations between people the basis of his theory; and third, to have opposed to the **negation** of the negation a positive moment grounded in itself as the real movement and history of humanity. Despite this, Marx was soon to find weaknesses in Feuerbach's own position. In *The German Ideology* (1845–1846) he argues that 'as far as Feuerbach is a materialist he does not deal with history, and as far as he considers history he is not a materialist'. Feuerbach, then, despite his advances on Hegel's philosophy, still remained trapped within idealist forms of thought. However, Marx therefore still had to find a way to transcend Hegel's dialectic materialistically.

The classic and most explicit statement where Marx says how he has accomplished this occurs nearly thirty years later in the Afterword to the second German edition of *Capital* **1** (1867). Marx asserts that his dialectical method is not only different from Hegel's but is its exact opposite because Hegel sees the world being created by the process of thinking through his notion of the Idea and the world itself as the external appearance of this Idea. In contrast, Marx sees this Idea as nothing more than the material world reflected in the minds of humans and then translated into forms of thought. So for Hegel, thoughts and abstract thinking dominate our understanding of the world, but for Marx such thoughts are a reflection of the real world. Hence, Hegel's dialectic is shrouded in **idealism** and therefore mysticism, whereas Marx's dialectic is rooted in the material conditions of human existence. However, Marx then makes the point that although the dialectic suffers from mystification in Hegel's thought, this does not stop him from being the first thinker to present its general forms of motion in a comprehensive and a conscious manner. Hegel simply stood the dialectic on its head, whereas it needs to be 'inverted in order to discover the rational kernel within the mystical shell'.

Marx argues that in its mystical form the dialectic simply endorses what exists, but in its rational form it is a scandal and an abomination to the **bourgeoisie** and their apologists. Marx's dialectic, whilst recognizing the positive moment in what exists, also recognizes the negation and destruction of the existing order. It is through this **contradiction** that his dialectic exposes the transient **nature** of all historically developed forms and grasps them in their movement and motion. As such, Marx's dialectic is in its very essence critical and revolutionary. To illustrate this briefly, Marx notes how **capitalist** society is full of contradictions that manifest themselves through the periodic industrial cycles of boom and bust that lead into **economic crises**. Indeed, he maintains that it is through the intensity and impact of such crises that his revolutionary dialectic is drummed into the heads of the bourgeoisie and forces them to confront the reality of **capitalism**. (See also **abstraction** and **theory and practice**.)

dictatorship of the proletariat   The term given by Marx to the political system to be adopted immediately after the **working class** has seized political power. In *The Class Struggles in France* (1850) he wrote that the workers involved in the June insurrection of 1848 had become so radicalized that they had set up the battle-cry of 'Overthrow of the **bourgeoisie**! Dictatorship of the working class!' Marx considered that the government of the time amounted to a 'dictatorship of the bourgeoisie', although in fact it derived its legitimacy from elections based on universal male franchise two months earlier. His use of the word 'dictatorship' should not be taken, therefore, as the simple opposite of '**democracy**'. At the time 'dictatorship' was normally associated with the device used in the ancient Roman republic, when a ruler would be granted or assume supreme power for a period of no more than six months in order to defend the republic. Later in the *Class Struggles* he endorses the dictatorship of the **proletariat** as a 'necessary intermediate point on the path toward the abolition of **class** differences in general'. He reaffirmed this view in a letter to Joseph Weydemeyer in 1852, arguing that the **class struggle** necessarily led to the dictatorship of the proletariat, and that this dictatorship is the transition to the abolition of all classes and the creation of a classless society. Although Marx was not inclined to speculate about the social and political forms that post-revolutionary society should or might take, in the **Critique of the Gotha Programme** of 1875 he re-states his conviction that the revolutionary dictatorship of the proletariat is the only **form** of transition from **capitalist** to communist society. His enthusiastic endorsement of the direct democratic practices of the **Paris Commune** of 1871 in **The Civil War in France** offers the clearest picture of what this sort of dictatorship might look like. Marx admired the fact that the Commune was a legislative and executive body staffed by elected delegates who could be recalled if they failed to carry out their mandates. Judges and magistrates were also elected, the army was replaced by a militia and public administration was performed by officials working for the average wage.

Doctoral Dissertation (1841)   Marx was awarded the degree of Doctor of Philosophy for his dissertation, *On the Difference between the Democritean and Epicurean Philosophy of Nature*, by the University of Jena in April 1841. It was a highly original comparison of the atomic theories of Democritus (460–371 BC) and Epicurus (341–270 BC). While both philosophers speculated – with amazing foresight – that the atom was the basic building block of the natural world, Democritus' determinism was criticized by Marx. In favouring Epicurus' view that the propensity of atoms to swerve lent spontaneity and unpredictability to **nature**, Marx hinted at much wider philosophical implications. First, in relating the swerve of atoms to the repulsion of atoms, Epicurus accepted the positive nature of an inner **contradiction**. In other words, there were early signs in his philosophy of nature that he had expressed the principle of the **dialectic** – the **negation** of the negation – later perfected by **Hegel**. Marx also thought that Epicurus extended this principle to his social views, as in the notion of a political contract bringing an otherwise fragmented people together. Second, Marx drew a parallel between Epicurus' breakthrough and the situation of German philosophy following Hegel. Epicurus philosophized at a time when most intellectuals considered that **Aristotle** had already had the last word in philosophy, but Epicurus overturned Aristotle's view that the heavenly bodies were fixed. In Marx's student days, the philosophical scene was dominated by Hegelian philosophy, but Marx speculated that it too was destined to be transcended. The thesis is therefore a very anti-deterministic work that reflects his enthusiastic embrace of Epicurus' insistence that humans can understand the world without the assistance of the gods.

—E—

Economic and Philosophical Manuscripts **(1844, posthumously published 1932)** Written in the spring and summer of 1844, the *Economic and Philosophical Manuscripts* contain the clearest expression of Marx's theory of **alienation** and his philosophical **humanism**, yet they remained unpublished until 1932. Even then they met a muted response in the world communist movement and it was not until the 1960s and 1970s that popular editions became available in a variety of languages. The work consists of a Preface and three manuscripts, although only the final four pages of the second manuscript have survived. The *Manuscripts* show Marx's first confrontation with the prevailing orthodoxy in **political economy**, mainly with the work of Adam **Smith**, but also David **Ricardo** and Jean-Baptiste Say. He also draws on a range of socialist sources to outline the appalling conditions endured by the **working class**.

The first manuscript begins with the **wages** of **labour** and goes on to address the role of **capital**, its drive for **profit**, its rule over labour, and the rent of land and the development of modern landed **property**. The final part of the first manuscript contains an important exposition of Marx's concept of alienation as it arises in the labour process. He describes four aspects of alienation (*Entaüsserung* or *Entfremdung*), beginning with the fact that the product of labour stands opposed to the producer as something alien, owned and controlled by the employer. The worker is also alienated from the process of **production**, for work is forced labour over which the worker has no control, leading to a 'loss of self'. The third element is alienation from human **essence** or **species-being** (*Gatungswesen*). Production is a defining feature of what it is to be human, but when the production process is alienated, humans are alienated from their essence. As a consequence, a fourth type of alienation occurs: the alienation of human beings from each other and from **nature**. Marx concludes that as private property is founded on alienated labour, the **emancipation** of society from private property is possible only through the emancipation of the workers.

The short second manuscript deals with social relationships in private property and complains that not only are workers turned into commodities but also into 'mentally and physically dehumanized' beings. The third manuscript begins with a discussion of the relationship between private property and labour and describes for the first time the relationship between capital and labour as a **contradiction** (*Widerspruch*), a 'vigorous relation ... driving towards resolution'. In the next section, on property and **communism**, Marx discusses the historical development of communism from the crude communism of sixteenth-century movements to modern communism that strives to supersede private property and liberate all the human senses and attributes. He also stresses the need for **equality** of respect between men and **women**. The manuscripts continue with a discussion of need, production and the division of labour. Marx observes that although the division of labour and **exchange** are regarded by the political economists as indicating the social nature of economics, in fact they reveal a contradiction – the domination of society by unsocial, particular interests. In the next section he talks about the corrosive power of **money**, making use of quotations from Goethe's *Faust* and Shakespeare's *Timon of Athens* to show the distorting effects that money has on all human relationships.

The final part of the third manuscript is a critique of Hegel's **dialectic**, focusing mainly on the *Phenomenology* but also containing some comments on the shorter *Logic*. It begins with an appreciation of **Feuerbach** as the 'true conqueror' of the idealist dialectic. He then criticizes **Hegel** for committing a double error. The first is dealing only in thought categories, so that alienation becomes merely a problem within thought to be resolved only in **consciousness**. The second is conceiving the categories of the objective world as spiritual entities, remaining within the realm of abstract thought, so that the identification of alienated relations is itself alienated from sensuous reality. Marx argues that the **naturalism** or humanism developed from Feuerbach's philosophy overcomes the limitations of Hegel's **idealism** without falling into crude **materialism**. Despite these objections, Marx praises Hegel for grasping the dialectic of negativity as the moving and producing principle, for conceiving the 'self-creation' of human beings as a process and for identifying alienation and its supersession (*Aufhebung*). He acknowledges that Hegel sees labour as the 'self-confirming essence' of human life, and also recognizes that the 'objective' being can be appropriated only through the supersession of its alienation.

economic crises   For Marx, periodic economic crises reveal the contradictory and unsustainable **nature** of the **capitalist mode of production**. In his mature critique of **political economy** Marx explains the underlying instability that makes crises possible in his work on the **tendency of the rate of profit to fall** and offers more direct explanations of crises in his ideas on over-production and disproportional investment. However, even before he engaged in detailed analysis of economic phenomena he recognized that economic crises were an indicator of the instability of **capitalism**. In **The Communist Manifesto** (1848) crises are regarded as manifestations of a tension between modern productive forces and the **property** relations within which they are developed. At times of economic crisis capitalists are unable to sell their products, a situation of over-production that would have seemed an absurdity in all previous historical epochs. In response, many productive forces are closed or destroyed, but the capitalists will then attempt either the conquest of new markets or the more intensive **exploitation** of old ones. However, in doing this they pave the way for more serious crises in the future, indicating that crises were systematically unavoidable and would recur with increasing intensity.

  In the **Contribution to the Critique of Political Economy** (1859) Marx rejects the general theory of equilibrium set down in Say's Law, whereby every purchase was a sale and supply equals demand. In reality, the development of credit means that purchase and sale become separated, and that separation establishes the possibility of crisis. Capitalists make their investments on the basis of an estimate of the potential **market**, but if they all overestimate, a glut will result. The underlying instability of the system is brought out by Marx in his theory of the tendency of the rate of profit to fall, first set down in the **Grundrisse** (1857–1858) and then more clearly in **Capital 3** (1864–1865). Marx argues that the rate of **profit** depends on the relationship of the amount of **money** expended as **wages** on living **labour** (variable **capital**) and the amount expended on raw materials and the means of production (constant capital). When a greater portion is expended on constant capital there is an increase in the organic composition of capital and the rate of profit declines. As **competition** constantly drives capitalists to spend proportionately more on constant capital in order to increase productivity, the tendency is for the rate of profit to fall over time. Marx describes this as 'in every respect the most important law of political economy', and he links it to the contradictions which reveal themselves in 'crises, spasms, explosions, cataclysms'. Although he argues that this is the actual tendency of capitalist production, it could be delayed by counteracting factors. Nevertheless, these are not sufficient to resist the long-term tendency, which is carried along by the expansionist dynamic of the system. Marx argues that this dynamic necessarily involves massive and regular dislocations, and any periods of equilibrium are won only after the violent purge of a major crisis.

However, as Marx argues in **Theories of Surplus Value** (1861–1863), the possibility of crises implies only that a 'framework for a crisis' exists, which is different from explaining why crises occur at a particular phase of the system's development. Marx considers two more specific causes of crises: under-consumption or over-production and dispropor-tional investment. Under-consumption refers to the problem that although capitalism has a tendency to unlimited **accumulation**, the basis of capitalist production ensures that there is a limit to that accumulation, namely the ability of consumers to purchase the goods. Capitalist production is based on exploitation, the extraction of **surplus value**, but this means that there will never be sufficient effective demand to 'realize' surplus value. In *Capital* 3, Marx writes that the ultimate **reason** for all real crises always remains 'the restricted **consumption** of the masses'. However, this might lead us to expect protracted stagnation and it fails to explain why there are periods in which there is effective demand.

Marx himself expresses doubts about the adequacy of under-consumption as an explanation of crises in his critique of **Ricardo** in chapter seventeen of *Theories of Surplus Value* and also in chapter twenty of **Capital** 2 (1863–1878). He considers why expansion occurs and why it periodically collapses, and in explanation introduces his disproportionality thesis. He contends that a sudden switch of capital, perhaps caused by raw materials becoming scarcer, can have dramatic knock-on effects, producing over-capacity in some sectors of the economy and under-investment in others. Expansion into foreign markets can be offset by the increased competition for the benefits of that expansion, as, for example, in the imperialist scramble for territory that occurred towards the end of Marx's life. Marx recognizes that cycles of boom and bust were related to surges of investment in major capital projects, and he correctly forecast the crisis of the late 1870s that lasted until 1896. Significantly, he argues that perfectly rational investment decisions could result in unexpectedly high shifts in demand, throwing the whole productive system into imbalance, and in this respect he anticipates what later became known in economics as the 'accelerator principle'.

Marx considers an economic crisis to be a 'reconciliation of contradictions' brought about by the violent fusion of disconnected factors. Crises do not lead to the collapse of the entire economic system, but bring about a dramatic reorganization of the economic structure that contributes to the development of even more serious crises in the future, more 'industrial earthquakes'. Marx also notes, in *Capital* 2, the volatility produced when credit is extended by merchants who are themselves reliant on credit, although he regards this apparent crisis on the money market as a reflection of 'anomalies' in the production and reproduction process itself. For Marx, there is always pressure on the money market, but in capitalist society 'social rationality' only asserts itself after a crash, and 'major disturbances can and must occur'.

As for the social impact of economic crises, Marx was always clear that the hardships would fall first and most severely on the **working class**. In his economic writings he goes into great detail of the normal hardships of life as a worker, with long hours, minimal wages and appalling conditions in work and in lodgings, but in times of crisis the situation is worsened by unemployment or short-time working. In **Wage Labour and Capital** (1849) he comments that 'the forest of uplifted arms demanding work becomes even thicker, while the arms themselves become even thinner'. He also considers that crises can destroy many small businesses and marginalize the **petty bourgeoisie**, pushing many of them into the ranks of the workers.

education Free public education for all children was one of the practical demands set down in **The Communist Manifesto** (1848), along with the demand for the abolition of child **labour** in factories and also the call for education to be combined with work experience. Marx reiterated this view in his advice to delegates of the 1866 Conference of the **First International** (1864–1872), stating that in a 'rational' **state** of society this work experience should begin at nine years of age. He added that child labour under **capitalism** was 'distorted into an abomination'. Marx gave a speech on education to the General Council of the International in 1869, and although he called for free national education guaranteed by the state, he did not want the state to be the direct provider of teaching. In the *Critique of the Gotha Programme* (1875) he deplored the programme's demand for elementary education to be provided by the state, insisting that the state should not be the educator of the people. He accepted that the state may set laws to ensure the qualification of teachers and other standards, but apart from that, both government and church should be excluded from all influence in schools. Marx was also concerned with the political education of the workers, noting in a letter to the leaders of the German socialists that bourgeois 'converts' were welcome only if they brought 'real educative elements' to the movement and recognized the inevitability of the **class struggle**.

The Eighteenth Brumaire of Louis Bonaparte **(1852)**   The curious title refers to the calendar adopted after the great French Revolution. Marx was parodying the *coup d'état* of Louis Bonaparte, in December 1851, as a pale imitation of the seizure of power of his uncle, Napoleon Bonaparte, in 1799. Marx's book provides a masterly analysis of the political struggles that led up to his seizure of power, covering the brief history of the French Second Republic from its inception at the February **revolution** in 1848 until the *coup*. It was published in the United States, but few copies reached Europe, and it was not until the second edition of 1869 that it became widely available.

Marx linked the various political parties of the Republic with particular **class** interests. He argued that although the parties in opposition adopted political positions that did not appear to be determined by class interest, at times of political crisis their class interests prevailed and political principles became expendable. Perhaps the best example was the party of the 'Pure Republicans' that led the opposition to King Louis Philippe, initially identified not in terms of their class interests, but in terms of their opposition to monarchy and their support for political and civil liberties. However, when the June uprising of the Paris **working class** threatened their power and their **property**, the Pure Republicans introduced strict press censorship and attacked **freedom** of association. The republicans were heavily defeated in the election of May 1849, leaving the majority party in the Second Republic, the Party of Order, in the hands of supporters of the two rival royal families. Finally, in 1850, the republicans agreed to the abolition of the universal male franchise that had been established in 1848.

The *Brumaire* contains valuable insights into Marx's views on social class and its political expression, and on the nature of the **state**. On social class, it is clear that Marx does not see the **class struggle** in the simplified working-class-versus-**bourgeoisie form** predicted in *The Communist Manifesto* (1848). The bourgeoisie was divided into three factions, representing industry, land and finance. Their failure to act in concert created the vacuum that enabled the President, Louis Bonaparte, to usurp power. Bonaparte was elected by the overwhelming majority in France, the **peasantry**, but this was a class only in so far as its members shared a common lifestyle: it was unable to represent its own interests, let alone impose them on a political leader. The working class, threatened with destitution when the closure of the national workshops was announced, plunged into a revolution that was bloodily suppressed in June 1848. Nevertheless, by the following year, working-class and urban petty bourgeois interests were represented in the National Assembly by a group termed 'social **democracy**' by Marx, who was dismissive of their efforts. The other class dealt with by Marx was the **lumpenproletariat**, comprising those on the margins of society such as pickpockets and vagabonds – *la bohème* – fit only to become the 'bribed tool of reactionary intrigue'. A minority were mobilized by Louis Bonaparte, prompting Marx to call him a 'princely lumpenproletarian'.

In terms of the state, the idea expressed in the *Manifesto* that the state represents the interests of the bourgeoisie appears to be contradicted in the *Brumaire*. At one point Marx observes that under Bonaparte the state seems to have attained 'a completely autonomous position'. In fact, Marx argues, Bonaparte represented the peasants who had voted for him in their millions, but as the peasantry was a disorganized class it meant that Bonaparte and the state machine he controlled had a great deal of independent power. Eventually he used that power to abolish the National Assembly, abolish representative government and re-establish an autocratic empire. However, his own power ultimately rested on his ability to deliver what was good for French **capitalism**, and to do this he would have to placate the various competing interests in society, something Marx considered to be an 'impossible' task.

emancipation   Used by Marx to refer to the achievement of freedom from all forms of oppression. Although he supported emancipation struggles against national subjugation and **slavery**, his primary concern was with emancipation from the scourge of class rule. He made a crucial link between the liberation of the working class and the liberation of humanity as a whole. This was first set down in a **Contribution to the Critique of Hegel's Philosophy of Right: Introduction** (1844), when he argued that the working class, or **proletariat**, was the class that suffered no particular wrong but wrong in general, a class whose condition appeared as the 'total loss of humanity' and whose self-liberation can only lead to the 'total redemption of humanity'. Marx consistently reiterated this conviction, emphasizing repeatedly that the emancipation (*Emanzipation*) of the working class could be achieved only by the working class itself. He considered **communism** to be the movement of this self-emancipation through which the class would gain **consciousness** of its historic mission. Marx made an important distinction between political emancipation and human emancipation (*menschliche Emanzipation*) in **On the Jewish Question** (1844). The achievement of a democratic republic would be a major step forward, but this political emancipation would only create the means through which the **class struggle** could be fought out openly. Only with the abolition of private **property** and the establishment of a classless society could we think in terms of human emancipation. However, Marx was reluctant to talk about what the emancipated future might look like. In political terms, the participatory democracy adopted by the **Paris Commune** (1871) offered a model for a new society. In more general terms, his depiction of the realm of **freedom** in **Capital 3** (1864–1865) makes it clear that **production** in society would be organized in a rational way by the associated producers using the least onerous methods and reduced working hours. Only on this basis could the real realm of freedom begin, conjuring up an image of conscious reciprocity and boundless creativity.

Engels, Friedrich (1820–1895)   Marx's closest friend and collaborator, Engels was co-author of **The Holy Family** (1845), the unpublished **The German Ideology** (1845–1846) and **The Communist Manifesto** (1848). After Marx's death he was responsible for editing and publishing **Capital 2** (1885) and **Capital 3** (1895).

They first met in 1842 when Marx was editor of the *Rheinische Zeitung*, but their association blossomed the following year when Engels wrote

'Outlines of a Critique of Political Economy' for Marx's new journal, the *Deutsch-Französiche Jahrbücher*. The essay appeared in the final edition of the journal in February 1844 and it made a deep and lasting impression on Marx. In this engagement with British political economy, Engels exposes its callous disregard for the social cost of the inexorable advance of capitalism, but he goes further than that, arguing that the progress of the system erodes its own foundations and paves the way for its transformation. He predicts that private property will eventually be superseded by a more rational system, reconciling humankind with nature and with itself. He concludes by lambasting the 'despicable immorality' of the system and the brazen hypocrisy of the economists. The article confirmed Marx in his conviction to proceed with his own critical analysis of political economy, and he outlined his own thoughts on the nature of **exploitation** as **alienation** in the ***Economic and Philosophical Manuscripts*** (1844). Engels went on to write his masterpiece, *The Condition of the Working Class in England*, published in 1845, and his detailed descriptions of working-class life provided a template that Marx was to adopt when writing ***Capital* 1** more than twenty years later.

Engels joined Marx in Brussels in 1845, working together in the Brussels Correspondence Committee, developing networks that eventually led to the creation of the Communist League in 1847. Their collaboration on the unpublished ***The German Ideology*** in the winter of 1845–1846 marked a vitally important moment in the development of the interpretation of history that served as their theoretical framework. When Marx eventually summarized this interpretation in the 1859 **Preface to *A Contribution to the Critique of Political Economy***, Engels reviewed the work and labelled it the 'materialist conception of history', though Marx never used this term. In an 1890 letter to Joseph Bloch, Engels offered a new name for the theory – **historical materialism**. The most famous collaboration between Marx and Engels came when they were asked to write a programme for the Communist League, resulting in the publication of ***The Communist Manifesto*** in January 1848. Although Marx wrote the final draft himself, he made use of two earlier programmatic pieces by Engels, *Draft of a Communist Confession of Faith* and *Principles of Communism*. Within weeks of the publication of the *Manifesto*, revolutions erupted across Europe. Engels helped Marx edit the *Neue Rheinische Zeitung*, for which he wrote more than 150 articles. As well as working for the goal of a unified democratic German republic, they pushed for radical reform in favour of the working class, set down in *The Demands of the Communist Party in Germany*. These demands included universal franchise, nationalization of banks and key industries, free education and the introduction of a progressive income tax. Engels took part in fighting for the democrats against the Prussian army in Elberfeld and in Baden before being forced to flee Germany. Like Marx, he migrated to England, basing himself in Manchester, where he drew a regular income by working for his family firm. Marx relied overwhelmingly on Engels' financial support to enable him to continue with his theoretical work.

The correspondence between the two friends during their long exile was invaluable for the development of Marx's thought. Engels was always the first to receive Marx's insights and opinions and their extensive exchange of views helped both men to clarify their ideas. The correspondence is also a valuable source for tracing the development of Marx's thought. Engels played a decisive role in presenting Marx's social theory to the world at large as their shared worldview. He published *Anti-Dühring* in 1877–1878, part of which became published as *Socialism, Utopian and Scientific* (1880), an immensely popular book that could be regarded as the founding text of 'Marxism'. Engels gave the graveside oration at Marx's funeral, praising Marx for introducing two outstanding scientific advances: the discovery of the 'law of development of human history' and the 'special law of motion' governing the capitalist mode of production. Engels extended the application of dialectical philosophy to nature in the *Dialectics of Nature*, published shortly after his death in 1895. This work on nature and the codification of laws of dialectics that came with it were quickly assimilated into the new '**science**' of Marxism as 'dialectical materialism', although there is no evidence that Marx approved such views.

equality   Marx argues that in bourgeois society equality is formal rather than real and he shows this in a number of ways. In *Capital* **1** (1867) he says that at the level of **exchange** when the worker, the seller of **labour power**, confronts the **capitalist**, the buyer of labour power with **money**, **capital** appears to be the 'realm of **freedom**, equality, **property** and Bentham', one of the founders of utilitarianism. They are free because both have free will and as free persons they are equal before the **law**. They are equal because they are exchanging commodities that are equivalent to each other. They have property because they are selling what belongs to them and they are Bentham because they both look only to their own advantage in the transaction. Both worker and capitalist therefore appear to be equal members of society and both appear to enjoy equally the **rights** of that society. However, Marx argues that in reality their relationship is one of inequality, and only formal equality exists in the realm of exchange. In the hidden abode of **production**, the capitalist, through his or her control over the means of production, engages in the **exploitation** of the worker through the extraction of **surplus value**. The unequal relations at the heart of the production process are therefore concealed in the appearances of equality in the realm of capitalist exchange. Rectifying the inequalities that operate in the realm of production therefore take on a particular importance for Marx.

In the **Critique of the Gotha Programme** (1875) he argues that any distribution of the means of **consumption** is only a consequence of the distribution of the conditions of production themselves. Hence, proposals for redistribution tend to centre on the redistribution of income, but ultimately this still leaves people within the capitalist system of exploitation. Marx's main concern is about inequalities in production and thus the need to transcend capital by bringing the means of production under common ownership and control. Once this has been achieved he then considers the nature of redistribution in the early and higher phases of communist society. He points out that in the early phase the society will still bear many of the hallmarks of capital and the workers would expect to get in return the equal amount of what they have put into the work they have done. However, he sees this equal right of all, what he also calls a bourgeois right, to be an unequal right for unequal **labour** because it does not account for differences in skills, strength, intelligence or the number of dependents the workers may have. Yet all these factors affect the capacity of individuals to work and so determine the rewards that society can give them. Once a higher stage of **communism** is reached, Marx suggests that there will be more real equality because the rule that will govern society will be: from each according to his or her ability, to each according to his or her **needs**. So, equality for Marx is not treating everyone the same, but instead involves a careful scrutiny and appreciation of their different needs and capabilities.

essence   In terms of his **method**, Marx contrasts essence as reality with the mystifications of **appearance**. He contends that we cannot properly understand things simply by observing them because they need to be analyzed carefully to reveal their essence. As he says in **Capital 3** (1864–1865), 'all **science** would be superfluous if the outward appearance and the essence of things coincided'. Scientific truth itself is also paradoxical because it seems to go against our everyday experience of things. As examples Marx gives the paradox that the earth moves round the sun and that water consists of two highly inflammable gases. So if we can be deceived by observable reality in this way, we must subject things to further scrutiny and analysis and not assume that they are necessarily as they seem. Consequently, we need to uncover the essences of phenomena and grasp their relation to each other. In relation to **capital**, for example, it appears as an open and free system, but further investigation reveals its essence as a class society based on the **exploitation** of the workers.

Essence also relates to what makes us **human** and is linked to Marx's notion of **species-being**. Essence can only be discerned in creative social activity manifest in society, what Marx calls in the sixth **Theses on Feuerbach** (1845) the 'ensemble of the social relations'. Hence, it must be understood not simply in **abstraction**, but instead from the historical development of how humans make and create the world. In capital, the **form** this essence takes is one of **alienation** rather than what it should be: a true community of human beings in their authentic existence of social activity and social enjoyment.

exchange   In the **Grundrisse** (1857–1858) Marx discusses exchange as having a dialectical relationship to **production**, **consumption** and distribution. He argues that exchange is present in and constitutes the production process through the exchange of activities and abilities, through the exchange of products in terms of finishing them and making them fit for direct consumption, and through the exchange of commodities between dealers. Exchange only appears independent from production in the final phase where the product is exchanged directly for consumption. However, exchange in all its moments is either directly comprised in, or determined by, production for three reasons. First, there can be no exchange without a division of **labour**. Second, private exchange presupposes private production. Third, the intensity of exchange, as well as its intention and its manner, are determined by the development and structure of production. This is not to deny that exchange itself can impact on production. If there is an expansion in the **market** for a particular product, for example, then that will certainly cause a growth in production, but Marx sees these determinants of production as being one-sided, when the key is to understand these relations through their mutual interaction as an organic whole.

The realm of exchange also acts as the realm of **appearance** in **capital**, and so disguises the real relations that take place in the realm of production. In **Capital 1** (1867), for example, in his discussion of the buying and selling of **labour power**, Marx refers to the sphere of circulation or **commodity** exchange as presenting itself as a Garden of Eden that contains the **rights** of all. Its appearance is as a realm of **freedom**, **equality**, **property** and Bentham, one of the founders of utilitarianism. Freedom is present because the buyer and seller of labour power contract as free persons who are equal under the **law**. Equality and property occurs because each exchanges his or her own property, one of labour power and the other of **money**, as equivalent for equivalent, and Bentham is included because as an advocate of maximizing utility he would expect both parties to look only to their own interests. What brings the seller and buyer together in the realm of exchange is therefore the selfishness, gain and private interest of each, and yet in doing so it appears that they work together for mutual advantage and in the common interest of society. However, Marx contends that really to understand what is happening in the sphere of exchange, it is necessary to enter the hidden abode of production to discover that this relationship is actually based on **exploitation** and **alienation**, and is a far cry from the way capital presents itself to us.

exploitation   The extraction of unpaid surplus **labour** in a process of **class struggle**. Marx states in **Capital 3** (1864–1865), in a succinct passage on the **nature** of exploitation, that the 'specific economic **form** in which unpaid surplus labour is pumped out of direct producers, determines the relationship of rulers and ruled'. On the basis of this antagonism of the relations of **production** arises both an economic community and its specific political form. By focusing on the way people come together to produce in any society, therefore, Marx suggests that its exploitative nature can be exposed and that will then reveal the economic and political forms that society will take. Surplus labour itself, as Marx states in **Capital 1** (1867), exists wherever a section of society controls the means of production and makes the workers, whether free or unfree, add an extra amount of labour time to that which is necessary to reproduce themselves. This extra time is used to produce the means of subsistence for the owners of the means of production. These owners can be traced back through history from the Athenian and Roman aristocrats, Norman barons, American slave-owners and modern landlords or capitalists. However, Marx observes that in pre-capitalist societies in particular, the pumping out of surplus labour will normally be more limited because they are concerned with producing for use **value** rather than **exchange** value. That is, they are mainly preoccupied with creating useful goods for **consumption** rather than for sale on the **market**. With the onset of a **world market** and the beginning of **capital**, production for exchange value takes precedence over production for use value and a more intense pumping out of surplus labour, and thereby exploitation, begins.

In a slave society, for example, the surplus labour is produced by the slave who works beyond the amount of time necessary to reproduce him or herself. The master takes this unpaid surplus labour for his or her own consumption, even though it is the slave who has produced the goods and completed the work. So the way in which this unpaid surplus labour is pumped out determines the relation of the ruler, the master as slave owner, to the ruled, the slave. Society economically and politically will therefore reflect and support this relationship through its laws and practices.

Similarly, in **feudalism**, the serf who works on the land for the lord has to work more than the time necessary to reproduce him or herself. In feudalism this form of exploitation is clearly visible because the serf works a certain number of days producing for his or her own **needs** and the needs of his or her **family**, and then another certain number of days producing a surplus for the lord. The way this surplus is pumped out again determines the exploitative relationships between ruler and ruled and is enshrined in the economic and political structure that is appropriate to such relations, which in feudalism means that the **state** and **civil society** are merged with each other.

Within the appearances of **capitalism**, exploitation takes a more hidden form, because the worker, as the seller of **labour power**, and the **capitalist**, as its buyer, seem to be engaging in a free and equal exchange with each other. Moreover, unlike the slave who was tied to a master, or the serf who was tied to the lord, the worker is now free to choose an employer. The separation of civil society from the state reflects this new social relation that has again emerged economically and politically out of the pumping out of surplus labour. New forms of exploitation require new forms of legal and political practices to regulate them.

In the apparently free realm of capitalism, when the workers engage in exchange with capitalists they seem to offer equivalent for equivalent in their transaction. The worker gets a wage and the capitalist gets the worker's labour power. However, once the capitalist puts the labour power into motion as actual labour, the worker creates more than is necessary to satisfy his or her subsistence needs, and the labour beyond that level is the surplus labour that is taken by the capitalist in the form of **surplus value**. What obscures the process of exploitation here is the payment of **wages** and the fact that that the necessary labour and surplus labour appear mingled together. However, in **essence** the splitting up of the **working day** into necessary and surplus labour is present here just as it is in feudal relations of exploitation. Wages pay only for that part of the day that forms necessary labour, and the worker remains unpaid for that part of the day that forms surplus labour. Breaking through the appearances of capital allows Marx to expose that fact and the persistence of exploitation in previous and current history as a history of class struggle. Such exploitation, the pumping out of unpaid surplus labour, is therefore characteristic of all **class** societies where a minority, through their control over the means of production, put the majority to work for them. Societies only differ in the form this exploitation takes whether it is based on **slavery**, feudalism or capitalist relations of production.

—F—

family   In **_The Communist Manifesto_** (1848) Marx launched a strong attack on bourgeois hypocrisy when it comes to the veneration of the family. While preaching about the importance of the parent–child relationship, the **bourgeoisie** presides over an economic system that destroys **working-class** family life through child **labour**. He accuses bourgeois men of treating their wives as 'mere instruments of **production**' (whereas communists would remove that status), for taking sexual advantage of working-class wives and daughters, and of widespread use of prostitutes. In chapter fifteen of *Capital* **1** (1867) he returns to the theme of how the family life of the working class is destroyed by the employment of whole families in dreadful conditions for extraordinarily long hours on minimal **wages**. He quotes the concluding report of the Children's Employment Commission of 1866, which blamed working-class parents for the **exploitation** of their children. Marx points out that it was not the misuse of parental power that created the exploitation of children by **capital**, but rather the **capitalist** system that was responsible for the 'terrible and disgusting dissolution of the old family'. Despite this appalling reality, he argued that bringing **women** and young people into employment created a 'new economic foundation for a higher **form** of the family and relations between the sexes'. Towards the end of his life he made copious notes from a variety of anthropological sources on various forms of family life. He was scornful of the writers who considered the patriarchal family to be the original form, ignoring more communal forms such as the clan. He was particularly interested in those societies in which women played a more powerful role than in modern bourgeois society.

feudalism   The historical period and **mode of production** that emerged after ancient Roman society and immediately preceded **capitalism**. In *The Communist Manifesto* (1848) Marx points out that the main social relations that prevailed in ancient Rome were a **class struggle** between the patricians, those who controlled the land and held **state** power, the plebeians, those who were citizens who were free but did not have full civic **rights**, and the slaves. Feudalism emerged out of this class struggle. As he notes in *The German Ideology* (1845–1846), the decline of the Roman Empire allowed conquest by the barbarians, who destroyed a large part of the productive forces of that society, leading to a decline in agriculture, industry and trade. Out of this situation, the need to develop productive forces asserted itself, and the model for this was a form of martial organization that came from Germany and introduced feudal social relations.

   Marx describes feudalism as a society where the social relations of **production** predominantly take the **form** of an antagonistic relationship between lords and serfs or peasants. The lords own the means of production, which is the land, and the serfs or peasants are therefore forced to work the land to satisfy their own **needs** and those of the lords. The lords take the surplus **labour** of the serfs in the produce they create in a process of **exploitation** and class struggle.

In the *Economic and Philosophical Manuscripts* (1844) Marx examines the **nature** of the state and **civil society** in feudalism, arguing that they appear to be separate because the state was the preserve of the monarch, and the lords and serfs existed outside this realm in civil society. However, he contends that civil society is directly political because all the elements of civil life, such as **property**, **family** and the nature of work, are overseen and regulated by the lord. Feudalism is therefore characterized by legal and customary bonds that exist between lords and serfs. Labour is not, as in capital, free labour, to be exploited by any owner of the means of production. Rather it is tied to production under the jurisdiction of the lord who controls the manor. For Marx, therefore, feudal landownership represents the domination of the earth as an alien power over human beings. However, the relationship between lord and serf is not a relationship of **alienation**, as is the case between a **capitalist** and a worker, because there is no pretence of **equality** and there is also still some semblance of an intimate connection between the lord and his land of which the serfs are a part.

Feudalism is also typified by a lower level of technological development of the productive forces compared to capital. Each society will therefore have social relations that closely correspond to their productive forces. As Marx argues in *The Poverty of Philosophy* (1847), 'the hand-mill gives you society with a feudal lord; the steam-mill, society with the industrial capitalist'.

In part eight of *Capital* 1 (1867) Marx shows how the movement from feudalism into capitalism was a violent and bloody process that involved the expulsion of the peasants from the land, and in particular the enclosing of common land, in a process of primitive **accumulation**. Again, as Marx elucidates in the *Manuscripts*, the breaking down of these feudal relations also results in the separation of civil society from the state and allows agricultural labour to take the form of labour in general in capital.

Feuerbach, Ludwig (1804–1872)   German philosopher, a pupil of **Hegel**, one of the **Young Hegelians** and author of the hugely influential *The*

Essence of Christianity (1841), *Provisional Theses for the Reform of Philosophy* (1842) and *Principles of the Philosophy of the Future* (1843). Feuerbach's **materialism**, critiques of **religion**, **idealism** and the **dialectic** of Hegel had a profound influence on Marx. Even Marx's crucial concept of **species-being** had its origins in Feuerbach's thought, as did his notion of **commodity fetishism**. In a letter to Feuerbach in 1844, Marx declared his love and respect for him, not least for providing a philosophical basis for **socialism**.

In the *Essence* Feuerbach offers a humanist critique of religion to expose how real human **needs** and desires are projected in an alienated **form** into religious beliefs. Whilst Marx was sympathetic to such arguments, which influenced his own understanding of religion, he was more impressed with Feuerbach's discussion of Hegel in the *Theses*. This work enabled Marx to invert Hegel's dialectic and informed his own discussion of this issue in the *Critique of Hegel's Philosophy of Right* in 1843. Indeed, the following year, in the *Economic and Philosophical Manuscripts* (1844), Marx praises Feuerbach for being the only person to offer a serious and critical attitude to the Hegelian dialectic, and such adulation of Feuerbach allowed Marx to be identified simply as his disciple. In the *Theses on Feuerbach* (1845) Marx even adopts the aphoristic style that Feuerbach had employed in his *Principles* and *Provisional Theses*. However, it is in the *Theses* that Marx develops a far more critical attitude towards Feuerbach. He rejects his materialism for being ahistorical and still imprisoned within the abstractions that Feuerbach had himself exposed within idealism. In *The German Ideology* (1845–1846) Marx also accuses him of both accepting and misunderstanding existing reality by believing that being coincides with essence. Feuerbach wrongly assumes that humans or non-human **animals** in their existence and 'mode of life' are realizing their essence, and where this is not the case then he assumes it to be an 'unavoidable misfortune, which must be borne quietly'. Yet, as Marx indicates, humans can make their being and essence coincide by changing the world to overcome such 'misfortune' rather than passively accepting such an intolerable situation.

Despite all these criticisms, Marx's debt to Feuerbach cannot be doubted. In a letter to a fellow German communist, Johann Baptist von Schweitzer, on 24 January 1865, Marx stated that while Feuerbach is certainly poor compared to Hegel, he nevertheless was epoch-making after Hegel because he laid stress on certain points that were disagreeable to the Christian

consciousness but important for the progress of criticism, points that Hegel had left in mysticism.

fictitious capital   Money used in the credit system that is not related to the **production** of actual commodities. In *Capital* **3** (1864–1865) Marx argues that when money is used as **capital** it is lent out with the intention of realizing interest. This is in contrast to money that is used as capital that is invested in the means of production in order to realize **surplus value**, through the **exploitation** of **labour**. Money capital is therefore fictitious in the sense that it is not related to the reality of producing actual commodities and so has no solid basis in reality. It is instead a claim on the future production of surplus value, and this creates a tension between these different forms of capital. Fictitious capital is therefore parasitic on capital employed in the production process and so gives rise to a new kind of parasite, a financial aristocracy in the **form** of company promoters, speculators and directors. As such, 'a colossal system of gambling and swindling' emerges in relation to the promotion of companies, issues of shares and share dealings. This gap between the real side of the economy and the fictitious side can give rise to financial crises if there are barriers to surplus extraction and credit is expanded to overcome this. Such mounting debt becomes unsustainable and the fictitious nature of the capital is therefore exposed.

First International (1864–1872)   The name commonly given to the International Working Men's Association, comprising **individual** members and branch affiliates from all the major European countries and the United States. It was set up at the initiative of French and British **working-class** leaders at a meeting in St Martin's Hall, London, in September 1864 and Marx, excited by its potential, played a leading role from the outset as a member of the General Council. He wrote the Inaugural Address, which was published as a pamphlet, and also the Provisional Rules, which were confirmed at the Geneva Congress in 1866. The Address declared that the conquest of political power was the great duty of the working classes, while the first Rule stated that 'the **emancipation** of the working classes must be conquered by the working classes themselves', leading to 'the abolition of **class** rule'. During its eight active years it had tens of thousands of individual members and affiliates. Its support for workers involved in industrial struggles led to notable victories in Paris, Geneva and Lyon, and it gave financial assistance and supportive publicity to workers in dispute in Europe and the United States. The principal factions within the International at first included the anarchist supporters of **Proudhon**, followers of Giuseppe Mazzini, the Italian nationalist revolutionary, moderate British trade unionists, and Marx and his followers. Inevitably, there was considerable disagreement over both goals and tactics, and the situation polarized after 1868 when **Bakunin** and his anarchist followers joined the International. In general the anarchists were opposed to participation in parliamentary **politics** and suspicious of policies like nationalization that might enhance the power of the **state**. They did not support the idea that the workers should seize state power, but instead favoured the state's immediate abolition. The antagonism between the Marx and Bakunin camps divided the International, and Marx was concerned that the apocalyptic and insurrectionary rhetoric of the anarchists obstructed the development of legal activity by political parties and **trade unions**. The International's support for the **Paris Commune** (1871) led to it being banned in France and governments throughout Europe arrested socialists and closed their publications. Two prominent British trade unionists withdrew from the General Council in protest at its support for the Commune. In this volatile situation, Bakunin wanted to wrest power in the International away from Marx and his allies. Marx, fearing that the International risked being converted into a clandestine organization preaching insurrection or even terrorism, engineered the transfer of its headquarters to New York at the 1872 Hague Conference, effectively ending its active life. It was formally dissolved in Philadelphia in 1876.

form Crucial for tracing the internal relation between phenomena so that we can discover the antagonistic relationship between **capital** and **labour**. This antagonistic relationship always expresses itself in fetishized forms, such as the value-form, money-form, state-form etc. It is through dissolving these forms that the social relation they deny can be unearthed. For example, in *Capital* **1** (1867) Marx uses the notion of form to distinguish his **method** from the method of classical **political economy**. He praises all the economists since the time of William Petty for investigating the 'real internal framework of bourgeois relations of **production**, as opposed to the vulgar economists who only flounder around within the apparent framework of those relations', whilst 'proclaiming for everlasting truths, the banal and complacent notions held by the bourgeois agents of production about their own world, which is to them the best possible one'. Previous classical political economy made a real contribution because it did try to analyze the internal framework of phenomena. Its best representatives, for example **Smith** and **Ricardo**, attempted to analyze capital scientifically by investigating the **commodity** and its **value**. However, their chief failing, according to Marx, was in not asking the important question of why this content has assumed that particular form. That is to say, they did not ask why labour is expressed in **value** and why the measurement of labour by its duration is expressed in the magnitude of the value of the product. Had they done so they would have seen that labour is expressed in value because people are separated from the means of production in a commodity-producing society, and the only way to find out whether the independent labours expended on a commodity have been worthwhile is through its validation on the **market** as socially necessary labour time. As Marx indicates, these outcomes show that capital is a particular type of social production that has been created, and thereby can be uncreated, where the system controls humans rather than humans controlling the system. Attention to form therefore reveals the true nature of **capitalism** and also its transitory character.

Consequently, form is an essential aspect of Marx's method and his critique of conceptual approaches that take things at face value. This becomes even clearer in Marx's 'Notes on Adolph Wagner' (1879–1880), where he states explicitly that he does not start out from concepts, such as the concept of value, for example. Instead, his starting point for analysis is the simplest social form in which the labour-product is presented in contemporary society, the commodity. He therefore analyses it, and right from the beginning, in the form in which it appears.

free trade Marx identified both destructive and progressive consequences in free trade. In a speech in January 1848, he made it clear that the advocates of free trade were solely concerned with the most ruthless **exploitation** of all markets, but he concluded that free trade should be supported because it hastened the 'social **revolution**'. Its further development marked the triumph of the **bourgeoisie** against the old conservative forces and set the scene for the final **class struggle** between the bourgeoisie and the **working class**. However, in that speech Marx was speaking of free trade primarily as the removal of tariff barriers and other protective measures. In a newspaper article in August 1852 he recognized that the commitment of the free traders in Britain was not simply to the 'unfettered movement of **capital**', but also to the removal of any 'political or social restrictions, regulations or monopolies'. Marx consistently berated this doctrinaire resistance to all forms of regulation, praising the **trade unions** for their part in securing restrictions on the **working day** and other protective regulations. In the Inaugural Address to the **First International** (1864–1872) he praised the part that organized **labour** played in winning the Ten Hours Act in Britain in 1847, declaring it a victory for the '**political economy** of the working class' over 'the political economy of the middle'. In the chapter on the working day in *Capital* **1** (1867), Marx noted with satisfaction that **state** regulation was imposed to overcome the scandalous conditions in the baking trade, without any regard for 'His Holiness' Free Trade. He also pointed to the hypocrisy of those free traders in Britain who had argued that the abolition of the protectionist Corn Laws would benefit the working class and who then protested at efforts to reduce the working day. He frequently mocked the tendency of bourgeois writers and orators to equate free trade with **freedom** itself. In *The Communist Manifesto* (1848) he argued that free buying and selling can only be related to freedom in general if we compare it with the feudal system, but in a free **market** system the vast majority of people have no **property**. In other words, bourgeois 'freedom' was freedom only for a small minority of people, and only **communism** could bring social freedom through the abolition of private productive property.

freedom Marx's work was driven by a strong commitment to freedom, but he rejects the unlimited freedom to private **property** valued in the liberal tradition. In his 1848 *Speech on Free Trade* he appeals for people not to be deluded by the abstract word 'freedom', demanding to know 'Whose freedom?' He argued that **free trade** did not mean the freedom of one **individual** in relation to another, but rather 'freedom of **capital** to crush the worker'. In *The Communist Manifesto* (1848) Marx responds to critics who accused the communists of wanting to abolish the right of personally acquiring the fruits of their **labour**, the 'alleged' groundwork of all personal freedom, activity and independence. He insists that although communists did not want to deprive people of the right to appropriate the products of society, they did want to deny the right of people to subjugate the labour of others by this appropriation. For Marx, the reality behind the 'brave words' of the **bourgeoisie** about 'freedom in general' is that modem bourgeois property condemns the mass of workers to **poverty**, thereby depriving them of their substantive freedom. The abolition of private productive property is therefore seen as a prerequisite for the goal of a classless society, an association 'in which the free development of each is the condition for the free development of all'. This insistence on reciprocity is key to Marx's conception of freedom.

In order to achieve true freedom, political freedom in the shape of political **democracy** is needed, but from as early as 1843, when he wrote *On the Jewish Question* (1844), Marx stressed that the political **emancipation** delivered by democracy should not be confused with human **emancipation**. Human freedom begins only with the dissolution of **class** society. In terms of positive freedoms, from his first confrontation with practical social issues as editor of the *Rheinische Zeitung* (1842–1843), Marx consistently supported freedom of the press, freedom of association and freedom of assembly. His views on the political arrangements that would help to achieve freedom become clearer when he reported on the participatory democracy of the **Paris Commune** (1871), endorsing it with enthusiasm in *The Civil War in France* (1871). Here Marx sees for the first time a **working-class** government unconstrained by the power of economic elites or the interventions of the **bureaucracy** and the army, the unelected elements of the **state**. The need to make the government properly accountable is stressed in the *Critique of the Gotha Programme* (1875), where he writes that 'freedom consists in converting the state from an organ superimposed on society into one thoroughly subordinate to it'. As to the means to achieve it, in a speech in Amsterdam in 1872 he stated that it was possible for workers to achieve their goals through peaceful means in countries that were moving towards political democracy, but kept open the possibility of revolutionary force in autocratic states.

In chapter forty-eight of *Capital* **3** (1864–1865) Marx speaks in uncharacteristically visionary terms of what the 'realm of freedom' might look like. It begins only where labour determined by necessity and external expediency ends, and lies 'by its very **nature**' beyond the sphere of material **production** proper. Socialized human beings can govern production in a rational way 'in conditions worthy and appropriate for their **human** nature', but that work process still remains in the realm of necessity. Only once that is taken care of, on the basis of greatly reduced working hours, can the true realm of freedom flourish, where individuals can choose to do what they want, provided that it does not impair the freedom of others. In terms of the subjective experience of freedom, there are occasional uses of the terms 'self-actualization' and 'self-realization' (*Selstbetätigung*) to invoke the feeling that individuals could experience in communist society. In *The German Ideology* (1845–1846) Marx speculates that only when the working class 'rids itself of everything that still clings to it' from its previous position in society can self-activity coincide with material life, developing individuals into complete individuals and 'casting off all natural limitations'. In the *Grundrisse* (1857–1858) he again talks about labour in communist society transforming itself into 'liberating activity' or 'self-realization'.

—G—

The German Ideology* (1845–1846, posthumously published 1932)**   Written in collaboration with **Engels** in the winter of 1845 and 1846 but unpublished in their lifetimes, *The German Ideology* is significant as the first expression of Marx's conception of historical development, later known as **historical materialism**. In an article published in the *Deutsch-Brüsseler-Zeitung*, the 'Declaration Against Karl Grün', in April 1847, Marx revealed that he and Engels had written a document entitled *The German Ideology* critiquing the work of **Feuerbach**, Bruno Bauer and Max Stirner as well some of the 'prophets' of German **socialism**. In the 1859 **Preface to *A Contribution to the Critique of Political Economy he commented that they had abandoned the manuscript of the two-volume critique of the 'ideological' views of post-Hegelian philosophy, having achieved their goal of 'self-clarification'.

By far the most significant part of the book is the first part, the fragments set down under '1 Feuerbach', although it is doubtful that this was intended to be part of the planned book mentioned above. Here it is argued that human **consciousness** develops as part of the life-process, and the best way to understand the development of this life-process is to focus on the ways in which human beings produce and reproduce their material life. The history of humanity must therefore always be 'studied and treated in relation to the history of industry and **exchange**'. Once a social division of **labour** develops under private **property**, social classes emerge, and with them the **state**. Political battles are seen as 'illusory' forms in which the real struggles of the different classes are fought out. Different ways of social organization accompany the development of the forces of **production** and a number of modes of production are identified – tribal, ancient, **feudal** and 'advanced', the latter referring to **capitalism**. The various stages of capitalism are then described, from the early development of industry in response to the **appearance** of gold and silver from America, through the phase of colonial monopolies, and then into the era of large-scale industry and universal **competition**. Marx argues that although social revolutions will take on 'subsidiary forms' such as the battle for ideas and political struggles, all collisions in history have their origin in the **contradiction** between the productive forces and forms of intercourse. This is the first formulation of what came to be known in the 1859 Preface as the contradiction between the forces of production and the relations of production. In capitalism this contradiction takes on the **form** of a **class struggle** between the **bourgeoisie** and the **working class**, the **class** that can achieve **emancipation** only by abolishing labour itself and ushering in a classless society. Marx talks about the development of a communist consciousness, involving the 'alteration' of people 'on a mass scale' through revolutionary activity. There are confident predictions that the workers will develop this consciousness and become 'world historical' figures, conscious of their position and determined to achieve liberation in an international **revolution**. However, it is also acknowledged that the ideas of the **ruling class** are the ruling ideas and that people are often not aware of the material causes of the divisions in society. The competition between different groups of workers can obstruct their development into a 'community of revolutionary proletarians'.

The rest of *The German Ideology* is devoted to critiques of works by **Young Hegelians**. In the first volume there is a short attack on Bauer's attack on Feuerbach followed by a very long critique of Stirner's *The Ego and his Own* (1845). There is also a short second volume criticizing the

German 'true socialists'. The critiques can be seen as a continuation of the work done in **The Holy Family** (1845) and the beginning of serious interventions in economics and **politics**.

Commentators differ on the extent to which Marx's evident frustration with the abstract philosophical discourse of his recent past involved a conscious renunciation of substantive philosophical positions held in 1844, in particular the idea of **alienation** from human **essence** or **species-being**. Marx certainly complains about the misuse of 'essence', but these comments are directed to specific errors of Feuerbach, Stirner and Karl Grün and do not entail a retraction of his own position in the **Economic and Philosophical Manuscripts** (1844). For example, Marx disapproves of Feuerbach's view that a person's being is at the same time his or her essence because this implies that millions of impoverished workers are experiencing their essence. Marx declares that their anger tells us that they are not, and he concludes that only through revolution would the workers be able to bring their 'being' into harmony with their 'essence'. Marx had clearly wearied with philosophical discourse of this kind, as is indicated elsewhere in the book, when he declared that 'philosophy and the study of the actual world have the same relation to one another as masturbation and sexual love'. Nevertheless, there is no repudiation of the substantive philosophical positions adopted in 1844.

Greek mythology   Refers to the myths created by the ancient Greeks to explain and think about existence in its various forms. Marx delighted in Greek mythology, as he did in all forms of **art**, and he saw it as being significant in a number of ways. In the Foreword to his **Doctoral Dissertation** (1841) he refers to Prometheus as the eminent saint and martyr of the philosophical calendar. He approvingly quotes and endorses Prometheus' confession, as reported by the Greek tragedian Aeschylus – whom Marx ranked along with **Shakespeare** and Goethe as his three favourite poets – in his play *Prometheus Unbound* that he hates all gods. Marx also adds that whether gods are heavenly or earthly, if they do not acknowledge human self-consciousness as the highest divinity, then we should be against them. Prometheus was tied to a rock for his defiance of the gods, and Marx again quotes and thereby praises Prometheus for his fortitude in saying he would rather continue to be tied to the rock he was on than be the servant of the gods. So Greek mythology in this sense, through the character of Prometheus, is praised by Marx for its defiance of authority.

In his ***Contribution to the Critique of Hegel's Philosophy of Right: Introduction*** (1844) Marx again refers to Greek mythology and in this instance he sees it as helping us understand developments in political history. Marx notes how, historically, the period of Greek tragedy captured so well by great writers such as Aeschylus had to pass away and turn instead to comedy and, in particular, the writings of Lucian. Marx's contention is that history chooses this course so that humanity can leave its past behind in a cheerful spirit. Greek mythology was therefore the way in which the peoples of antiquity lived their history in their imagination, and comparing literature in this way can inform us about the **nature** and historical development of a society.

In the ***Grundrisse*** (1857–1858) Marx takes this issue further by considering how certain periods of art are out of all proportion to the general development of society. He considers the relation of Greek mythology to his own time of the mid-nineteenth century and rhetorically asks if such myths are now possible given the development in technology that has taken place in society. For example, how can Greek mythology be relevant in a world of self-acting mule spindles, railways, locomotives and electrical telegraphs? Is Achilles possible to contemplate now we have powder and lead, when he only had sword and shield? Can the very story of him in Homer's *Iliad* now be possible given the development of the printing press? Marx's answer is that they are relevant because they give us artistic pleasure and even act as a norm and unattainable model of what another world might be like. Greek mythology, therefore, is like an historic childhood of humanity in its most beautiful unfolding, and whilst it is never to return it will always exercise its eternal charm.

Grundrisse* (1857–1858, posthumously published, 1953)**   Written by Marx during the winter of 1857–1858, mainly for the purpose of self-clarification, the manuscript, which had been lost, was eventually published in German in a limited edition in 1938 and 1939 and as an accessible edition only in 1953. It is seen as a forerunner for the three volumes of ***Capital and consists of seven notebooks in rough draft that have been ordered into four main sections, comprising the Introduction, chapters on **money** and **capital**, and a final section devoted to the political economists Bastiat and Carey. Within each of these chapters is a wealth of material that spans over some 800 pages examining the theories of a diverse number of thinkers such as **Proudhon** and his follower Alfred Darimon, and Say, **Smith** and **Ricardo**, amongst others.

The Introduction is of particular importance because Marx discusses his dialectical **method**, which still displays the continuing influence of **Hegel**. Marx also contrasts his own superior method with the inferior method of **political economy** and explores this through the different moments of **production**, distribution, **exchange** and **consumption**. He also outlines his understanding of what he thinks constitutes an **individual**.

The chapter on money considers issues such as **economic crises**, **value**, **price** and different examinations of money in all its different forms. The chapter on capital has substantial sections that consider the production process of capital, the notions of **surplus value** and **profit**, the circulation process of capital, the way surplus value becomes surplus capital, the original **accumulation** of capital, theories of surplus value and the transformation of surplus value into profit. In a miscellaneous section, Marx examines a diverse number of topics, one of which is the concept of **alienation**, and so shows a clear link with the **humanism** expressed by him in the early *Economic and Philosophical Manuscripts* (1844). The *Grundrisse*'s importance also stems from the wide variety of topics it discusses under all these sections mentioned above. Some of the most notable are the **world market**, the **state**, the international division of **labour** and **machines**, in which Marx considers how automation could be used as a way to liberate people from work. Moreover, the manuscript is also crucial for showing us how Marx engages in his actual work process, in reflecting and examining on his own concepts, and offering a critique of the concepts and arguments of others.

—**H**—

Hegel, G. W. F. (1770–1831) German philosopher who had a profound influence on Marx, although the extent of this influence has been controversial because Marx himself was ambivalent in his attitude towards Hegel's philosophy throughout his life.

Marx's first contact with Hegel's thought was when he went to the University of Berlin in 1836. Once there, Marx found two groupings that had emerged after Hegel's death, the radical **Young Hegelians** who stood in direct opposition to the more conservative old Hegelians. Marx aligned himself with the Young Hegelians but he was eventually to transcend their thought. In his *Doctoral Dissertation* (1841) Marx defended Hegel by stressing how his Young Hegelian disciples could and should explain what took for him the **form** of esoteric or hidden aspects of his thought and so reveal their radical **nature**. However, such a radical interpretation of Hegel was not actually present in Marx's own first systematic analysis of Hegel's writings, his *Critique of Hegel's Philosophy of Right* (1843). Here he depicts Hegel as a mystical idealist who reverses the relation between subjects and what is said about them, predicates. For Marx, Hegel errs in beginning his analysis not with an actual existent, a real subject, but with predicates of universal determination, which manifest themselves as subjects through the vehicle of the mystical Idea. Hegel mistakenly interprets social institutions, such as the **state**, as the manifestation of the Idea, and thereby envelops them in mysticism. Consequently, Marx argues for a materialist rather than an idealist philosophy that roots its analysis in human individuals and which does not consider these individuals to be the mere playthings of such a mystical divine Idea.

Marx replicates this theme in the *Economic and Philosophical Manuscripts* (1844) where he critically considers Hegel's *Phenomenology of Spirit*. He praises Hegel for conceiving the self-creation of humans as a process through which they affirm themselves through their **labour** in the form of estrangement. Hegel's problem, however, is that he recognizes this labour as only abstract mental labour and regards human **production** and their creation of objects as mere entities of thought. Similarly, Hegel regards entities such as **wealth** and the state, for example, as estranged from humans, but only in abstract, philosophical thought. All forms of estrangement, therefore, are imprisoned within the realm of **abstraction**, resulting in a mystifying criticism. For Marx, then, Hegel fails to locate **alienation** in people's material existence because he offers only a **dialectic** of pure thought.

In the *Grundrisse* (1857–1858) Marx continues his early depiction of Hegel as being a philosophical idealist trapped within the realm of thought, and begins to make a more explicit enunciation of his own materialist dialectical approach to the world. In doing so, he declares how a re-reading of Hegel's *Logic* had been of great use to him, and expresses his desire to write a short book on the value of Hegel's dialectic shorn of its mysticism, even though he never did. In the *Grundrisse* Marx emphasizes the differences between his own dialectic compared to that of Hegel. He develops his own dialectical approach to the study of **political economy** by making a distinction between a general and determinate abstraction, and again Marx uses Hegel as a point of contrast to indicate the incorrect **method** for analyzing phenomena. According to Marx, Hegel fell into the illusion of conceiving the real as the product of thought concentrating itself, probing its own depths and unfolding itself out of itself, by itself. Instead, Marx argues, the movement from abstract to concrete is simply the way thought duplicates the concrete, or the material world, in the mind. Hegel mistakenly thinks that this movement from abstract to concrete is the way the concrete comes into being. He therefore understands the conceptual world as the only reality and forgets that the real subject retains its autonomous existence outside the realm of thought.

The ambivalence of Marx's attitude towards Hegel re-appears in his later writings in the Afterword to the second German edition of **Capital** 1 (1867), where he emphatically declares that his dialectical method is, in its foundations, not only different from the Hegelian, but exactly opposite to it. Again, Marx rebukes Hegel for supposing that the process of thinking is the creator of the real world, and the real world is only the external **appearance** of the idea. In Hegel's hands the dialectic becomes mystified, which means that it must be inverted in order to discover the rational kernel within the mystical shell. However, it was Marx himself who at the time was accused of being something of an idealist in a review of *Capital* 1 by the Russian economist I. I. Kaufmann. Whilst Marx agreed that his method could appear to be idealist because he presents his arguments moving from the abstract to the concrete, in reality it was thoroughly materialist because his investigations of phenomena always begin with the concrete, from which he then makes abstractions. Despite all of these criticisms of Hegel, Marx nevertheless insists that there is still much to be said for Hegelian philosophy, and especially for Hegel's commitment to dialectics. In the Afterword Marx openly avows himself a pupil of Hegel, whom he calls a 'mighty thinker', and reveals that he had 'coquetted with the mode of expression peculiar to him' in the chapter on value in *Capital* 1. He also praises Hegel for being the first to present the general forms of motion of the dialectic in a comprehensive and conscious manner. For Marx, then, Hegel had made a crucial contribution to the development of a dialectical approach to the world, despite his mystical **idealism**.

historical materialism   The term most commonly employed to describe Marx's theory of historical development. It was first used by Engels in a letter to Bloch in 1890, in which it appears along with his previous formulation, the **materialist conception of history**, although neither term was ever utilized by Marx.

The starting point for understanding historical materialism is Marx's contention in *The German Ideology* (1845–1846) that the analysis of any society must be rooted in the way that its members come together to produce to satisfy their **needs**. Marx states that this is the first premise of all human history and thus the first historical act along with the development of new **needs** and human reproduction, which all exist simultaneously throughout history from the origin of humanity down to today. Such activities suppose the coming together of people in forms of social **cooperation**, which itself is a productive force that relates to a certain **mode of production** or stage of industrial development. Hence the history of humanity must always be studied in relation to the history of industry and **exchange**. It is from this basis that Marx suggests we can understand the movement from a different historical epoch into another and the change from one mode of production to another through these moments and through developments in the division of **labour** of each society. These epochs have moved from the tribal through to ancient slave-holding societies, then feudal society, and eventually to modern bourgeois society. It is out of the social processes of **production** that social and political structures evolve and humans develop their material relations with each other. As Marx states, it is not **consciousness** that determines life, but life that determines consciousness. A materialist understanding of history therefore grasps the consciousness of humans, not as they think they are, but as real living individuals whose thinking emanates from the actual world they are in and so forms *their* consciousness. Such an approach thus avoids understanding history incorrectly as either a collection of dead facts, as empiricists do, or as the imagined activity of imagined subjects, as is the case with **idealism**.

Ideas are formed from practice and not the other way around. Consequently, for Marx, human liberation can take place only in the real world and not in the mind, through real means, so that, for example, **slavery** cannot be abolished without the steam engine and the mule jenny, serfdom cannot be abolished without improving agriculture, and people in general cannot be liberated without being provided with adequate food, drink, housing and clothing. In short, humans must be in a position to live in order to make history and the productive forces must be developed to a very high degree and on a world scale in order to do this. However, Marx argues that as the productive forces develop there comes a stage where they come into conflict with the relations that operate in production and this causes the development of a **class** in opposition to existing social relations. Marx concludes that such a development can bring forth both an international **proletariat** that is directly linked with world history itself and has the capacity to develop a communist consciousness through the fact that it suffers the burdens of society without enjoying all of its advantages. Such an alteration of humans on a mass scale, Marx suggests, must take place in a practical movement that engages in a **revolution** to overthrow the **ruling class**. In that way, the **proletariat** succeeds not only in 'ridding itself of all the muck of ages', but also becomes totally 'fitted to found society anew'.

In *The Communist Manifesto* (1848) Marx famously claims that 'the history of all society up to now is the history of class struggles' and he cites past struggles between freeman and slave, patrician and plebeian, lord and serf, and guild-master and journeyman. Under **capitalism**, society is tending to split into two great major camps – the **bourgeoisie** and the proletariat. The volatile **nature** of the economic system, allied to the emergence of an exploited **working class**, points to the eventual – indeed 'inevitable' – demise of the rule of the bourgeoisie and the triumph of the working class. The class is tasked with winning the battle for **democracy**, abolishing private property and inaugurating the classless society. When Marx gives a concise summary of his conception of history in the 1859 **Preface to *A Contribution to the Critique of Political Economy***, his account of the 'guiding principle' of his studies places the emphasis on structural change rather than **class struggle**. Using the metaphor of **base and superstructure**, Marx describes the economic structure as the base on which arises a legal, political and cultural superstructure: 'the **mode of production** of material life conditions the general process of social, political and intellectual life'. However, at a certain point in the development of the economic structure the existing relations of production come into contradiction with the forces of production, and a social revolution takes place, leading to a new historical epoch. Marx describes the successive modes of production, this time with Asiatic rather than tribal, followed by ancient, feudal and modern bourgeois, the latter designated the 'last antagonistic social **form**'. He boldly states that its demise will draw to an end 'the prehistory of human society'. However, there is an important proviso in this account of revolutionary change, for Marx stipulates that 'no social order is ever destroyed before all the productive forces for which it is sufficient have been developed, and new superior relations of production never replace older ones before the material conditions for their existence have matured within the framework of the old society'.

Although Marx's conception of historical development has been criticized by some commentators for being excessively deterministic, at various times in his life he warned against using this theoretical framework as a substitute for empirical analysis. In *The German Ideology* he emphasized that these abstractions served only to guide the arrangement of historical material and should not be used as a 'schema or recipe' for 'neatly trimming the epochs of history'. In an 1877 letter to the journal *Otechestvenniye Zapiski*, he stressed that a general conception of history served only as a guide to help empirical and comparative work establish the truth, and that 'one will never arrive there by using as one's master key a general historical-philosophical theory, the supreme virtue of which consists in being supra-historical'. The substance of the particular issue addressed here was the possibility of the communal farming system in Russia becoming a basis for **socialism** without going through capitalism, which Marx dealt with in a flexible way in his correspondence with Vera **Zasulich**. Nevertheless, his confident predictions of the end of capitalism and the triumph of communism indicate an underlying **teleology** in his conception of history.

***The Holy Family* (1845)**   A polemical attack on Marx's former friends in the Young Hegelian movement, the book was sub-titled *Critique of Critical Criticism: Against Bruno Bauer and Company* and was his first collaborative work with **Engels**. Marx had grown impatient with the Young Hegelians' failure to follow him down the path of 'profane **communism**' and denounced their 'spiritualism' and 'speculative **idealism**' as the most dangerous enemy of 'real **humanism**' in Germany. Philosophically, the book is interesting for its restatement of the **alienation** theme that had been central to the *Economic and Philosophical Manuscripts* of 1844. One development of this is the acknowledgement that the propertied **class** also suffered from alienation, but whereas those with **property** feel strengthened and at ease with this alienation, for the **working class** it means an inhuman condition, a '**contradiction** between its **human nature** and its condition of life'. Marx reiterates that this loss of humanity can be recovered through revolutionary action, and he also claims that a large part of the French and German working class had already developed a **consciousness** of its historical emancipatory task. He predicts that the working class will be 'historically compelled' to engage in the struggle against all the inhuman conditions of life. Marx also developed his criticism of the illusory **nature** of **freedom** in **civil society**. This appears to offer the greatest freedom and independence to the **individual**, no longer constrained by common bonds, but this surrender to **market** forces instead produces a new **form** of 'fully developed **slavery** and inhumanity'. The reality of the individualistic slavery of civil society stands in contradiction to the communal ideal of a democratic representative **state**.

human nature   In the course of his discussion of **alienation** in the *Economic and Philosophical Manuscripts* (1844), Marx considers what distinguishes humans from other **animals**. In depicting alienation from the product of **labour** and from the process of **production**, he observes that work in modern industry is so oppressive that the worker feels free only in functions we share with other animals, such as eating, drinking and making love. Marx thinks that human beings should be able to develop all the human senses, including their aesthetic capabilities. In discussing alienation from **species-being**, he enlarges on the difference between humans and animals, arguing that 'conscious life activity' distinguishes humans from animals, for whereas animals are 'one' with their life activity, humans make their life activity the object of their will and **consciousness**. Central to this life activity is production, the ability to create products for each other in a consciously planned way. He argues that, in creating a world of objects by practical activity, human beings prove themselves to be conscious species-beings.

Marx's emphasis on our productive capacity, combined with his insistence that humans are always social beings, presents a view of human **essence** as social creativity. Full realization of this essence would involve free **cooperation** between equals, but historically, cooperation in labour has often been imposed by external discipline, whether through direct coercion, as in **slavery**, or by contract, as in the modern factory system, in which the workers have no creative input. Although the modern industrial system denied **freedom** to the mass of producers, it nevertheless showed the immense capacity of human creativity. Marx conceived the development of industry in dialectical terms, as presenting both the 'open book' of people's 'essential powers' and the simultaneous perversion of that essence through alienation. The development of technology opened the way for human **emancipation** by offering the prospect of material abundance, even though its immediate effect was to create **dehumanization**. Only through the abolition of private **property** can we achieve the 'complete emancipation of all human senses and qualities'.

In **The German Ideology** (1845–1846) Marx sketches an anthropological account of human development, describing three aspects of social activity that have been evident since the dawn of history and continue to assert themselves in history: the production of material life itself, the creation of new **needs** and the reproduction of the species. He argues that although humans can be distinguished from animals by consciousness or **religion**, they themselves establish their distinctiveness by producing their means of subsistence, for in doing so they are 'indirectly producing their material life'. In developing their material production and forms of **exchange**, human beings change not only the material world but also their thinking and the products of their thinking. Marx concludes, in contrast to idealist philosophy, 'it is not consciousness that determines life, but life that determines consciousness', a formulation repeated in his 1859 **Preface to A Contribution to the Critique of Political Economy**.

In chapter seven of **Capital 1** (1867) Marx returns to the difference between humans and other beings. He talks about labour as an exclusively human characteristic, for although a spider makes webs that resemble the work of a weaver, and a bee would put many a human architect to shame by the quality of its honeycombs: 'what distinguishes the worst architect from the best of bees is that the architect builds the cell in his mind before he constructs it of wax'. Humans 'realize' (*verwirklicht*) their own purpose in working on the materials of **nature**. The less the worker finds his work attractive, the more strict external discipline has to be imposed. Human beings therefore need to take control over production and distribution to enable them to express their true humanity. An important footnote in chapter twenty-four of *Capital* 1 shows that Marx was well aware of the distinction between human nature 'in general' and 'human nature as historically modified in each epoch'. He chides Jeremy Bentham with failing to understand that to apply the principle of utility it would be necessary to have a view of human nature, just as to know what was useful for dogs would involve an investigation of the nature of dogs.

humanism At various times in 1844 and 1845 Marx described his philosophical outlook as humanist and defended 'real humanism' as the logical basis of **communism**. He acknowledges the critical role played by Ludwig **Feuerbach** as the instigator of modern humanistic and naturalistic criticism. Feuerbach's humanism turned on his critique of **religion** and his materialist critique of Hegel's idealist philosophy. Feuerbach viewed religion as an ideological construction of humanity, a projection of the ideal human personality on to God, who is then worshipped as the omniscient creator. Humanity needed to overcome this **alienation** and claim its place as the liberated subject of the social world. Marx was excited by the focus on religion as the primary example of alienated existence, but he wanted to complete the analysis of alienation by showing that humans were effectively dehumanized as a result of the processes of modern **production**. The only way to overcome that was for the **working class** to become conscious of their **exploitation** and transcend it by social **revolution**. Communism is characterized in the ***Economic and Philosophical Manuscripts*** (1844) as 'the true appropriation of the human **essence** through and for humanity', and it is explicitly equated with **naturalism** and humanism. In ***The Holy Family*** (1845) Marx describes his viewpoint as 'real humanism' and argues that French and English **socialism** and communism represent **materialism** and humanism 'in the practical domain'. Marx became frustrated at the refusal of Feuerbach and the **Young Hegelians** to extend their humanism into communism. In the fifth of the ***Theses on Feuerbach*** (1845) he complained that although the latter is not satisfied with abstract thinking and appeals to 'sensuous contemplation', he failed to conceive sensuousness as practical, human-sensuous experience'. The *Theses* attack Feuerbach's theorization of abstract individuals for failing to analyze social relations or assist 'revolutionary practice'. Marx still terms his materialism the standpoint of 'associated humanity' in the tenth thesis, but by the time ***The German Ideology*** was written (1845–1846) he was prepared to mock the limitations of the Young Hegelian emphasis on human essence. This disdain towards the earlier humanist discourse is repeated in ***The Communist Manifesto*** (1848), when he ridicules the German socialists for responding to French criticisms of the economic function of **money** by talking abstractly about the 'alienation of humanity'. Despite this departure from his earlier philosophical discourse, Marx's humanism is evident in his later **political economy**, particularly in the persistence of the alienation motif in the ***Grundrisse*** (1857–1858) and ***Capital* 1** (1867), and the famous passage on the realm of **freedom** in chapter forty-eight of ***Capital* 3** (1864–1865). In a magazine questionnaire in 1865 Marx listed his favourite maxim as '*nihil humani a me alien puto*' – 'nothing human is alien to me'. Originally written by the poet Terentius (185–159 BC), this was also Feuerbach's motto for his 'new' philosophy, announced in the *Principles of the Philosophy of the Future*.

idealism   The philosophical doctrine that sees perceptions and ideas as the ultimate reality. Marx's main engagement with idealism begins with his ***Critique of Hegel's Philosophy of Right*** (1843). In this work, Marx accuses **Hegel** of falling into a mystification of the **state** because he does not start with real subjects that are its basis, and instead treats it as an idea that then infuses these subjects. The subjects then appear as the result of the idea, as ideality, rather than the idea appearing as the objectification of the subjects. Consequently, Hegel wrongly sees ideas as the driving force in society, when in fact it is real living people through which these ideas emerge.

Marx continues with this theme in the ***Economic and Philosophical Manuscripts*** (1844) where, in a consideration of Hegel's *Phenomenology of Spirit*, he initially approves Hegel's observation that entities such as

wealth, the power of the state and the way humans objectify themselves through their **labour** can all take alienated forms. However, this critical insight is marred because Hegel can only see these forms of estrangement taking place in abstract, philosophical thought rather than in reality, and so results in what Marx calls uncritical idealism. As Marx points out further in **The German Ideology** (1845–1846), Hegel turns the whole material world into the world of ideas and the whole of history into the history of ideas. Indeed, Marx sees this rule of ideas over actuality as infecting the work of both Bauer and **Feuerbach**. This leads him to refer to them as sheep posing as wolves, whose 'bleating merely imitates in a philosophic **form** the conceptions of the German middle **class**', within which all change takes place in the realm of pure thought.

In Marx's later writings, with his theory of **materialism** now clearly established as the basis for his understanding of society, he makes some further points in relation to idealism, with Hegel again the main target. In the 1859 **Preface to _A Contribution to the Critique of Political Economy_** he reiterates how his studies of Hegel from 1844 led him to the conclusion that legal or political relations could not be understood either by themselves or on the basis of the development of the human mind. Instead, they must be understood in the material conditions of life that constitute, what Hegel calls **civil society**, through the analysis of **political economy**. Similarly, in the Afterword to the second German edition of **Capital 1** (1867), in his discussion of his **dialectic**, Marx again shows how Hegel's idealism leads him to posit incorrectly the process of thinking as the creator of the real world. Hegel encapsulates this with his notion of the Idea and thus transforms the latter into an independent subject, and so sees the real world itself as simply the external **appearance** of this Idea. For Marx, the opposite is the case in that the notion of the Idea is nothing but the material world reflected in the minds of people and translated into forms of thought. However, he still praises Hegel for grasping this fact, even if he did so in a mystified and contradictory form. (See also **method**.)

ideology Used by Marx both critically, to describe a distorted set of ideas, or descriptively, to refer to ideas in general. The concept was originally developed by Destutt de Tracy early in the nineteenth century in his _Elements of Ideology_ to describe a proposed **science** of ideas, which sought to apply **reason** to explain the origin and meaning of concepts. Although Marx was familiar with de Tracy's work, he did not use ideology in this positive sense. Marx's descriptive use of ideology can be found in the 1859 **Preface to *A Contribution to a Critique of Political Economy***, in which he refers to the 'ideological forms' of **law**, **politics**, **religion**, **art** and philosophy. These are conceived as the forms of **consciousness** through which the clashes of material interests are articulated. The dominant ideological forms reflect the dominant economic interests. In ***The German Ideology*** (1845–1846) he asserts that the ideas of the **ruling class** will always be the ruling ideas, and in ***The Communist Manifesto*** (1848) he reiterates that 'the ruling ideas of each age have ever been the ideas of its ruling class'.

More critically, in *The German Ideology* Marx uses ideology and ideological in a pejorative sense to denote the hidden bias in the works of various philosophers. The main thrust of the attack against the ideology of the **Young Hegelians** is that it grants too much autonomy to the world of ideas, suggesting that simply by thinking about the world in a different way we can change it. For example, **Feuerbach**, in resolving the religious world into its secular basis, idealized that secular basis rather than going on to analyze the power struggles within it. He accused Feuerbach of 'deceiving himself', and self-deception is an important feature in Marx's conception of ideology. Indeed, the first sentence of the Preface to *The German Ideology* begins with the assertion that 'men have always formed wrong ideas about themselves, about what they are and what they ought to be'. Marx sought to uncover these illusions and show how particular perspectives reflected specific material interests. For example, in ***The Eighteenth Brumaire of Louis Bonaparte*** (1852) he argues that the ideological differences between the followers of the rival royal families were genuinely felt, and that the individuals concerned imagined that their feelings of loyalty were the 'real determinants' of what kept them apart. However, he then shows that it was really their different material interests that prevented them from reaching a compromise. He draws an analogy with private life, in which we make a distinction between what a person thinks and says about him or herself and what that person really is and does. The same analogy is found in the 1859 Preface when he comments that it is not possible to understand social transformation purely by its consciousness, just as 'one does not judge an **individual** by what he thinks about himself'.

Marx was determined to debunk the ruling ideas of his day, particularly in **political economy**, the science that dealt directly with how we organize the material conditions of our existence. His own political economy can be seen as an extended critique of bourgeois ideology. In criticizing bourgeois political economists like **Smith**, **Ricardo** and Mill, he acknowledged their scientific advances but exposed the falsity of their claims that the economic system can operate in equilibrium. He accused them, like other ideologists, of fostering illusions. However, he pointed out that what made the ideology of bourgeois political economy so powerful was that in the **capitalist mode of production** it really does appear as though the power of inanimate **capital** creates all the **wealth**, rather than **labour power** in harmony with nature. It also appears as though **money** creates wealth and that private **property** is the basis for **freedom**. In other words, ideology is most effective when it is able to offer an account of reality that appears to be consonant with our experience. (See also **appearance**, **commodity fetishism** and **reification**.)

individual   For Marx, the key to understanding any notion of an individual emerges out of his developmental **method** of properly grasping the abstract and the concrete. In his early work on **Hegel** both in the *Critique of Hegel's Philosophy of Right* (1843) and the *Economic and Philosophical Manuscripts* (1844) Marx rebuked him for beginning his analysis with abstract concepts rather than real subjects. In doing so, Hegel abstracts from **nature** and real people and is therefore completely indifferent to all real determinateness. It follows then that for Marx to grasp properly this real determinateness, we must avoid abstract theorizing separately from it. Such an abstract/concrete dichotomy is what Marx perceives to be a fundamental flaw in Hegel's philosophy because instead of understanding things as themselves, Hegel instead understands things as emanations of abstract concepts. Marx develops this further in relation to his critique of Ludwig **Feuerbach** where he now begins to give an indication of how an individual should be understood. In the sixth of the *Theses on Feuerbach* (1845), for instance, Marx berates Feuerbach for not realizing that the **essence** of humans 'is no **abstraction** inherent in each single individual'; rather, in its reality, it is the 'ensemble of the social relations'. For Marx, Feuerbach therefore puts forward only an abstract-isolated-human-individual that is divorced from the historical process. Feuerbach fails to realize that the abstract individual that he analyses belongs in reality to a particular **form** of society.

Marx develops this argument more explicitly in the Introduction to the *Grundrisse* (1857–1858) while discussing his method. He makes the distinction between general and determinate abstractions. General abstractions are where we abstract from concrete social circumstances to focus on a common universal element amongst phenomena. Determinate abstractions are when we analyze the movement from the general to the concrete or particular form. One illustration of the power of Marx's method here is in his example of understanding the notion of the individual in contrast to that of **Smith** and **Ricardo**. Marx argues that both Smith and Ricardo remain at the level of general abstraction by having a concept of the individual as an isolated hunter and fisherman that exists throughout time. But the general abstraction they make is based on their own assumptions about **human nature** rather than on the forms individuals take in particular historical circumstances. For Marx, Smith's and Ricardo's independent individual is projected back into the past as an ideal, rather than as a result of the end of feudal relations and the development of **capital**.

Marx asserts that the more we look back into history the more we see an individual as being dependent and belonging to a greater whole. This is exemplified in the movement from the **family** to the clan and then to different communal forms of organization through the interrelations of the clans. With the onset of **civil society** in the eighteenth century, individuals suddenly appear as isolated and preoccupied with pursuing only their self-interest. Smith and Ricardo, then, belong amongst the unimaginative conceits of the eighteenth-century 'Robinsonades' by positing as a norm the rare exception of an isolated individual producing outside society in the manner of Daniel Defoe's novel *Robinson Crusoe*. Indeed, even when this rarity occurs it is normally where an individual is, like Crusoe, cast into the wilderness, but already possesses aspects of civilized society in terms of the products he salvages from the ship and the social relations he has previously formed. For Marx, therefore, a human being is a 'political animal, not merely a gregarious animal, but an animal which can individuate itself only in the midst of society'. He rejects any notion of an abstract individual separate from its concrete form. Individuals must be understood in their social setting as part of a community and as historically developed in different ways. The Robinsonade nature of Smith's and Ricardo's notion of the individual, which they assume as a general abstraction true for all time, must therefore be rejected.

internationalism   Marx was a committed internationalist throughout his life. Because **capitalism** was a global **mode of production** it was clear to him that it could be replaced only through concerted international action. In ***The German Ideology*** (1845–1846) he argues that the international development of productive forces implies the development of world-historical individuals who would be able to emancipate themselves only through simultaneous revolutions in all the major nations. In ***The Communist Manifesto*** (1848) he specifies commitment to the 'union and agreement of democratic parties of all countries' as one of the defining features of communist action. He also stipulates 'united action' in at least the 'leading civilized countries' as one of the first conditions for the **emancipation** of the **working class**. The formation of the **First International** in 1864 provided the opportunity for socialists to put into practice their commitment to internationalism, but the organization contained many factions and was effectively abandoned by Marx in 1872 because he feared that it would become dominated by the anti-political **anarchism** of **Bakunin** and his followers. Marx regarded the International as 'only the first attempt' to create a central organization to lead the international struggle. In the ***Critique of the Gotha Programme*** (1875) Marx expresses his anger at the vapidity of the proposed article on the 'international brotherhood of all peoples' in the programme of the newly unified German Social Democratic Workers Party. It contained no details of the international role of the German working class, and Marx remarks scornfully that there was more content about internationalism in the programme of the liberal **Free Trade** party. He added that the official newspaper of the German government was right to conclude that the new party had renounced internationalism. He stresses that national parties needed to specify their commitment to international action in order to counter the internationalism practised by the **bourgeoisie**.

—J—

justice   Although Marx frequently used moralistic **language** to denounce **exploitation** and oppression, he took great care to avoid arguing that

capitalism was unjust. He considered that appeals to justice were impotent and diverted attention away from analyzing the real power relations in the great social struggles of his day. An example of his disdain towards rhetorical appeals for justice occurs in a circular letter to leaders of the German socialists in 1879 in which he complained that 'when the **class struggle** is rejected as a disagreeable "coarse" phenomenon, nothing remains as the basis of **socialism** other than "true love of humanity" and empty phrases about "justice"'. In *The Communist Manifesto* (1848) Marx was dismissive of the idea that justice was an 'eternal truth', arguing that it merely changed **form** with every change in the form of private **property**. This relativist view is confirmed in the *Critique of the Gotha Programme* (1875) in which he argues that the bourgeois claim that the existing system of economic distribution is 'just' (*gerecht*) is defensible because under **capitalist** relations of **production** it is the *only* just system. For Marx, legal concepts of justice are determined by economic relations, not the other way round. However, the relativist conception implies that a communist society would operate with a different standard of justice. This is illustrated in a remark in *Capital* **3** (1864–1865) in which he states that in a 'higher' phase of society the private ownership of land will come to be regarded as absurd in the same way that the idea of **slavery** appears to people in liberal societies. It is clear that Marx would prefer a standard of justice that reflected a classless society, and there is, therefore, a **moral** component implicit in his work. However, largely for tactical reasons, Marx scrupulously avoided arguing for 'justice'. (See also **morality** and **rights**.)

—**L**—

labour   The process by which humans, through their own actions, mediate, regulate and control the metabolism between themselves and **nature**. For Marx, labour is part of our **essence** as humans and is the fundamental basis of society, because without labour humans would cease to exist. In much of his discussion on labour he contrasts what labour should be like in its most positive sense, which is what it would be like in communist society, with what it is really like in its most negative sense, which occurs in **capitalism**. In his early writings, such as the ***Comments on James Mill's Elements of Political Economy*** (1844) and the ***Economic and Philosophical Manuscripts*** (1844), Marx argues that when humans engage in labouring activity they have a continuing dialogue with nature, of which they are a part, and that must continue if they are not to die. Nature is therefore something that should be preserved and not simply plundered irrespective of the consequences of using its material for labouring activity.

When humans labour, this should involve the fulfilment of their person-ality, and the realization of their natural talents and spiritual goals. Labour should be the free expression, affirmation and enjoyment of life, through which a person affirms his or her own individuality, his or her authentic and communal nature, and his or her **species-being**, 'conscious life activity', through creating an object that satisfies the need of another human being. Indeed, the object of labour itself is to objectify the species-life of human beings not only intellectually, in their **consciousness**, but actively and actually, so humans can contemplate themselves in a world they have created. This is why humans are universal beings because whereas non-human **animals** also produce – they build nests and dwellings, for example – they do so only when immediate physical need compels them to, whereas humans produce even when they are free from such need, and indeed truly produce only in **freedom** from such need. As Marx says in chapter seven of ***Capital* 1** (1867), 'what distinguishes the worst architect from the best of bees is that the architect builds the cell in his mind before he constructs it in wax'. So at the end of every labour process a result emerges that had already been conceived by the worker before undertaking the task. This leads Marx to posit three elements of the labour process: 'purposeful activity', which is the work itself; the object on which the work is performed; and the instruments used in that work. He contends that such labouring activity should be the 'free play' of the worker's 'physical and mental powers' for it to be as fulfilling as possible. Just how free humans can be when engaging in the labour process is developed further by Marx in chapter forty-eight of ***Capital* 3** (1864–1865) where he makes a distinction between the realm of necessity and the realm of freedom.

Marx argues that the realm of freedom really begins only where labour determined by necessity ends and it lies by its very nature beyond the sphere of material **production** proper. Freedom in this sphere can consist only in this, that socialized humans, the associated producers, govern the human metabolism with nature in a rational way, bringing it under their collective control instead of being dominated by it as a blind power; accomplishing it with the least expenditure of energy and in conditions most worthy and appropriate for their **human nature**. But this always remains a realm of necessity. The true realm of freedom, the development of human power as an end in itself, begins beyond it, though it can only flourish with this realm of necessity as its basis. The reduction of the **working day** is the basic prerequisite.

For Marx it is therefore self-evident that all societies have to reproduce themselves to survive; they have to satisfy their natural **needs**. The labour performed in doing this is not totally free labour because it does not involve the development of human powers as an end in themselves. Rather, such labour is a means to an end, the end of satisfying the essential natural needs of all of society. The only way an element of freedom can exist in this sphere of necessity is to accomplish these necessary tasks with the minimum of effort and in pleasurable surroundings. However, even if humans meet these conditions they are still in the realm of necessity and not true freedom. Only in the latter realm can human powers develop as ends in themselves and not just as a means to satisfy natural needs. The path to the true realm of freedom begins, therefore, with a reduction in the working day – a reduction in necessary labour. This allows us to pursue activities that we want to pursue as human beings, and not as mere cogs in a production process. The satisfaction of our natural needs is a constant burden but its diminution is possible with the development of the productive forces. As Marx explains in the ***Grundrisse*** (1857–1858), such a reduction of necessary labour time corresponds to the artistic and scientific development of the individuals in the time set free. Such free time, which is both idle time and time for higher activity, has naturally transformed its possessor into a different subject who then enters into the direct production process as this different subject.

Even with the development of the productive forces to high levels of automation, humans will still have to enter the realm of natural necessity to perform necessary labour to satisfy the social needs of society. This is still the realm of unfreedom, but we perform labour there as a different subject. We realize we are satisfying the needs of others who in turn are satisfying our needs as fellow human beings. Marx, though, perceptively points out that the capacity for technological developments means that even this minimal *direct labour* ceases to be the basis of production because it is transformed more into a supervisory and regulatory activity. The onset of automatic work processes means that human involvement in the realm of necessity and unfreedom will be very minimal indeed. Necessary labour is therefore not free labour and must be decreased. True labour, labour that involves the development of human powers as ends in themselves, stands above and beyond such necessary labour and becomes 'a living, form-giving fire'.

However, as Marx notes from his early to later writings, in **capital** where labour takes the **form** of wage-labour, all these positive aspects of labouring activity are turned into their opposite through the intense imposition of the division of labour process, particularly in the factory system. Through the repetitive activity of doing one particular task, the workers' labours are machine-like and the workers themselves are reduced to the level of a machine. Human labouring activity is therefore not an end in itself, because it is reduced to nothing more than the maintenance of physical existence, a mere means to the end of ensuring a worker's physical survival. As labouring activity is also forced labour, it simply becomes a torture for the workers, and **alienation** is the end result. (See also **abstract labour** and **labour power**.)

labour power   The capacity to **labour**, which the worker sells to the **capitalist** in **exchange** for a **wage**. In *Capital* **1** (1867) Marx argues that when the capitalist buys the labour power of the worker he or she is buying something that is potential rather than actual. Labour power therefore only becomes real, as actual labour, which is its use **value**, once it is put into making a **commodity**. Its exchange value is the socially necessary labour time required to reproduce itself at a certain standard of living. What Marx means by this is that a worker expends various degrees of effort both physical and mental into his or her labour, and for this process to continue the worker must get the means necessary to replenish both himself or herself and their dependents, future labour power, to re-enter the **production** process.

Once a capitalist purchases labour power her or she can put it to work over a certain length of time that constitutes the **working day** and the working week. Indeed, as Marx ironically identifies, it is the custom in capitalist societies for capitalists not to pay for labour power in advance, which means that the worker is actually extending credit to the capitalist. The **price** of labour power that the capitalist will eventually pay in the **form** of the wage is determined by a contract and Marx assumes such a price is the going rate. So the capitalist is not cheating the worker in any way when buying labour power, but paying exactly what it is worth, which is the socially necessary labour time required to produce it. However, once we leave the sphere of the **market** and enter what Marx calls the hidden abode of production, a different relationship between the worker as the owner of labour power and the capitalist as the owner of **money** and its buyer is exposed.

The capitalist puts the worker to work and finds that labour power as a commodity has the characteristic of not only being a source of value but, even more importantly, of being able to produce more value than it has itself, which takes the form of **surplus value**. This has arisen in the process of production and not in the sphere of circulation or market exchange. So, for example, if the working day was set at eight hours the worker could stop working after, say, four hours because by that time he or she would have performed the labour necessary for his or her reproduction. However, the capitalist makes the worker work the full eight hours and so pockets these hours as surplus labour or surplus value, which takes the form of **profit**. Understanding labour power as the capacity to labour therefore allows us to uncover the secret of profit-making and so exposes **capital** as a system of **exploitation**.

labour theory of value   The theory that the value of any **commodity** is given by the socially necessary labour time expended on it. The classical **labour** theory of **value** contends that the value of a good is the result of the labour expended in producing it. This is *not* the view of Marx. That it has been interpreted as such has caused much confusion over Marx's own value theory. Classical political economists attempted to discover the origin and measure of value leading them to posit labour as the prime factor. However, the labour theory of value was fundamentally modified by Marx. He praised those political economists who examined labour as the basis of value, but suggested that their error lay in not properly analyzing the **form** of value. For Marx, unlike the classical political economists, **exchange** relations are the social form through which the labour of independent producers can be co-ordinated to satisfy social **needs**. Classical political economists such as **Smith** and **Ricardo** saw exchange as an institution where prices are mechanically derived from labour time. In contrast, Marx showed how exchange is a system of social relationships that is peculiar to a commodity producing society such as **capitalism**.

Value is therefore a social relation that expresses the portion of the total labour time of society allocated to producing a particular commodity – its socially necessary labour time, and *not* the labour time embodied in a commodity. For Ricardo, value expressed the labour of the **individual** producer, but for Marx it expressed the labour of the producer as a member of society. What Marx means by this is that **capital** is a system where there is no conscious social regulation of **production**. As capital is based on private **property** and private labour, economic decisions are therefore not consciously co-ordinated to meet people's needs. Instead, many different firms produce commodities in isolation from each other in the hope that they will satisfy demand and make a **profit**. However, they do not know whether the labour expended on making commodities is socially necessary until they appear on the **market** and are sold. So, for example, if a firm produces shirts on the basis that people need them and there should be a demand for them, this does not mean that these particular shirts will be bought. People might buy other shirts from their competitors instead, for instance. If some are not bought, or they are sold at a loss or below the average rate of profit, then it is clear that the labour time expended on making the shirts was not socially necessary and this has been a waste of labour time for society as a whole.

Marx's value theory argues that what regulates the reproduction of **capitalist** relations is socially necessary labour time. Consequently, Marx is offering not a technical labour theory of value in the classical **political economy** sense, but is instead showing why labour takes the form it does in capital. Marx's theory does not therefore state that prices will be directly proportionate to quantities of socially necessary **abstract labour**, which is value. On the contrary, value and prices must differ due to the fact that there is disequilibrium inherent in a system where production is anarchic and not consciously planned, and their relationship to each other is therefore a complex one. The laws of supply and demand are therefore simply the outward appearances of the operations of capital, whereas the **law** of value exposes its inner **essence**. Moreover, this process is also shrouded in **commodity fetishism**, which again distinguishes Marx's value theory from previous political economy. Economists who try to reject Marx's value theory on this basis are therefore trapped within the fetishized appearances of capital and the fetishized relations that permeate the system. As Marx says in a famous letter to fellow communist Ludwig Kugelmann in 1868, '**science** consists in precisely determining how the law of value asserts itself'. So Marx does not start with a definition of value and then analyze real social relations to see whether they confirm to its laws. On the contrary, it is through investigation that its laws are discovered to show how it imposes itself on human beings through **class struggle**, **alienation**, **exploitation**, **accumulation** and **economic crises**. Value theory is therefore crucial for comprehending capital because it uncovers the real relations of the system and so exposes its internal contradictions.

landlord   The owner of land and appropriator of rent. Also referred to as a landowner. In the ***Economic and Philosophical Manuscripts*** (1844) Marx quotes approvingly the classical political economists Jean-Baptiste Say and Adam **Smith** who contend that the right of the landlords for their ownership of land can be traced back to robbery. Additionally, such ownership allows landlords to extract a rent from the natural produce of the land to make **money** from land that they may never have worked on. Hence, they 'love to reap where they never sowed'. However, whilst these writers grasp the parasitic nature of the landlord's actions, they make the error of reducing the rent of land to the degree of the fertility of the soil, and in doing so incorrectly see the latter as being an attribute of the landlord. As Marx asserts, this is another example of how concepts become perverted in **political economy** by showing the exact opposite to what is actually the case. He argues that once we consider the rent of land as it is actually formed, we see that it is established through the struggle between landlords and tenants. The main concern of landlords is to increase their **wealth** by raising house rents, which also involves a rise in the interest on the land on which the house stands (that is, ground rent). Landlords can demand more rent when tenants pay out less **wages** to day-labourers, and the more rent the landlords demand, the more the tenants push down wages, resulting in the distress and misery of the rural **population**. Consequently, Marx suggests that the landlords' interests are just as opposed to the farm labourers' interests, as the capitalists' interests are opposed to the interests of the factory workers.

Marx observes that as industrialization progresses the landlords of large-scale landed **property** reduce their own workers to total misery and drive the majority of them off the land into factory **labour**, thus creating and increasing the power of their enemy, **capital** and industry. So a large part of the landlords are forced to take over from the tenants who themselves fall into the realm of the **proletariat**, but given many of the landlords are not capable of agricultural management, they either fall into ruin or the tenants take possession of their land. The outcome is the increased development of capital, but as Marx states later in *Capital* **3** (1864–65), the landlords still remain as one of the three classes, along with wage-labourers and industrial capitalists, that confront each other and constitute the framework of modern society. He refers to these three classes as forming what he calls the trinity formula of capital-profit, land-ground rent and labour-wages, and suggests these hold all the mysteries of the social **production** process. (See also **capitalist**.)

language   The expression of practical, real **consciousness** arising from and developing with our social interaction. In the anthropological passages of *The German Ideology* (1845–1846) Marx discusses the significance of language in human development and argues that it evolves as humans engage in increasingly sophisticated ways of producing their material life and creating new **needs**. He contends that our language changes to reflect the dominant relations of **production** so that the advance of the commercial world gives us a language dominated by words such as possession and **value**. In other words, social relations are sustained by language, and language is a social product. In the *Comments on James Mill* (1844) he remarks on the phenomenon of an everyday discourse that has become focused on objects that we own and **exchange**. In a system of private **property**, we would struggle to understand a 'truly human' language in which we ask for things and offer things freely, according to our needs and our anticipation of the needs of others. To ask for things in this way would be like begging, so that the one who asks feels humiliated and degraded, while the one who is asked thinks of it as impertinence or lunacy. Marx concludes that we are so alienated from our human **essence** that 'the direct language of this essential **nature** seems to us a violation of human dignity', whereas the 'estranged language of material values' is, paradoxically, regarded as the justified and self-confident assertion of human dignity.

law   Marx uses law in two senses: first, in a juridical sense (*Recht*) to refer to the body of rules enforced by the **state**; second, to a general rule (*Gesetz*) in his **political economy** used to explain the development of the economic system. In the first sense, Marx asserts that legal (*juristischer*) forms are one of the aspects of social life shaped by the dominant economic structure. In the 1859 **Preface to *A Contribution to the Critique of Political Economy***, law is allocated an epiphenomenal position as part of a social superstructure conditioned by the economic **base**. Marx originally developed this understanding of law when his duties as editor of the *Rheinische Zeitung* obliged him to investigate issues such as press censorship and the law on theft of wood. In the first part of *The German Ideology* (1845–1846) Marx declares that law (*Recht*) has always changed in accordance with the **needs** of the dominant economic **class**. Whenever new forms of business develop, 'the law has always been compelled to admit them'. In *The Communist Manifesto* (1848) he reiterates the position that law changes according to the progress of class struggles, dismissing out of hand the argument that law has existed throughout history and that certain principles of **justice** are common to all societies.

   Although Marx argues that the law reflects the interests of the dominant class, the relationship is not one of simple determination, as competing interests within the economic structure fight out their differences in many forms, including legal ones. He describes in his economic writings how the development of the **bourgeoisie** is accompanied by a series of legal struggles to sweep away the barriers to **production** and trade, culminating in Britain in the abolition of the Corn Laws in 1846. He also describes the punitive use of laws against 'the expropriated' that had operated since the end of the fifteenth century, devoting chapter twenty-eight of *Capital* 1 (1867) to various pieces of legislation that sanctioned the whipping and imprisoning of vagabonds and the forcible reduction of **wages**. However, he also notes that legal change can sometimes benefit the exploited class. For example, he regarded the successful struggle to secure a legal limitation on the **working day** as a victory of 'the political economy of the **working class**' over that of the middle class. Marx does not discuss what would take the place of law in the higher phase of communist society.

   In the second sense, Marx formulates general rules in **political economy** that describe the working of the system, such as the General Law (*Das allgemeine Gesetz*) of **Capitalist Accumulation**. However, although he uses 'law' in this way in the Preface to the first edition of *Capital* 1, he qualifies it by offering 'tendency' (*Notwendigkeit*) as an alternative. He does the same thing in **Capital 3** (1864–1865) when discussing **the tendency of the rate of profit to fall**. The law posits that when the rate of **surplus value** is constant and the organic composition of **capital** is rising, the rate of **profit** must fall. However, Marx qualifies this by stating that although this is a real tendency in the system, there are various counteracting factors that needed to be taken into account. When discussing those factors he qualifies the word 'law' by commenting that a tendency is 'a law whose absolute realization is held up, delayed and weakened'. In general Marx was wary of presenting either his theory of historical development or his analysis of the dynamics of **capitalism** as laws that could offer over-simplified conclusions and predictions.

lumpenproletariat   Marx used this word in a disparaging way to describe the **class** of urban poor who did not seek regular employment but survived by a variety of illegal or parasitic means. In **The Communist Manifesto** (1848) he argued that although the lumpenproletarians may be swept up into the movement of the workers' **revolution**, it is more likely that they will become the 'bribed tool of reactionary intrigue'. He describes them as a 'passively rotting mass', although the additional insult of 'social scum' in some of the English versions has been added by the translator. In **The Eighteenth Brumaire of Louis Bonaparte** (1852) he accuses the lumpenproletariat of joining the Mobile Guards to crush the workers in the revolution of June 1848 as well as providing the troops of the Society of December 10, a paramilitary group supporting Louis Napoleon. He provides a long list of lumpenproletarian occupations, including vagabonds, discharged soldiers, discharged prisoners, pickpockets, tricksters, gamblers, pimps, organ-grinders, knife-grinders and beggars. Marx's negative view of the lumpenproletariat was not shared by the anarchists, who were optimistic that this desperate class could be mobilized in the revolutionary struggle against the existing power structures.

—M—

machines   Defined in chapter fifteen of **Capital 1** (1867) as 'a mechanism that, after being set in motion, performs with its tools the same operation as the worker formerly did with similar tools'. Marx understands machines in both a positive and negative manner. The negative interpretation relates to the way machines are used in **capital** against **labour**, and the positive interpretation is how they can be used to reduce working hours and increase **production** in favour of labour and against capital in a different **form** of society.

In the **Economic and Philosophical Manuscripts** (1844) Marx notes how capitalists use machinery to expel workers from the production process, forcing them into barbarous forms of work or back on to the labour **market**. For those workers that remain, their work is reduced to a monotonous form as the division of labour is increased and intensified. The endless and repetitive tasks the workers are forced to engage in means that while they work *through* machines they also seem to work *as* machines. Marx observes how in the spinning and cotton mills, **women** outnumber men in this process of degradation, and even children are used in place of machinery, thus turning them into machines. Additionally, Marx relates the ironic fact that through **capitalist** greed, workers are also forced to work even longer hours despite the machinery being labour-saving.

In the **Grundrisse** (1857–1858) Marx gives a short overview of the historical relation between labour and machinery. He notes that in the move from feudal to capitalist relations of production machines stand in opposition to living labour as an alien and hostile force because they confront the workers as capital. This occurs because the means of labour goes through different metamorphoses, which culminate in the machine, then a system of machinery, and, in its highest form, an automatic system of machinery that is set in motion by an automaton, a moving power that moves itself. The machine now seems to take on a life of its own in place of the worker, who is reduced to responding to its movement in a mere **abstraction** of activity. Living labour itself, therefore, does not govern the process of production, but instead becomes governed by it through the operation of the machine as objectified labour, and as a power in the form of capital.

In *Capital* 1 Marx repeats many of these themes and deepens his understanding of the **nature** of machines. He states that the main aim of their application in capital is as a means for producing **surplus value**. He argues that their introduction resulted in increasing the number of workers regardless of age or sex into the process of **exploitation**, so that the capitalist now appropriates the surplus labour of the whole **family**: mother, father and children. The workers are therefore transformed into mere machines for the production of surplus value. The result is a process of the deskilling of labour, **competition** among the workers, and the creation of a reserve army of unemployed labour that is expelled from the production process and replaced by machines.

For capitalists, the introduction of machinery allows them to revolutionize the forces of production and increase productivity, thereby making their commodities in a faster time. An **individual** capitalist who can undercut his or her competitors in this way will accrue more surplus value. Other capitalists will also attempt to follow suit and introduce machinery in the same manner, to try and undercut that capitalist. So the introduction of machinery is part of the whole process of capitalist competition and **accumulation**. Nevertheless, Marx argues that although an individual capitalist can increase his or her surplus value in this way in the form of increased profits, he maintains that it is only **labour power**, what he also calls variable capital, which is the source of this **profit**. Machines are constant capital or dead labour and do not create any new **value**. When an individual capitalist introduces machinery, expels labour and then accrues more profit with less labour power, it seems that the machines are responsible for this, rather than the source being the expenditure of labour power. However, Marx's point is that surplus value is not always accrued where it has been created. It therefore follows that for capitalists in general their profits will decrease due to the actions of this individual capitalist, as there will have been less surplus value created across the economy. Consequently, there is a fall in the general rate of profit due to the increase of machinery into the production process and the expulsion of living labour, which can lead to **economic crises** through the **tendency of the rate of profit to fall**.

Overall, then, as Marx says in the *Grundrisse*, even though machines are agencies of social production, in a system founded on wage labour they do not belong to the workers and the workers come to serve them rather than the other way round. However, he then maintains that under the rule of the associated workers where the machines do come under their control they will still be agencies of social production, but they will be used in the interests of and in harmony with labour rather than against it, as is the case in the capitalist **mode of production**.

Manifesto of the Communist Party   (See *Communist Manifesto*)

market   In **capitalism**, the market is a place people are compelled to enter in order to buy and sell commodities to satisfy their means of subsistence. Marx's understanding of the market is in stark contrast to the bourgeois understanding of it as a place that allows the opportunity for buying and selling. In **capital**, the market appears as though it is a free place because people maximize their utility in the purchasing and selling of goods, and the **price** mechanism ensures that supply and demand are met through a process of self-regulation. However, the reality is quite different. What distinguishes the operation of the market in capital is the extent to which it turns all social relationships into relations between things in a process of **commodity fetishism**. So while markets have obviously existed in previous historical periods, what distinguishes the market in capital is the way in which people are excessively dependent on it in order to live. Such a dependence, and hence unfreedom, is therefore directed by the logic of the **capitalist** system, which asserts itself through **competition**, **accumulation**, profit-maximization and new forms of **exploitation**. All human relationships come under the rule of the market and the alienating activities that go with it in a **commodity**-producing society such as capital.

In *The Communist Manifesto* (1848) Marx describes how out of **class struggle** and the need to find new ways to increase **surplus value**, **feudalism** gave way to an emerging capitalist system, and along with it the modern **bourgeoisie** that ushered in the movement from a national market to a **world market**. Driven by the need for a constantly expanding market for its goods, the bourgeoisie scours the globe subordinating all social relationships to the logic of the market and capitalist social relations. Marx argues that through its exploitation of the world market, the bourgeoisie has given a cosmopolitan character to **production** and **consumption** in every country by making industries not just dependent on materials available in their own country, but on materials drawn from some of the remotest parts of the globe. The rapacious **nature** of capitalist development means that all countries are forced to adopt the bourgeois **mode of production** and so become bourgeois themselves, subject to the dictates of the market. The market is also the place where capitalists try and realize the surplus value they have taken in the production process.

materialism Marx's materialism emphasizes the importance of uniting theory with practice and sees human beings not simply as passive receivers of the material world but active participants in its creation and development. It avoids remaining in the abstract realm, as is the case with **idealism**, and overcomes the tendency to slip into contemplative thought that is typical of previous forms of materialism, even including the most sophisticated variant in the work of **Feuerbach**. Marx's materialism is also part of his dialectical **method** of rooting his analysis in the real world, through the interplay between the abstract and the concrete moments of phenomena.

In the philosophic tradition, materialism refers to treating the material world as the ultimate reality and dates back to ancient times. Marx's concern with this tradition is evinced in his choice of topic for his ***Doctoral Dissertation*** (1841), which examined the philosophy of **nature** through a comparison between the theories of the Greek philosophers Democritus and Epicurus. In favouring Epicurus, Marx not only endorses a more dynamic view of the movement of atoms, but approvingly links it to a wider anti-deterministic philosophical outlook.

In ***The Holy Family*** (1845) Marx gives an overview of the development of materialism from Descartes onwards and begins to develop his own form of materialism as being inextricably related to **humanism** and acting as the logical basis to **communism**. He argues that if humans are shaped by their surroundings, then their surroundings must be made human. Moreover, if humans are social by nature, then they will develop their true nature only in society. However, Marx has not quite escaped the influence of Feuerbach's materialism, and it is with his ***Theses on Feuerbach*** (1845) that Marx brings his own materialism to the fore and shows it to be a decisive advance on all its previous forms. From this point on Marx's materialism is at the basis of his analysis of society and history as encapsulated particularly in the three volumes of *Capital*. (See also **historical materialism**.)

materialist conception of history   A term created by **Engels** to describe Marx's theory of historical development, although not used by Marx himself. Engels first employed it in an 1859 anonymous review of Marx's **Contribution to the Critique of Political Economy** for the journal *Das Volk*. It was adopted by followers of Marx after Engels' use of the term in the enormously popular *Socialism: Utopian and Scientific* (1880). Engels also coined the term **historical materialism** in a letter to Bloch in 1890, and this became even more popular.

mediation   In dialectical philosophy, the act through which opposing concepts are reconciled, enabling further development to take place. In his **Critique of Hegel's Philosophy of Right** (1843) Marx was highly critical of Hegel's use of mediation in his justification of the structure of the Prussian **state**. Marx considered that Hegel's idealist **method** presented real differences of interests between social groupings as conceptual oppositions that could be easily mediated. In Hegel's view, the constitution was essentially 'a system of mediation' from the extreme of 'particularity' in the **form** of the monarch to the extreme of 'generality' in the form of **civil society**. The institutions of the state were described by **Hegel** as effecting checks and balances to ensure that the common good prevails over the material interests of any particular social group. For Marx, Hegel's mediations did no such thing, but rather disguised the fact that the state reflected the dominant socio-economic interests in Prussia. He berated Hegel for this 'absurdity of mediation' and argued that real extremes cannot be mediated precisely because they are real extremes. For Marx, the state always represents **class** interests, and attempts to legitimate it through conceptual mediations are illusory. Only with the achievement of political **democracy** can these interests be openly fought out as an 'unconcealed' **contradiction**.

Marx found the Hegelian approach invaluable as a methodological device to analyze contradictions occurring within the economic system. In **A Contribution to the Critique of Political Economy** (1859), when discussing the circuit of **capital**, he argues that the formula C-M-C (**commodity-money**-commodity) 'can be reduced to the abstract logical syllogism P-U-I, where particularity forms the first extreme, universality characterises the common middle term and individuality signals the final extreme'. This reversion to Hegelian logic helped Marx to build up his picture of the **capitalist mode of production** as a series of mediated contradictions that simultaneously allow it to expand while undermining the possibility of its stable development. In the *Grundrisse* (1857–1858) Marx indicates that the mediating term assumes greater power than the concepts that are mediated, and he draws an analogy between **religion** and economics. In religion Christ, as the mediator between God and 'man', takes on, as their unity, the greater role of 'God-man'. In economics, money assumes the greater role between exchanged commodities, the banker assumes the greater role as mediator between manufacturers and merchants, and the wholesaler becomes more important than the manufacturer and the retailer. This is all related to money in **capitalism** becoming transformed from a means to an end, adding to the volatility of the system as a whole.

metaphysics   A branch of philosophy that from the time of **Aristotle** has been concerned with the study of what cannot be accounted for by the senses, but is referred to by Marx as philosophy that deals with concepts in the abstract and separate from reality. Marx made this criticism of metaphysics when he was 19 and at the University of Berlin in a letter to his father, where he talks about studying **law** and philosophy. In the letter, Marx refers disparagingly to the metaphysics of law that he himself mistakenly had subscribed to, and which he characterizes as the basic principles, reflections, definitions of concepts that are divorced from all actual law and every actual **form** of law. Instead, Marx argues, it is the object under investigation, whether it is the law or the **state**, for example, which needs to be focused on to grasp its contradictions and inner development.

Similarly, in *The German Ideology* (1845–1846) Marx notes how the **production** of ideas is inextricably linked with the material activity and material interaction of human beings with the productive forces prevalent in any society at a given time. Mental production, of which metaphysics is a part, is therefore the outcome of these interactions, rather than the starting point of them. Proper investigation therefore begins with the material production of people and it is from this that what they think and say arises. Otherwise, all that is left are abstractions that are divorced from real history and as such have no real explanatory power. Marx's initial target here is Ludwig **Feuerbach**, whom he accuses of being 'a materialist who does not deal with history, and in so far as he deals with history he is not a materialist'.

Marx continues with a similar line of criticism specifically against Max Stirner, whom he sees as turning the actual relations of people into metaphysical relations. As one example, Marx notes how Stirner sees people as having formed a concept of what it is to be a human, and on that basis people have won **freedom** for themselves by realizing this concept. However, in reality, as Marx points out, people won freedom for themselves not by postulating a concept of what it is to be human but through their interaction with the real productive forces of society in the satisfaction of their needs and in opposition to those who would deny this. Hence the **class struggle** throughout history that has taken place between masters and slaves, lords and serfs and now the **bourgeoisie** and the **proletariat**. Again, the critique against metaphysics is a rejection of the mistaken assumption that concepts are the driving force of history when in actuality it is real, living human beings in their material production that drive history forward and furnish the basis for the conceptual understanding of that process. Marx reiterates these arguments in *The Holy Family* (1845), where he contends that metaphysics will be defeated forever by his own materialist **method**. (See also **idealism**, **materialism** and *The Poverty of Philosophy*.)

method   Intrinsically linked with Marx's **dialectic** and his **materialism**. One of the best expositions of his method occurs in the Afterword to the second German edition of *Capital* **1** (1867) in response to a review of *Capital* by the Russian economist I. I. Kaufmann, who criticizes Marx for having a philosophically idealist method of presentation and a realistic method of inquiry. Marx uses the review to refute such a contention. Kaufmann notes how Marx is concerned to find the laws of phenomena that have a definite **form** and mutual connection within a given historical period. Even more importantly, he realizes that Marx wants to understand phenomena in their transition from one form into another, from one series of connections into a different one. Marx stipulates that this is exactly what his method is, namely understanding phenomena as having inner connections with each other. However, Marx still has to respond to Kaufmann's criticism concerning the idealistic presentation and the realistic form of inquiry. Marx argues that presentation and inquiry must indeed differ. The method of inquiry has to appropriate the material in detail, to analyze its different forms of development and to track down their inner connection.

The method of inquiry is therefore nothing other than the analyzing of forms. The phenomena under consideration are subject to a critique that attempts to find their inner relation. The phenomena are thereby understood as forms, modes of existence, which should not be considered distinct and separate from one another but intrinsically linked in a dialectical unity – unity in difference. Once this process has been accomplished the real movement can then be presented. Then the life of the subject matter is reflected back into the ideas. Marx realizes that this can give the impression of an *a priori* construction and this is what Kaufmann has mistakenly taken for the idealistic method of presentation.

What Marx is saying is that any investigation of phenomena must begin by a concrete analysis of the form they take. When this has been accomplished and the investigation is ready for presentation it is presented not as beginning with the concrete but with the abstract. The method of inquiry moves from concrete to abstract, but the method of presentation moves from abstract to concrete. As Marx asserts in the **Grundrisse** (1857–1858), the concrete is concrete because it is the concentration of many determinations, hence unity of the diverse. It appears in the process of thinking, therefore, as a process of concentration as a result, not as a point of departure, even though it is the point of departure in reality and hence also the point of departure for observation and conception. So any investigation of phenomena is faced with the concrete, which itself is complex. If we were to examine the concept of **money**, for instance, we would see that it takes many different forms in society. In its concrete manifestation it is a complex phenomenon. To thought, this concrete appears as a 'result', an end point, not a starting point: 'This is money. This is how money manifests itself in society.' Money *appears* to thought in this way, but in reality this **appearance** is not an end point but the point of departure. For observation and conception we actually begin with the result, the concrete form money takes in society. The method of inquiry must therefore begin with the forms phenomena take in society and subject them to analysis to find their inner connection. When this has been accomplished the method of presentation is from the abstract to the concrete, from general to determinate **abstraction**. Marx realizes that to begin an enquiry with a general abstraction would presuppose what was trying to be proved. Instead, the correct method is a dialectical approach that must begin with phenomena in actuality, with what is given in its appearance.

mode of production   Defined in the 1859 **Preface to *A Contribution to a Critique of Political Economy*** as relations of production that correspond to a definite stage of development of the productive forces. The term is therefore used to distinguish one historical epoch from another. Marx denotes four main modes of **production** in history: the Asiatic, ancient, feudal and modern bourgeois. He argues that these periods of history can be regarded as progressing the economic development of society. All these modes of production have at their basis an antagonism in the social conditions people enter into in order to produce. What Marx means by this is that the social relations of production in each epoch are composed of opposing forces, e.g. master and slave, lord and serf, and **capitalist** and worker. He sees the bourgeois mode of production as the last antagonistic **form** of the social process of production, and proposes that the productive forces that are present within this society will create the material conditions for a resolution of this antagonism and the end of bourgeois society.

Marx also contends that the mode of production of material life conditions the general process of social, political and intellectual life. Consequently, Marx argues that it is not the **consciousness** of humans that determines their existence, but their social existence that determines their consciousness. So in a mode of production that is capitalist, for example, all aspects of society will reflect the **ideology** of **capital**. The pursuit of self-interest, the rule of the **market** and **competition** that are symptomatic of capitalist values therefore permeate society and penetrate the consciousness of human beings. Although Marx can be seen to be determinist here, it must be remembered that it is only through the development of **class consciousness** in a process of **class struggle** that he thought we could break through such ideology.

Marx also uses the term mode of production to analyze different types of production in a society. In ***Capital* 1** (1867), for example, he notes how the transformation of a mode of production in one sphere of industry necessitates similar transformations in other spheres. As an example, Marx gives the instance of how machine-spinning made machine-weaving necessary and this led to a mechanical and chemical **revolution** being compulsory in bleaching, printing and dyeing. On a grander scale, he notes how changes in the modes of production of industry and agriculture necessitated a revolution in the means of communication and transport. As pre-capitalist agriculture along with its subsidiary domestic industries and urban handicrafts was small scale, communication and transport were therefore totally inadequate to those required for the **needs** of a rapidly developing manufacturing sector of the economy. Consequently, there was a transformation in the means of transport and communication that gradually adapted themselves to the new mode of production of large-scale industry by the development of a system railways, river steamers, ocean steamers and telegraphs. However, the period of manufacture itself was incapable of constructing the **machines** that were needed for these developments and so large-scale industry had to take over the machine itself and so produce machines by means of machines. The mode of production understood in this way therefore grasps the dynamic basis to social and economic development. (See also **base and superstructure** and **historical materialism**.)

money In its simplest **form**, a medium for the **exchange** of goods. Marx considered that although money had been used in many earlier modes of **production**, it only reached its 'intensive' form in **capitalism**. He argued that beyond the apparently neutral function of enabling commodities to circulate, money had significant social repercussions. Although the social character of production is expressed in money, instead of affirming the power of the producers, money itself appeared to be the creative power. Marx first developed this view in the ***Comments on James Mill*** (1844), and it remains central to his argument on **commodity fetishism** in his mature **political economy**.

In his discussion of Mill on money he argues that the social act of exchange in which the products of people mutually complement one another is mediated by a material thing, money, as a result of which the products themselves become an attribute not of our fellow producers, but of money itself. Humanity has therefore created a power outside and above humans, leaving people lost and dehumanized. Originally, money has value because it represents products, but in a fully developed money economy the products possess value only because they represent money. This reversal of the relationship between producers and their products is likened by Marx to the development of **religion**, in which the human mind creates God and then accords it with the status of creator. In this analogy, Christ as a mediator between humanity and God is likened to money as **mediation** between producer and product, and in both cases the subject of the process becomes the object. Marx opposed any idea that the emergence of paper money and credit dispensed with all the problems caused by the hoarding of gold and silver, and he considered credit to be particularly deceitful because it gave the **appearance** of trust, when in fact it is based on a cold calculation of the security of the loan. The elevation of creditworthiness to the status of moral recognition is regarded by the young Marx as an immoral vileness, and as long as credit would only go to those who already had money, it would sharpen the opposition between **capital** and **labour**, and also between small and large capital. A money economy meant that people produced not for each other but for **individual** gain, and he thought of it as the sensuous and even objective existence of **alienation**.

In the ***Economic and Philosophical Manuscripts*** (1844) Marx developed the argument that money has contradictory effects, both increasing economic activity and objectively bringing people together, and at the same time forming the lifeblood of a system of production that was inherently unsocial and divisive. He uses quotes from Shakespeare's *Timon of Athens* and Goethe's *Faust* to emphasize how money can pervert human qualities, enabling the rich to buy the appearance of being brave, powerful and attractive, while those with no money are unable to develop their natural abilities. This perversion of human qualities does not occur through the misuse of money or through a technical flaw in the medium of exchange. Rather, money makes contradictions 'embrace' as a direct and inevitable result of its role in promoting **capitalist** relations of production.

Marx made extensive notes from virtually all the available literature on money in 1851, and it is the subject of the long first chapter of the ***Grundrisse*** (1857–1858). He rejected arguments that new forms of distribution, such as labour-time certificates, could revolutionize the system of production. Some forms might work better than others, but a money economy would still be assailed by contradictions. Money originally appears to facilitate production, but as the producers become dependent on exchange, the rift between product as product and product as exchange value appears to widen, leaving us with the 'the apparently transcendental power of money'. Marx also considers that money comes between purchase and sale by selling a commodity (C) for money (M) to buy another commodity (C), (C-M-C), and buying in order to sell where money (M) is used to buy a commodity (C) to get more money (M), (M-C-M). The separation of the two acts in space and time invites economic instability.

This is made even more acute with the development of a separate finance capital independent of the **commodity** producers. The *Grundrisse* repeats many of the examples about the power of money to pervert social relationships present in the 1844 *Manuscripts*, including the quotation from *Timon of Athens*, the reference to money standing as an alien power over the producers, and the analogy with God, a human creation that stands over human beings as their creator. Most of the arguments find their way into the **Contribution to the Critique of Political Economy** (1859), but Marx now rejects the idea that money is a symbol. It appears to be the originator of the productive system, but this 'perverted appearance' is 'prosaically real and by no means imaginary'. Changing the form of money, for instance by experimenting with 'labour money', cannot resolve the problems inherent in commodity production.

The discussion of money in **Capital 1** (1867), particularly its role in commodity fetishism, comes very close to the arguments in the *Manuscripts* and the *Grundrisse*. The argument concerning the perverting power of money is repeated, this time backed up by quotations from Columbus, who had written that gold enabled souls to enter Paradise, and Sophocles' *Antigone*, where it is stated that 'nothing so evil as money ever grew to be current among men'. Commodity fetishism is inseparable from money fetishism, for commodities find their value is expressed by another commodity, money, which exists 'outside but also alongside them'. Money becomes the object of production, and in the process the social bond between people gives way to 'purely atomistic' relations 'independent of their control and their conscious individual action'. The functions of money described by Marx – universal equivalent, means of exchange, measure of value, means of deferred payment and means of accumulating values – all bring with them potential instability even though they were necessary for the system's development. Deferred payments, for example, even when operating in a developed banking system, could still provoke a financial crisis.

Capital 2 (1863–1878) is devoted to circulation, reproduction and extended **accumulation** and is famous for the reproduction schemas which pose the problem of how production can continue in a stable fashion. The first chapter is devoted to the circuit of money capital, emphasizing the instability that naturally accompanies interruptions between the sphere of circulation and the sphere of production. Perceptively, Marx notes that all capitalist countries 'are periodically seized by fits of giddiness in which they try to accomplish the money-making without the mediation of the production process'. He looks at the various independent forms of money capital in part five of **Capital 3** (1864–1865). His discussion of the emergence of a separate money **market** shows that production itself can be seen to be incidental to the process of making money, and he predicts that the system will be rocked by such things as fluctuations in the money market, surges in large-scale investments and the difference in the speed of turnover of money capital in different sectors of the economy.

Marx's technical analysis of money and the circulation of money capital is impressive, but it is important not to lose sight of its philosophical significance. That is why the *Grundrisse* is so valuable, for it brings that philosophical significance to the fore, revealing money as the key **mediation** that reproduces the alienation inherent in the capitalist **mode of production**. (See also **fictitious capital**.)

morality   Before 1845 there was a strong moral thrust to Marx's central argument that **capitalism** is rooted in **alienation** and has a dehumanizing impact on the producers. In the *Economic and Philosophical Manuscripts* (1844) it is clear that he wants to see the flowering of human potential, conceived in terms of the realization of human **essence**. However, in *The German Ideology* (1845–1846) he expresses impatience with all moral discourse, announcing that 'communists do not preach morality at all'. This was part of a wider theoretical shift that rejected abstract philosophical argument in favour of critical analysis of the **capitalist mode of production**. In arguing that it is not **consciousness** that determines life, but life that determines consciousness, Marx denied the need for the independent study of morality, **religion** or **metaphysics**. In *The Communist Manifesto* (1848) he argues a relativist position on morality, viewing all moral, religious and philosophical ideas as reflections of the conditions of material existence, so that 'the ruling ideas of each age are the ideas of its **ruling class**'. He anticipates the objection that morality itself has persisted throughout history, despite historical modifications, and that therefore if **communism** rejects 'eternal truths' it runs the risk of acting in **contradiction** to all past historical experience. In response he argues that since all the history of past society has been one of **class** antagonism, the common forms of consciousness must reflect, in various ways, the exploitative **nature** of class society. Only with the abolition of class antagonisms can these common forms of consciousness be left behind, so that communism involves the most radical rupture with traditional ideas. He then abruptly ends the discussion and urges the **working class** to win the battle for **democracy**.

Marx concedes that the communist society of the future will have its moral ideals, but he refuses to countenance how those ideals develop in the struggle against capitalism. At one stage in **Capital 3** (1864–1865) he imagines one aspect of what a communist moral viewpoint would look like when he states that the private ownership of land will come to be regarded as just as absurd as the idea of **slavery** appears to us in liberal society. However, this is an isolated instance of thinking about what a communist morality might look like or how it might develop. Instead, all is left to the revolutionary struggle, informed by theoretical analyses of the economic and political conditions. Marx's moral reticence flowed from a conviction that focusing on the fairness or otherwise of existing conditions detracted from the urgent priority of analyzing the material conditions confronting the working class, in order to identify the most propitious ways of organizing and intervening politically. At this relatively early time in the development of socialist thought, most of the contributions were moralistic or utopian, setting down ideal alternatives without due consideration of how revolutionary social movements could develop under existing conditions and circumstances. However, it is important to recognize that Marx was making a tactical choice in shunning moral argument, rather than repudiating the idea that communism has a moral dimension. In other words, his denunciation of specific moral positions should not be taken to mean that all moral utterances are nonsense.

A good example of Marx denouncing bad moralizing that does not entail a rejection of all moral thinking is found in those parts of the **Critique of the Gotha Programme** (1875) in which he criticizes the demand for 'a just distribution of the proceeds of **labour**'. He reiterates his relativist position by stating that the **bourgeoisie** would claim that the present system of distribution is just, and that they would be right to do so within the present relations of **production**. However, Marx makes it clear that by 'just' he refers to a legal concept of right, thereby leaving open the possibility that it may be considered unjust by some socialist standard that anticipates a postcapitalist future. The moral claims made by the programme are dismissed by Marx as 'obsolete verbal rubbish', but he does concede that these ideas 'may have made some sense at a particular time'. He is, however, anxious that the realistic outlook that he favoured should not be 'perverted' by 'ideological, legal and other humbug'. He adds that it any event it was theoretically mistaken to focus on distribution rather than production. Marx was guided here by a tactical judgement, and this did not prevent him from announcing a moral principle of distribution for the future communist society: from each according to ability to each according to **needs**.

Along with Marx's aversion to moral discourse, then, is an acknowledgment that moral statements can make sense and that moral ideals are an inevitable part of **class struggle**. When he wrote the Provisional Rules of the **First International** in 1864, he included a commitment that the members of the International 'will acknowledge truth, **justice**, and morality, as the basis of their conduct towards each other, and towards all men, without regard to colour, creed, or nationality', followed by a claim for the **rights** and duties of man and **citizen**. In a letter to **Engels** in November 1864, Marx revealed that he had been 'obliged' to insert these sentences by the sub-committee, adding that 'these are so placed that they can do no harm'. Not only was he quite willing to put his name to these moral commitments, but in his own Inaugural Address to the International he urged the working class to apply the 'simple laws of morals and justice' that ought to govern private relationships when judging the foreign policies of their national governments. In his preamble to the programme of the French Workers' Party in 1880, he begins by asserting that 'the **emancipation** of the producing class is that of all human beings without distinction of sex or **race**'. (See also **human nature**.)

—**N**—

nation   Regarded by Marx as a naturally evolved entity, he used the term interchangeably with people or peoples. Theoretical discussions about the nature of nationalism did not develop until after his death, following the appearance of Ernest Renan's seminal essay *What is a Nation?* in 1882, but Marx made important observations about national **consciousness** and relations between nations. In **_The Communist Manifesto_** (1848) Marx argued that with the development of international **capitalism** comes a 'universal interdependence of nations' that produces a situation in which 'national one-sidedness and narrow-mindedness become more and more impossible'. Because of this economic integration, national differences and antagonisms between people were 'vanishing'. Defending the principle of communist **internationalism**, Marx claims that the workers have no country, adding that 'we cannot take from them what they have not got'. In other words, since workers own nothing and have no political **rights**, they should feel no loyalty to an alien entity. Marx acknowledged that the **working class** of each country would have to establish its political supremacy within each nation and argued that overcoming **class** antagonism would bring with it the end of hostilities between nations. The *Manifesto* ends with an appeal to proletarians of all countries to unite.

In his Inaugural Address of the **First International** in 1864, Marx recognized the threat posed to the 'fraternal concurrence' of the international working class by the deliberate promotion of 'national prejudice' (*Nationalvorurteilen*) in foreign policy. He pointed to outstanding examples of working-class solidarity in foreign affairs, such as the support of the English working class for the struggle to abolish **slavery** during the American Civil War, and European working class opposition to the Russian suppression of the Polish independence movement. He saw these as examples of fighting for an ethical foreign policy – 'vindicating the simple laws of morals and **justice**' – as a necessary part of the struggle for the **emancipation** of the working class.

Marx recognized the baleful consequences of one nation oppressing another. He was particularly supportive of the national struggles of Ireland against Britain and Poland against Russia. In the case of British rule in Ireland, in a Confidential Communication to German socialist leaders in 1870 Marx likened British policy to what had happened on a monstrous scale in ancient Rome, concluding that 'any nation that oppresses another nation forges its own chains'. Marx had originally thought that only the triumph of the working class in Britain would resolve the problem in Ireland, but in a letter to **Engels** in 1869 he argued that the opposite was true, and that 'the English working class will never accomplish anything before it has got rid of Ireland'. This judgement rested not only on sympathy for the historical wrongs committed against the Irish, but also the divisive effects of **competition** for jobs between British and Irish workers in England. Elsewhere in the Confidential Communication he noted that this antagonism was fomented by the **bourgeoisie** to bolster its own rule.

naturalism   A term used in the early writings, along with **humanism**, to designate Marx's philosophical outlook, in distinction from **idealism** or crude **materialism**. In the *Economic and Philosophical Manuscripts* (1844) Marx describes **communism** as 'fully developed naturalism, equals humanism' and vice versa. This position was influenced by **Feuerbach**, who sought to restore **human nature** to its powers of will, **reason** and affection. Naturalism in this sense refers to the unfolding of humanity's true **nature**. However, Marx was already going much further in linking the development of this naturalism to the struggle against private **property**. Despite the claim in the *Manuscripts* that 'only naturalism is capable of comprehending the process of world history', he drops the term once his differences with Feuerbach become clearer. In the sixth of the *Theses on Feuerbach* (1845) he criticizes the latter's notion of the human **essence** as a 'mute general character which unites the many individuals in a purely natural way' rather than understanding it as 'the ensemble of the social relations'.

nature   Marx referred to nature as both the environment external to human beings and also to human potentials that transform the relationship between humans and their environment. In the *Economic and Philosophical Manuscripts* (1844) he argues that external nature is part of human **consciousness**, sometimes as the object of **science**, sometimes as the object of **art**, when it appears as our spiritual nourishment. The universality of humans is expressed in making all nature our 'inorganic body' by relying on it as our direct means of life and by acting on it as the instrument of our own life activity. He also emphasizes that when we satisfy our bodily and spiritual **needs** in our interaction with our natural environment we become part of nature. Only when humanity annuls **production** based on **private property** will society be able to appreciate our environment as the foundation of human existence, so as to experience the 'complete unity of humanity with nature'. In *The German Ideology* (1845–1846) he argues that much of non-human nature has been shaped by human beings, citing the example of sheep and dogs who, in their present **form**, are part of a historical process 'in spite of themselves' as a result of selective breeding organized by humans. Marx makes it clear that the part of external nature untouched by humans is shrinking with every advance of industry. He offers the example of the freshwater fish, which loses its '**essence**' of freshwater when the river becomes polluted with chemical dyes or waste products. However, he does not consider such pollution as inevitable or irreversible, and maintains that we have it in our powers to conduct our production in less damaging ways.

Although Marx's chief concern was for human **emancipation**, he was fully aware that this would require assuming responsibility for nature as a whole, both human and non-human. His criticisms of the nature cult of Georg Friedrich Daumer in 1850 were not based on the latter's veneration of external nature, but rather on the fact that Daumer was explicitly using his environmental concerns to dismiss the importance of **class struggle** and even to oppose democratic reforms for exciting the envy of the 'lower' classes. Marx was alert to the terrible damage done to human and non-human nature by a system of **accumulation** driven solely by the pursuit of **profit**. In respect of the damage to non-human nature, in chapter fifteen of *Capital* **1** (1867) he asserts that all progress in **capitalist** agriculture is progress in the art of not only robbing the worker but also robbing the soil; short-term progress in increasing the fertility of the soil was achieved only at the cost of ruining the long-term sources of that fertility. The scientist cited by Marx here was Justus von Liebig, among the first to write on the destructive side of modern agricultural methods, and he also praised the work of Karl Nikolas Fraas, the first to identify the disastrous unintended consequences of deforestation on cultivation. Marx certainly believed in using nature productively, but he knew that where production was driven by profit maximization, the results for nature and for long-term sustainability would be disastrous.

In a rare glimpse of how he envisioned communist society, in the *Grundrisse* (1857) Marx makes it clear that control over nature meant control over both 'so called' nature and also our own **human nature**, implying the assumption of responsibility for a harmonious relationship in which all aspects of nature were to be respected. The prefix 'so called' was Marx's way of reaffirming his view that much of what we think of as nature is not pristine but has already been developed through interaction with humanity. In chapter forty-six of *Capital* **3** (1864–1865) he envisages that in the future communist society the ownership of land will appear as absurd as **slavery** does in liberal society, emphasizing that neither individuals nor societies own the earth but simply act as stewards 'to bequeath it in an improved state to succeeding generations'.

needs   Prevalent throughout all Marx's writings, needs can only be understood by grasping the **form** they take in society. Marx's starting point as part of his **materialism** is to analyze how a society comes together in order to produce, and he deduces that all societies have to satisfy what he calls their natural needs for food, clothing, shelter etc. As **capital** is a system of private **property**, the workers cannot immediately satisfy their natural needs, so they have to sell their **labour power** first. The concrete forms that natural needs begin to take are mediated through the sale of labour power. As Marx says in *Capital* **1** (1867), the cruel nature-imposed necessity is that workers have to sell their labour power to satisfy their natural needs. Once the natural needs take on this form, a further **mediation** arises – the **value** of labour power. The latter is determined by the socially necessary **labour** time required for workers to reproduce themselves. However, the wage the workers receive can be above or below this level, depending on **class struggle**. It is here that natural needs take on the more concrete form of what Marx calls necessary needs. So if the wage or **money** received is greater than the value of labour power, the workers' necessary needs increase. This may allow a new form of luxury needs to come into existence and be satisfied. If the converse happens, then the workers could be forced back on to the lower limit of necessary needs. If they cannot sell their labour power, they could fall even further to the level of natural needs proper. Natural needs therefore take the form of necessary needs, which in turn take the form of luxury needs.

Those needs considered as luxury at one time can, with social development and increased **wages**, become necessary, and due to changing circumstances, necessary goods may even become luxury goods. Similarly, depending on societal development, necessary needs could become natural needs. New needs are socially created through developments in the **production** process, and these appear on the **market** in the form of luxury needs. The total or collective expression of need takes two forms: social and true social need. The former appears on the market in the form of effective demand, whilst the latter remains hidden as a potential level of need that people could satisfy if prices, and their own incomes and living conditions were different. In this sense, the market and bourgeois **political economy** do not recognize true social needs.

Marx also discusses higher needs. As people offer themselves on the market as a **commodity** in order to satisfy their natural needs, moments of human needs emerge. They can become manifest in an estranged form as egoistic needs or in their own right as moments of self-valorization. When such activity poses a threat to the **capitalist** system then human need takes the form of radical need. Analyzing forms of need, therefore, reveals the inner connection between these phenomena. The implications of Marx's argument for any theory of needs are therefore quite substantial. He would reject any privileging of either universal or particular conceptions of needs. Instead, it is the dialectical interaction between the two that has to be the focus. For Marx, needs can be posited as universal, but this is by subjects themselves in their interaction with other human beings and the natural world. In positing a universal need the particular mode of existence of its satisfaction can take many different forms. So the constant interaction of universal and particular, both alienated and human, reverberates in and against the capitalist system. For humans, the potential for subordination to a very miserable level of need-satisfaction exists alongside the potential for a much greater level of enjoyment. Technological developments offer increased free-time from necessary labour, and the opportunity for humans to become rich in needs and their satisfaction, just as they also offer the opportunity for degrading labour and unemployment. Hence Marx's theory of needs can highlight the positive moments within the negative manifestations of humans' contradictory development in their interaction with each other and the natural world. In this way, a movement beyond capital into a realm where human needs are properly satisfied can become a real possibility.

negation   A term derived from **Hegel** that means both to annul something whilst at the same time bringing out something positive from it, in a process of becoming. Negation is therefore an aspect of the **dialectic**.

In the ***Economic and Philosophical Manuscripts*** (1844) Marx criticizes Hegel's idealist application of the negation of the negation as a 'hollow abstraction' because it remains confined within pure thought. He also exposes how even the materialist use of negation in the critique of religion by the **Young Hegelians** suffers further weaknesses. They used atheism to negate God, but the affirmation of human power in their German theoretical socialism lacked real commitment to revolutionary change. For Marx, communism is the new, materialist negation of the negation through which human emancipation can take place. He argues, therefore, that the negation of the negation is the confirmation of true being through the negation of apparent being where humanity truly recovers its own **essence**.

In chapter thirty-two of *Capital* **1** (1867) Marx offers another example of his use of negation in relation to the historical development of **capitalist accumulation**. He detects in the move from **feudalism** to **capitalism** a major development of the 'immanent laws of capitalist **production** itself', which can lead to the downfall of the system. He argues that these developments result in the centralization of capitals as one capitalist eliminates many others and so dominates the **market**. However, such developments also bring the **working class** together as an organized grouping that is antagonistically present within the production process. Marx argues that it is through the growing 'revolt of the working class' that capitalism contains within itself not only the negation of the system of private **property** on which it is based, but also the negation of that negation where the capitalist 'expropriators are expropriated', the system is overcome, and **cooperation** and common ownership is introduced.

—O—

On the Jewish Question **(1844)**   An essay in two parts written in 1843 and later published in the journal *Deutsch-Französische Jahrbücher* in response to two articles by Bruno Bauer. In the first part of the essay Marx argues for religious toleration in a democratic, secular **state** and makes an important distinction between political **emancipation** and human emancipation. It contains a powerful critique of liberal conceptions of **rights** and is one of Marx's most important contributions to political theory. The second part reaffirms his conviction that it is unreasonable to demand that Jews renounce their **religion** before they be granted political rights, but he also equates Judaism with financial and commercial power, conforming to a prejudiced stereotype.

The issue was the demand for Jews to be given full civil rights in the Prussian state. Bauer had argued that the Jews should not be granted civil rights until they renounced their religion, since only when society at large emancipates itself from religion can we achieve political emancipation. Marx's criticism turned on Bauer's failure to examine the relationship between political emancipation and human emancipation. When looking at what kind of emancipation is involved in achieving civil rights, Marx points to the example of the United States, a secular state exemplifying complete political emancipation where religious life is 'fresh' and 'vigorous'. The state here is emancipated from religion in general. Marx shares Bauer's dislike of the Christian state, but he endorses the democratic secular state that 'relegates' religion to the level of the other elements of **civil society**, thereby allowing religion to continue in existence.

Bauer had argued that the Jews could not claim universal human rights since they identified themselves as separate from other people, but Marx retorted that the rights set down in the great French **Revolution** were precisely the rights of the restricted, egoistic **individual**. Rights such as legal **equality** and the right to own **property** enabled citizens to compete with one another in an egoistic civil society. Marx claims that the political revolution, in destroying the civil associations set up in the feudal era such as the guilds, abolished the political character of civil society, rendering it completely materialistic and devoid of 'even the *semblance* of a universal content'. He concluded that political emancipation did not require the prior renunciation of religion. Rather it represents a paradox in which the egoistic life of civil society contrasts with the idealized life of the social **citizen**, the 'moral person'. Only by socializing our productive lives can this paradox be resolved and human emancipation achieved.

The second part of the essay begins by reiterating the unreasonableness of Bauer's insistence that the Jews should be denied their civil rights, noting that this is based on a purely theological view about whether or not Christianity or Judaism lends itself better to the dissolution of religion in general. However, when Marx goes on to define Judaism in terms of its everyday 'secular' **essence** he equates it with 'haggling' and '**money**'. He associates Judaism with financial power, stating that even when Jews do not have civil rights they exert a massive practical domination over the Christian world, presenting a 'contemporary anti-social element'. In general this reflects the fact that although political power is supposed to be superior to financial power, it is really 'in thrall to it'. He concludes by stating that the *social* emancipation of the Jew is the emancipation of society from Judaism by the abolition of the **market** economy, not through the renunciation of **race** or religion. Marx's characterization did not reflect the reality of life for the vast majority of European Jews not engaged in finance and ignores the historical factors that had given rise to Jewish involvement in finance, such as the usury laws and the bans on Jewish participation in a range of occupations.

Owen, Robert (1771–1858)   The leading figure of British cooperative **socialism** in the early nineteenth century, admired by Marx for his commitment to the idea of the collective ownership of the means of **production** and the insight that only by transforming the system of production can people develop their potentials. In *The Communist Manifesto* (1848) Marx classified Owen as one of the representatives of critical **utopian socialism** who had undertaken a radical attack on the principles of existing society and had given valuable ideas to the **working class**. In *Capital* **1** (1867) he praised Owen not only for calling for a maximum ten-hour **working day** but actually introducing it in his mill at New Lanark in 1810. He also approved of Owen's idea of combining work and **education** for children. However, he rejected Owen's belief in the reconciliation of **class** antagonisms and his paternalistic attitude towards the working class. Although Marx was sure that Owenite schemes such as cooperatives and **labour money** could never supplant **capitalism**, he acknowledged that Owen also recognized the limited viability of such ideas as long as the **capitalist** system continued to expand.

—P—

Paris Commune (1871) The revolutionary government that controlled Paris for two months in 1871 was hailed by Marx as 'the glorious harbinger of a new society' in *The Civil War in France* (1871). The Commune arose out of the chaos that developed following the military defeats suffered by the army of Napoleon III in the Franco-Prussian War. The Emperor's capture led to the declaration of a republic in September 1870. With Paris under siege from the Prussian army, the provisional government agreed an armistice in late January, quickly followed by a national election. This produced a right-wing government under Adolphe Thiers, who agreed to a humiliating peace treaty with the Prussians, which saw them occupy Paris for a few days early in March. The majority of Parisians, incensed by the surrender, forced Thiers and his ministers to flee Paris for Versailles, triggering civil **war**. Fresh elections took place in Paris, after which the Commune was proclaimed, on 28 March. Some of the Communards were members of the **First International** (1864–1872) but most were either left-wing republicans or members of independent socialist or anarchist groups. They held out for two months, but were eventually overwhelmed by government troops. It is estimated that more than 20,000 were massacred.

In a letter to **Engels** in September 1870, Marx warned against the 'planned stupidities' of the Paris Internationalists who favoured overthrowing the provisional government and declaring a Commune. In the Second Address of the General Council on the Franco-Prussian War, also in September, he commented that for the Paris **working class** to overthrow the provisional government with the 'enemy at the door' would be a 'desperate folly'. Nevertheless, when the civil war broke out Marx gave his wholehearted backing to the Commune, arguing that the new national government lacked democratic legitimacy, whereas the Commune practiced a radical **form** of **democracy**. He admired the measures taken to ensure that privileged bureaucratic and legal elites were unable to wield power. However, despite this unqualified public support for the heroism of the Communards, Marx privately considered that the Commune was not socialist and had little chance of success. This is clear in his 1881 letter to Domela Nieuwenhuis in which he opined that the Communards, if they had used a 'small amount of common sense', could have reached a compromise with the Versailles

government 'useful to the whole mass of the people', the only thing that
could be achieved in those circumstances.

peasantry   One of Marx's most pertinent discussions of the peasantry
occurs in *The Eighteenth Brumaire of Louis Bonaparte* (1852) in which
he argues that while the French peasants are certainly exploited in the sense
that they perform surplus **labour** that is appropriated by a **landlord**, they
are not a revolutionary **class**. Their inability to assert their class interest is
due to their lack of interaction with each other, even though they form a
huge number of people who live in similar conditions. They become preoccupied with their own smallholdings, and such isolation is reinforced by
poor communication and the **poverty** of the peasants in general. A lack
of a division of labour in cultivation with no **science** applied to growing,
and therefore severe limits on agricultural development, further limits any
possibility of creating interconnections between people in different areas
of the country. Marx concludes that the majority of the peasantry in France
is fragmented, and when they do come together it is by simple accretion,
'just as a potatoes in a sack form a sack of potatoes'. They are therefore
incapable of asserting themselves as a class. However, Marx is not saying
that they cannot play a revolutionary role in social and political struggles,
for their contribution to the French **Revolution** of 1789 is testament to
that, but their role needs to be aligned with the urban **proletariat** if the
bourgeois order is to be properly overthrown. This is also why in *The Civil
War in France* (1871), where Marx discusses the **Paris Commune** (1871),
he states that the Commune was perfectly correct in telling the peasants
that the Commune's victory was their only hope. The peasants' accommodation to Bonapartism was rewarded with betrayal by Napoleon III, who
inflicted suffering on them in terms of excess taxes and the authoritarianism
of the local guard. In contrast, the Commune's aim was to liberate the
peasants from this oppression. Hence Marx endorses the winning over of
the peasantry by the **working class**, but it is only through the working class
that all oppressed sections of society can be emancipated.

petty bourgeoisie   Described in *The Communist Manifesto* (1848) as a
new **class** emerging in modern civilization, 'fluctuating between the **proletariat** and the bourgeoisie and ever renewing itself as a supplementary part
of bourgeois society'. The petty bourgeoisie (*Kleinbürgerlicher*) comprised

the independent traders and artisans, an intermediate class threatened by the ongoing development of large-scale industry and commerce. Marx recognized that elements of the petty bourgeoisie would at times be drawn to the cause of the workers. However, in his analysis of parliamentary **politics** in France in *The Eighteenth Brumaire of Louis Bonaparte* (1852) he was suspicious that the petty bourgeois representatives would 'soften the antagonism' between **capital** and **labour**. Marx consistently warned against this fudging of the **class struggle** by petty bourgeois influences, and this is particularly evident in the *Critique of the Gotha Programme* (1875) and in his circular letter of 1879 to the leaders of the German socialists.

political economy   Defined by Marx in *Capital* **1** (1867) as covering the work of all those economists since the time of William Petty who have investigated the real internal framework of bourgeois relations of **production**. He sees Adam **Smith** and David **Ricardo** as the best representatives of this tradition. This is in contrast to those economists whom Marx terms 'vulgar', because they are basically using political economy in a crude and simplistic way as a **form** of apologetics for **capital**.

In the Afterword to the second German edition of *Capital* 1, Marx offers a useful overview of the development of political economy, particularly in England, and shows how these two tendencies emerged. He argues that classical political economy belonged to a period where the **class struggle** was undeveloped, and it was only really with Ricardo who started his investigations with the 'antagonism of **class** interests, of **wages** and profits, of profits and rent' that political economy came to the fore. Indeed, because of this Marx refers to Ricardo as political economy's last great representative, even though he mistakenly took these antagonisms as a social **law** of **nature**. After Ricardo's contribution, Marx suggests that the bourgeois **science** of economics had reached its limit, and even in Ricardo's lifetime political economists such as Sismondi were already criticizing his theories and expressing doubt in political economy itself.

Marx sees the period 1820 to 1830 as a pivotal period for political economy because it was during this time that Ricardo's theories were both vulgarized and extended. The reason for this was that large-scale industry was still not fully developed, and the class struggle between capital and labour took second place to the political conflict between the feudal

aristocracy and the bourgeoisie, and the economic conflict between aristo-
cratic landed **property** and industrial capital. With the political victory of
the **bourgeoisie** gaining power in both England and France in 1830, class
struggle became both more explicit and more threatening both in **theory
and practice**, and so brought to an end the scientific bourgeois economics
that was political economy. As Marx indicates, the quest for truth that was
part of classical political economy now became a mere apology for capital.
Instead of disinterested inquirers, there were now 'prize-fighters' who were
only concerned whether a theory was useful in supporting the system or
not, so the science of political economy became what Marx called vulgar
economics.

Marx explains that the advocates of political economy now split into
two factions. One was simply vulgar, represented by Bastiat, and served
the interests of prudent and practical businessmen. The other, more proud
of their professional dignity in relation to political economy as a science,
were represented by John Stuart Mill, who attempted to reconcile the irreconcilable – the conflict between capital and labour. Both therefore were
doomed to failure and would remain imprisoned within the logic of capital.

One other important variant within the political economy tradition is the
neo-Ricardian or pre-Marxian socialists consisting of Charles Hall (1745–
1825), William Thompson (1775–1833), Thomas Hodgskin (1783–1869),
John Gray (1799–1850) and John Francis Bray (1809–1897). These writers
in their different ways made important contributions by offering prescient
criticisms of industrial **capitalism** and Marx was an admirer of many of their
writings. However, they did not manage to break free from the weaknesses
in Ricardo's theory in the way that Marx was to accomplish in his own
critique of political economy.

Out of this critique Marx made a number of advances on the political
economy that had gone before him. Through his understanding of **surplus
value** he exposed how capital is only different in **form** from other class
societies in the way it exploits the majority in the interests of a minority. As
part of this discovery he made the important distinction between **labour**
and **labour power** to show how surplus value was created. In relation to
surplus value itself, he showed how **profit**, rent and interest all came from
that one source and so displayed how it was simply the money-form of the
historical and universal category of social surplus product or social surplus
labour. His focus on **accumulation** revealed how capitalists themselves are

prisoners of the very system they support, as they constantly have to revolu-tionize the means of production in order to undercut their competitors. He also exposed how capital is inevitably prone to **economic crises** through the **tendency of the rate of profit to fall**, thus grasping capital as a dynamic rather than a static system in the way bourgeois theorists attempt to understand it.

politics   The organized **competition** for political power is placed in the 'superstructure' in Marx's conception of history, as outlined in the **Preface to *A Contribution to the Critique of Political Economy*** (1859). Politics is conceived as being conditioned by the economic structure, reflecting the class struggles being fought out within society. Before 1843, Marx thought that achieving political **democracy** was the ultimate goal, but in ***On the Jewish Question*** (1844) he criticized Bruno Bauer for confusing political **emancipation**, in the **form** of representative democracy, with human emancipation. The latter could be achieved only by abolishing private **property**, the basis of **class** society. For this, the political organi-zation of the **working class** was required. In ***The Communist Manifesto*** (1848) he urged the working class to 'win the battle for democracy' and to seize political power from the **bourgeoisie**. It could then transform the relations of **production** by abolishing private productive **property**, thereby removing the conditions for class conflict. He supported **communist** partici-pation in working class parties and alliances with other progressive groups, depending on national conditions and circumstances.

In ***The Eighteenth Brumaire of Louis Bonaparte*** (1852) Marx presented a meticulous account of the political struggles in the French Second Republic, being careful to distinguish between the ideological positions of the various political parties and the class interests that they represented. At times of crisis their class interests prevailed over their principles so that, for example, republicans entered into coalition with royalist parties in order to nullify the threat from the working class. Republicans once anxious to introduce universal male franchise voted for its abolition when socialists began to achieve electoral success. Marx's account shows parliamentary politics to be impotent, with real power resting elsewhere – with the **state bureaucracy**, the army and the directly elected President. In analyzing the behaviour of the social democrats in France between 1849 and 1851 he was contemptuous of their over-reliance on rhetorical gestures, describing it as 'parliamentary cretinism'. He was so disillusioned with the parliamentary politics of the Second Republic that he considered Bonaparte's *coup d'état* might help the cause of the workers in the long-term by centralizing state-power, making it easier for the working class to destroy it at a later date. However, the despotism of the Second Empire was so oppressive that Marx came to recognize that a bourgeois republic was worth defending against a right-wing dictatorship, as he made clear in a letter to his friend Friedrich Sorge in relation to the constitutional crisis in France in 1877.

Marx's own most active involvement in politics was in his role as a leading member of the General Council of the **First International** (1864–1872). It was entirely in keeping with his **internationalism** that this organization pre-dated the emergence of nationally based socialist and labour parties in most countries, but Marx had to struggle against anarchist resistance to legal political activity. In a Resolution of the London Conference of the International in 1871, Marx warned that even at a time of violent reaction from the **ruling class**, in response to the **Paris Commune** (1871), the working class could only act 'by constituting itself into a political party, distinct from, and opposed to, all old parties formed by the propertied classes'. He added that the formation of working class political parties was 'indispensable' to achieving social **revolution** and the abolition of classes. In January 1873 he wrote an article, 'Political Indifferentism', for an Italian journal in which he attacked those anarchists who were 'so stupid or so naïve as to attempt to deny to the working class any real means of struggle'. He placed particular blame for this anti-political line on Pierre-Joseph **Proudhon**, accusing him and his followers of preaching indifference in matters of politics that only guaranteed the continued oppression of the working class.

Marx wanted the working-class parties to take advantage of the extension of the franchise. In a speech in Amsterdam in 1872, he reiterated the need for the workers to seize political power and 'overthrow the old politics which bolster up the old institutions'. However, he insisted that there would be 'different roads' to the achievement of their goal, involving 'peaceful means' in Britain, the United States or Holland, but requiring 'force' in the autocratic states. Marx was anxious that the working-class parties should maintain their commitment to **class struggle** and not be seduced into class compromise. In his discussions of the internal politics of the German socialists in the 1870s he was highly critical of moves that seemed to weaken the message of class struggle and its international dimension, particularly in the ***Critique of the Gotha Programme*** (1875). In a circular letter of 1879 to the new leaders of the German party, he advised them strongly not to collaborate with elements who were advocating a politics of class conciliation.

population In ***The German Ideology*** (1845–1846) Marx refers to population as being intrinsically related to the way in which people come together in order to produce both themselves and their society through the development of the productive forces present at any given time. The development of the productive forces depends on the division of **labour** both within and beyond the **nation** and the creation of new **needs**, all of which can lead to increases in population. Consequently, the history of humanity must always be understood in relation to **production** and **exchange** in a particular historical epoch.

Marx elaborates on this point further in his discussion of his **method** in the ***Grundrisse*** (1857–1858), where he considers the best way to understand population as a category itself. He observes that when we consider a particular country both economically and politically it seems correct to begin with its population as starting point for analysis. However, Marx contends that this is a mistake because the population as a concept is simply an **abstraction** if we leave out the classes that comprise it. These classes themselves are a further abstraction if we omit the relations on which they rest such as wage, labour and **capital**, which in turn imply a division of labour, prices and so on. So the correct way to understand a population, and any other notion for that matter, is not in abstraction, but in its most concrete **form**, and that will be rooted in the social relations of production of a society in any given time.

Such historical specifity is important because as Marx asserts in ***Capital*** **1** (1867) all modes of production have their own special laws of population. In the period of the **capitalist mode of production** the **law** that operates pertains to what Marx calls a relative surplus population, which is part of, and arises from, the **accumulation** of capital itself. This relative surplus population emerges from the fluctuations that occur as different spheres of production either shed labour or increase its intake in certain areas to the detriment of others. Marx argues that the relative surplus population acts as condition for the existence of the capitalist mode of production, as it creates an industrial reserve army of labour that is there to be exploited by capital when it needs it for further expansion, and also as a means for keeping **wages** low. Indeed, it is this understanding of the workings of the relative surplus population that led Marx to dismiss the population theory of Thomas Malthus, who in his infamous work *An Essay on the Principle of Population* (1798) argued that population growth would outstrip the growth in resources needed to feed it. Malthus concluded therefore that living standards must be kept at minimum level of subsistence for the masses to stop them having more children. This was then popularized by many capitalists and their apologists to justify paying only minimal wages to the **working class**. However, as Marx indicates, there is no relation between family size and the levels of wages and, as we have seen above, the creation of the surplus population is due to the accumulation process itself within which capital needs new **labour power** to exploit. Moreover, capital is also able to expand the food supply by modernizing agricultural production.

poverty   Understood by Marx in both absolute and relative terms to refer to a condition within which a person lacks sufficient means to live a full life. As editor of the *Rheinische Zeitung* in 1842, Marx confronted poverty in the Rhineland for the first time and wrote an article, 'Debates on the Law on Thefts of Wood', within which he defends the customary law of gathering dead timber against the rich who opposed such a practice so the wood could be used for the needs of industry. In his ***Comments on James Mill's Elements of Political Economy*** (1844) Marx discusses poverty further as an outcome of the credit system and as a **form** of **alienation**. He argues that the degradation suffered by the workers emanates from the fact that they are at the mercy of the rich person who can decide whether to extend credit or not. It follows that a person who has no credit has the judgement passed on him or her that he or she is both poor and a social outcast or a bad person. The poor person is also humiliated by having to make the request to a rich person in the first place, and is often reduced to obtaining credit through stealth and lies. Mistrust therefore reigns as the basis of economic trust as the person giving the credit will need to pry into the life of the recipients to make sure they can pay the credit back. Consequently, people's real communal **nature**, their real **species-being**, is turned into its opposite, and what should be the **wealth** of human activity is in fact nothing but poverty. Similarly, in the **Economic and Philosophical Manuscripts** (1844) Marx discusses poverty in relation to alienation and now also **private property**. He argues that humans are reduced to an absolute poverty by the fact that private property makes people's physical and intellectual senses subordinate to simply having something. So poverty in this sense is a form of alienation or a loss of self, and a misuse of our powers and faculties. However, Marx also says that he can see a situation where workers would increase their **wages** and thereby their standard of living and so reduce poverty relatively. His point here is that such an increase in wages and thereby an improvement in their material life, still leaves them as nothing more than wage slaves. Workers are human beings not mere commodities to be sold on the **market**, and for them to become truly human they need to go beyond the wage relation and not be imprisoned instrumentally within its alienating effects.

In **The Communist Manifesto** (1844) the absolute poverty of modern labourers is captured by Marx's assertion that they fall into pauperism and so become paupers as **capitalist** industry progresses. Marx sees such poverty as being widespread in society, which of course it was at his time of writing. However, he also realized that there could be exceptions to this process, which suggests a more relative understanding of poverty. For example, when discussing the development of industry he makes the point that this results in a reduction in wages to a low level 'nearly everywhere' and not simply everywhere. Similarly, he also notes that **competition** makes the wages of the workers 'ever more fluctuating' – that is, they can go up or down and therefore must be relative. The fact that Marx sees the determination of the wage as being bound up with the conflict between capitalists and workers in **class struggle**, a struggle that either side can at times win, indicates the possibility of a reduction in poverty. Additionally, Marx also points out that wages can and do decline relatively where capitalists increase **surplus value** and appropriate the majority of the surplus themselves as **profit**, rather than giving it back to the workers who have created it. To that extent the workers will always be suffering relative to capitalists irrespective of whether they have a high standard of living or not.

In **The Poverty of Philosophy** (1847) Marx discusses poverty as an outcome of the class struggle between the **bourgeoisie** and the **working class**. He argues that there is dual character to the operations of the bourgeoisie in that in the very relations in which wealth is produced for themselves, poverty is produced for the working class. Marx therefore lambasts the indifference to such suffering of the **proletariat** by fatalist political economists such as **Smith** and **Ricardo**, who are more concerned with showing how wealth is accumulated and developing laws and categories to further that activity. Poverty, for them, is simply a pang that accompanies every childbirth in nature, just as it does in industry, and a necessary consequence of the move away from **feudalism**. In a similar fashion, Romantic economists of Marx's own time repeat the developments of their predecessors and simply look on the working class, who are the creators of wealth, with utter disdain. The humanitarian school, although recognizing the bad side of these relations, seeks to ease its conscience by telling the workers to be sober, to work hard and have few children. The philanthropic school follows on from the latter because it denies that any such antagonisms are necessary and suggests that everyone can become bourgeois. Marx even criticizes those socialists and communists who are the theoreticians of the working class because all they see in poverty is poverty rather than its revolutionary, subversive side that can overthrow society.

In chapter twenty-five of ***Capital* 1** (1867) Marx also discusses poverty in relation to the lowest sections of society that **capital** ejects from the **production** process, the unemployed, the sick and old. This section of society certainly exists throughout the world today and is generally referred to, for better or worse, as the underclass. So despite the many material gains made by the working class, the continued presence of an impoverished underclass stands as an affront to all capitalist societies.

Overall, then, Marx was deeply concerned about the nature of poverty in society and located it in the operations of **capitalism** as a system of **exploitation** and alienation. His discussion of it in both absolute and relative terms raises an important issue within his thought. He realized that workers through class struggle could make progress within capitalism by raising their living standards, but his concern, as expressed in his report to the **First International** (1864–1872) and in his worries over the development of German social democratic movement, was that the workers might not then see the need to destroy capitalism and instead lobby for reforms within the system. Poverty therefore plays a problematic role in Marx's thought in general and for his theory of **revolution** in particular.

***The Poverty of Philosophy* (1847)**   The first published and systematic statement of Marx's conception of history, which Marx himself recommended as an introduction to **Capital**, and a sustained attack on Proudhon's *The System of Economic Contradictions or The Philosophy of Poverty* (1846), hence the ironic title of Marx's own critique. The work is divided into two chapters with the first, entitled 'A Scientific Discovery', dissecting Proudhon's **value** theory and the second, entitled 'The **Metaphysics** of **Political Economy**', offering a brutal assault on Proudhon's philosophical **method**.

In the first chapter, Marx criticizes **Proudhon** in a number of areas. One of the most important was Proudhon's notion of constituted value, which refers to the value constituted by the **labour** time incorporated in a **commodity**. Proudhon's claim to originality here was immediately dismissed by Marx, who showed that it was no more than a repetition of Ricardo's value theory. The only difference was that Ricardo's notion relates to the society of the time, whereas Proudhon was using it to create a new society based on **equality**. For Marx, this was a forlorn exercise because Proudhon was confusing measure by the labour time needed for the **production** of a commodity, with measure by the value of the labour, which is **individual** labour embodied in the product. Proudhon sees the latter as being equivalent to the worker's payment, but as Marx points out, the consequence of this is that **wages** therefore tend towards a minimum. Proudhon begins to realize this and becomes worried that it results in accepting current society rather than going beyond it. He then attempts to solve this problem by asserting that labour is not a commodity and does not have value, which contradicts his argument that began by taking the value of labour as a measure. Additionally, Marx also mocks Proudhon's attempt to expose how the labour time needed to create a commodity is indicative of how needed it is in society, so that things that were produced in the least time would be the most useful. Marx shows the fallacious basis to such an argument because it would imply, for example, that the widespread use of alcoholic spirits in society, because of their low cost of production, is conclusive proof of their utility. In contrast, Marx argues that it is their social use value that should determine the amount of time spent in the production of commodities. Finally, the overall idea that Proudhon had of trying to create a society based on individual **exchange**, where workers exchanged equal amounts of labour, ignores the fact that any society based on individual exchange will always have **class** antagonisms.

In the second chapter, Marx's critique continues by exposing the misuse of Hegelian categories, and even mistakenly imposing categories on **Hegel**, such as the schema thesis-antithesis-synthesis, which Hegel did not use. Marx is particularly critical of the way in which Proudhon sees real relations in society simply as the embodiment of theories and principles, when in fact the opposite is the case. To explain this, Marx shows how people enter into social relations and engage with the productive forces of society. When the productive forces in society change so do the social relations that people have entered into in order to produce. As Marx says, the hand-mill gives you society with the feudal lord and the steam-mill gives you society with the industrial **capitalist**. It is out of these real relations that principles, ideas and categories emerge that are not eternal but transitory, and historically specific to the time they are in. Consequently, Proudhon did not understand concepts such as the division of labour, **competition** and landed **property** as being historical, and instead saw them as eternal and everlasting. As such, he could not grasp the transient **nature** of **capital**, nor analyze its inner relations correctly. Marx then concludes on a revolutionary note by rejecting Proudhon's claim that striking for higher **wages** was meaningless as it results in higher prices. Instead, Marx sees such struggles as moments on the ultimate path that leads to the **emancipation** of the oppressed class and the creation of a new society.

praxis   In the ***Theses on Feuerbach*** (1845) Marx conceives praxis as consciously guided revolutionary practice, as distinct from practice (*praktisch*), meaning simply carrying out an action. It signified an important moment in Marx turning his back on the German philosophical tradition and establishing his new theoretical outlook. Praxis was already established as a concept among the **Young Hegelians**, referring to going beyond the analysis of relations between abstract philosophical categories in order to develop a more concrete understanding of the 'real' world. In particular August Cieszkowski, in *Prolegomena zur Historiosophie* (1838), coined the term the 'philosophy of praxis' and called for philosophy to descend from the heights of theory into praxis. However, he was not advocating revolutionary **politics**. In general Marx shared this zeal for bringing philosophical concerns down to earth, but his idea of what should constitute praxis began to diverge from those of the Young Hegelians from early 1843, culminating in the *Theses on Feuerbach*. Here he commends praxis no fewer than six times in the eleven short aphorisms. **Feuerbach** had thought that he was restoring full subjectivity to real human beings in sensuous reality, but for Marx this **materialism** was static and purely contemplative. In his view, what is required is an understanding of the social condition of humanity through careful examination of the material life process and a determination to act on this. In the eighth thesis he stressed the importance of the comprehension of this praxis (*Begreifen dieser Praxis*) as the rational antidote to all 'mysticism'.

Preface to *A Contribution to the Critique of Political Economy* (1859)   The Preface is famous for its succinct summary of Marx's interpretation of historical development, later known as **historical materialism**. There is also an informative description of how Marx had come to regard **political economy** as the master **science**. He revealed that he was embarrassed to find himself acting as editor of the *Rheinische Zeitung* and having to deal with social problems he knew little about. He then recounted how he engaged in a critique of Hegel's philosophy of **law** and through this arrived at the conclusion that law and **politics** could be properly understood only by grasping their origins in the material conditions of life; in **civil society**. The anatomy of this civil society has to be sought in political economy. Marx then summarizes his theoretical framework using the **base and superstructure** metaphor to explain that the economic structure of society, or **mode of production**, conditions the entire legal, political and ideological superstructure. At a certain stage in the development of the mode of production, the material forces of **production** come into **contradiction** with the relations of production and the system comes under stress. In other words, the existing relations of ownership are no longer able to develop the productive forces efficiently, and alternative forms of organizing production become apparent. This heralds an era of social **revolution**. Marx identified Asiatic, ancient, feudal and bourgeois modes of production, describing the latter as the last antagonistic **form** of production, solemnly announcing that 'the prehistory of human society accordingly closes with this social formation'. Marx declared that he had first set down the 'the guiding principle of my studies' in conjunction with **Engels** in 1845, referring to the unpublished manuscripts known as ***The German Ideology*** (1845–1846). He also points out that their viewpoint can be found in ***The Communist Manifesto*** (1848). However, the summary of his guiding thread in the Preface differs from the *Manifesto* in not referring to class struggles at all, offering instead a structural account of the rise and fall of modes of production.

price   Defined in *Capital* **1** (1867) as the money-form of commodities. Marx considers how prices become attached to commodities. He describes them in the first instance as being imaginary or ideal because when a person makes a **commodity** he or she has to assign a price to it for sale on the **market**, even though he or she does not know whether it will fetch that price. So a disparity takes place between this ideal price and the price the commodity will achieve on the market. Additionally, the market price itself is not the real **value** of the commodity, but the **appearance** of that value. The real value of any commodity is the socially necessary **labour** time that has been expended in producing it, but in **capital** this becomes hidden behind the price as the money-form of the commodity. The price of the commodity can therefore fluctuate in relation to supply and demand and also in relation to the magnitude of value. Values and prices do not therefore always coincide. However, through the operations of supply and demand an equilibrium price emerges that can be indicative of the average socially necessary labour time required to produce a commodity, that is, its value. Marx argues therefore that price is the money-name of the labour objectified in a commodity.

Marx also points out that just as the magnitude of value and its expression as **money** or price can differ, it can also be the case that a qualitative **contradiction** occurs where value is not expressed in price, even though money is the value-form of commodities. Marx says that, for example, things that are not commodities, such as conscience and honour, can be offered for sale and so take on the **form** of commodities through their price. So a thing can have a price without having a value, but Marx asserts that in this case the price is again imaginary. Conversely, Marx also contends that this imaginary price-form could also conceal a real value-relation as in the case of the price for uncultivated land, which has no value because no human labour has been expended on it. However, although a price can therefore be put on anything, this does not alter the fact that the real relations of capital are based on material **production** and the socially necessary labour time that regulates this process. Marx's concern therefore is not in developing a theory of relative prices as is the case in bourgeois economic theory, but in analyzing the dynamic process where prices tend towards an equilibrium that indicate the outward manifestation of the **law** of value. Additionally, he exposes how the disequilibrium of prices are symptomatic of the imbalance in the allocation of goods in an anarchical system such as capital, and even more importantly how such imbalances act as a threat to the system as harbingers of **economic crises**. It follows, then, that bourgeois economists who deduce their theories in the realm of market **exchange** with a focus on the operations of the price mechanism remain trapped within the appearances of capital and so miss the real inner laws of the system. (See also **money**.)

production In the *Grundrisse* (1857–1858) Marx observes that production is inextricably linked with **consumption**, distribution and **exchange**. He grasps these different moments dialectically by understanding them both as a totality and as having distinctions within a unity. However, although all these moments relate to each other in a unity of diverse moments, Marx asserts that production itself is the real point of departure and the predominant moment within these relationships. Given that bourgeois society is the most developed and the most complex historic organization of production it is clear why Marx sees the latter as so fundamental. Examining how a society produces to satisfy its **needs** therefore reveals the true basis of that society. Moreover, the categories that express the relations of bourgeois society give us an insight into the structure and relations of production of previous societies from which **capital** has emerged, just as human anatomy contains a key to the anatomy of the ape. However, these categories must be treated with caution because in the hands of bourgeois economists they see bourgeois relations in all previous forms of production and often caricature previous relations in an attempt to show how distinctive and advanced their bourgeois society is. Marx's contention is that when we try to understand a society we need to focus on how it produces and so identify that **form** of production that predominates over the rest. So in **feudalism** agricultural production dominates and this impacts on the rest of production in that society. In bourgeois society the opposite is the case, as agriculture becomes more and more a branch of industry and is dominated entirely by capital.

Marx makes this even clearer in *Capital* 3 (1864–1865) when he argues that the 'specific economic form in which unpaid surplus **labour** or **surplus**

value is pumped out of the direct producers determines the relationship of domination and servitude in any society. This grows directly out of production itself and reacts back on it in turn as a determinant and on this is based the entire configuration of the economic community arising from the actual relations of production, and hence also its specific political form.' A focus on production is therefore key to understanding the real nature of societies, especially such a mystifying one as capital. Indeed, this is even more imperative given, as Marx states in **Capital 1** (1867), that it is only in the hidden abode of production that the real relations of capital can be exposed, which is in contrast to the realm of exchange or the sphere of circulation, which only displays the outward appearances of the system.

Marx also makes the important distinction between the forces and relations of production in the 1859 **Preface to *A Contribution to a Critique of Political Economy***. He states there that when humans come together to produce for each other, they enter into relations that are independent of their will, and he calls these the relations of production. These relations correspond to the material forces of production and both of these moments together constitute the economic structure of society upon which arises a legal and political superstructure. Marx argues that at a certain stage of historical development the forces of production come into **contradiction** (*Widerspruch*) with the relations of production and this ushers in a new historical epoch. So in the movement from feudalism to **capitalism**, the productive forces change from a mainly agrarian basis to one of increased industrialization and the social relation of lord and serf becomes a fetter on these forces and so changes into the social relation of **capitalist** and worker. The contradiction between the forces and relations of production thus brings about a social **revolution** from the feudal to the capitalist era. Finally, Marx also uses the term 'means of production' to denote those factors that can be used in the production process such as land, raw materials, machinery and **labour power**. (See also **base and superstructure** and **mode of production**.)

profit   Defined by Marx in ***Value, Price and Profit*** (1865) as the **surplus value**, or that part of the total **value** of the **commodity** in which surplus **labour** or unpaid labour of the worker is realized. Profit is therefore the **form** surplus value takes in the realm of **exchange**. When capitalists realize unpaid surplus labour as profit they cannot keep all of it as they may have to pay one part of it to landlords as rent for the use of their land. Additionally, another part of the surplus value that has been realized may have to go on an interest payment to a money-lending **capitalist**, and so what remains is industrial or commercial profit. Marx argues therefore that rent, interest and industrial profit are only different names for different parts of the surplus value of the commodity, or the unpaid labour realized in it, and they are equally derived from this source and from this source alone. Marx contends that along with his distinction between labour and **labour power** this was the most important discovery he had made in demystifying **capital**. In *Capital* **1** (1867) Marx develops this even more systematically through his notion of **exploitation** and his focus on the **class struggle** over the **working day**.

In *Capital* **3** (1864–1865) Marx's concern turns from showing the origin of profit in surplus value to showing how surplus value transforms into profit, and how the rate of surplus value transforms into the rate of profit, with which he will expose capital to be an unstable system that is prone to **economic crises**. In doing this, Marx illustrates how the formation of a general rate of profit has consequences that mean that the total surplus value that has been created by workers is distributed in different proportions amongst competing capitalists of various kinds such as industrialists, merchants, bankers and landlords. Marx's point is that the surplus value that has been extracted will not end up where it was first produced because it gets redistributed amongst these competing capitalists in a process of **competition** and **accumulation**, which itself leads to a **tendency of the rate of profit to fall**.

Marx thought that capital was a system that persistently fell into a crisis of profitability. He explains this through his notions of constant capital, which refers to machinery and raw materials, variable capital as labour power and surplus value as unpaid surplus labour. The capital is constant because it does not add any new value to the commodity produced at the end of the **production** process. Labour power is variable because when it is put into action it not only reproduces the equivalent of its own value, but also an excess beyond this, surplus value, that may be more or less depending on the exploitative conditions that prevail in production. Capitalists are therefore concerned with how much they can get out of both constant capital and variable capital, collectively referred to as the organic composition of capital, because they are interested in the rate of profit they can accrue from a particular process of production. Marx argues that constant capital will get larger as capitalists continually introduce new machinery to try and increase the level of surplus value. He contends that as constant capital increases there is a tendency for the rate of profit to fall. Marx, though, says there is a *tendency* for this to happen, not that it will always happen or that **capitalism** will break down. He understands capital as a dynamic system based on class struggle, so when capitalists see a dip in their profit rates they will try and offset this by intensifying the rate of exploitation or by cheapening the elements of constant capital. Marx calls these strategies counter-tendencies. Consequently, this process of struggle between workers and capitalists over the nature of the production process and the intensification of work reveals the inner **essence** of the capitalist system and thereby the reality of the role of profit.

proletariat   Marx used this old Latin term interchangeably with **working class**. In ancient Rome it referred to the poorest **class** of people who owned no possessions. Marx first used the term in his introduction to the ***Contribution to the Critique of Hegel's Philosophy of Right*** (1844) when he identified the proletariat as the class whose struggle for **emancipation** entailed the emancipation of all other spheres of society and the dissolution of the old world order. He specifies that this class was not the 'naturally arising poor' but an artificially impoverished class created by the development of industry. The term had been used in radical circles since Louis-Auguste Blanqui (1805–1881) invoked it in the opening line of his defence speech at his trial in 1832, referring to all thirty million poor people in France. Blanqui and his followers in France continued to use it in that extensive way, but Marx applied it only to industrial workers. It had first been used in that way in Germany by Eduard Gans, one of his most significant lecturers at the University of Berlin, who, having visited England and read the works of **Smith** and **Ricardo**, predicted the coming struggle between the middle class and the proletariat as early as 1836. Marx may have favoured the term proletariat because it could be used in all countries and was therefore consistent with his view that the developing **class struggle** was fundamentally international in character. Even within the various European languages there were often a number of different terms to denote the working class at this relatively early stage of its development.

property   In *The German Ideology* (1845–1846) Marx gives a useful overview of the historical development of property, which itself is related to the various stages of the development of the division of **labour**. Marx argues that there are four forms of property that have existed throughout history, and he sees the first **form** as being tribal property, which corresponds to an undeveloped stage of **production** where there is a limited division of labour and great areas of land remain uncultivated. People live mainly through hunting, fishing and cattle-raising, and society is structured through patriarchal chieftains, members of the tribe and slaves. The second form of property is ancient communal and **state** property, which arises through agreement and conquest, out of the union of different tribes into a city, and is still accompanied by **slavery**. Private property begins to develop here, although at this stage it is still subordinate to communal property, and so too does the division of labour. Additionally, the opposition between town and country is present, which prefigures the opposition between these states that represent the interests of towns and those states that represent country interests. Even inside the towns themselves there arises a conflict of interest between industry and maritime commerce, and the **class** relations between citizens and slaves become completely developed. Marx argues that we find here for the first time the development of private property relations that will re-appear in a more extensive fashion when we reach the era of modern private property. The third form is feudal or estate property, and like tribal and communal property it is also based on a community, but the directly producing class is no longer slaves but serfs or small **peasantry** who are governed by lords who own the land. Marx argues that this form of feudal ownership was replicated in the towns in the form of corporative property, that is, the feudal organization of trades. Property here consisted in the labour of each **individual** and the development of the guilds or skilled craftsmen, journeymen and apprentices that began to filter into the towns. The fourth form of property is private property proper that is the framework within which the conflict between the town and the country emerges. Marx argues that individuals become restricted under the division of labour as a definite activity is forced upon them as either town-animal or a country-animal. Labour is therefore a power over individuals, and as long as this power exists, so too does private property. Such a development is the precursor to the emergence of **capital** that is independent of landed property. It is the beginning of property that has its basis only in labour and **exchange**, the **capitalist mode of production**. It follows, therefore, as Marx outlines more extensively in his *Economic and Philosophical Manuscripts* (1844), that private property is a form of **alienation** in that it divides individuals both from each other and even from themselves. The antidote to this is therefore **communism** where private property and self-estrangement becomes superseded and humans can appropriate their human **essence** as social beings through communal forms of property.

Proudhon, Pierre Joseph (1809–1865) French anarchist, author of *What is Property?* (1840) and *The System of Economic Contradictions or The Philosophy of Poverty* (1846), which Marx subjected to an extensive and fierce critique in *The Poverty of Philosophy* (1847). Marx first met Proudhon in Paris in 1844 and thus began a long and eventually heated debate between the two of them over a number of years. The dispute between them ranged over a number of issues and is seen as one of the reasons for the eventual split between the Marxist and anarchist sections of the **First International** (1864–1872).

In the *Economic and Philosophical Manuscripts* (1844) Marx briefly refers to Proudhon's *What is Property?* in a discussion of private **property**. Marx argues that **political economy** begins its analysis with **labour** as the real soul of **production**, but ultimately gives nothing to labour and instead sides with the right of private property. He considers that Proudhon's solution to this problem, deciding for labour against private property, keeps labour in a relationship of **alienation**, given that **wages** are identical to private property. So labour is forced to be a servant of those wages rather than being an end in itself. Proudhon's solution can therefore not escape the alienation of labour.

Marx makes a similar criticism of *What is Property?* in *The Holy Family* (1845), but he also accompanies it with a more charitable judgement on the work. He praises Proudhon for making a 'great scientific advance' that revolutionized political economy and made it 'for the first time' a 'real **science**'. The advance consists in exposing how political economy takes private property as an incontestable fact, which is assumed rather than explained. Moreover, Proudhon is also revered for showing how the movement of **capital** produces **poverty**. However, later in 1865, in a letter to a German socialist Johann Baptist von Schweitzer, Marx was in a more critical mode and pointed out that the major problem lay with the title of the book itself.

Marx contends that the question *What is Property?* is so poorly formulated that it is impossible to answer it correctly. This is because what Proudhon was actually dealing with was modern bourgeois property as it existed at that time. However, the question of what constitutes property can only be answered by a critical analysis of political economy, which grasps the totality of property relations historically. Proudhon makes the mistake of only considering the legal aspect of these relations when it is their real **form**, that is as relations of production, that need to be focused on. As Proudhon enmeshed all of these economic relations in the general legal concept of property, he could not get beyond the answer that property is theft. As Marx also indicates, Proudhon was therefore replicating the same answer that the theorist Brissot gave in a similar work published before 1789. Such an answer is inadequate anyway, because it implies that at best the bourgeois legal conceptions of theft apply equally well to the 'honest' gains of the **bourgeoisie** themselves. Conversely, an action can only be classified as theft if there exists a system of private property prior to the action taking place. So Marx was exposing a tautology, as theft presupposes property. Proudhon therefore entangles himself in all sorts of fantasies, obscure even to himself, about the true **nature** of bourgeois property relations.

—R—

race   Marx bemoaned the fact that ethnic prejudice jeopardized the unity of working people. In an article for the Austrian newspaper *Die Presse* in November 1862, writing about the situation in the American Civil War, he reports that 'the Irishman sees in the negro a dangerous competitor' and also notes the racism of white farmers in the Midwest. In chapter ten of **Capital 1** (1867) he comments that independent workers' movements had failed to develop in the United States as long as **slavery** 'disfigured' a part of the republic. He concludes that '**labour** in a white skin cannot emancipate itself where it is branded in a black skin'. When Marx wrote the Provisional Rules of the **First International** in 1864 he included a commitment that the members of the International 'will acknowledge truth, **justice**, and **morality**, as the basis of their conduct towards each other, and towards all men, without regard to colour, creed, or nationality'. He introduced the programme of the French Workers' Party in 1880 by declaring that 'the **emancipation** of the producing **class** is that of all human beings without distinction of sex or race'. (See also **nation**.)

reason   'Reason has always existed, but not always in a reasonable **form**,' declared Marx in an 1843 letter to his friend Arnold Ruge, later published in the *Deutsch-Französiche Jahrbücher*. What he meant was that even when arguments appealed to reason and were internally consistent, they nevertheless reflected particular material interests. At this point in his intellectual development he considered that the adoption of representative **democracy** would provide the forum in which reason would prevail in 'all social struggles, **needs** and truths'. In *The German Ideology* (1845–1846) he argued that each new **ruling class** is compelled to present its interests as the common interest of all the members of society. It has to give its ideas the form of universality and present them as the 'only rational, universally valid' ones. Much of his mature work in **political economy** was devoted to exposing how purportedly scientific explanations of economic phenomena served to justify the existing relations of **production** and failed to show the contradictory **nature** of the system. Rational decisions made by **individual** capitalists in pursuit of **profit** produce unintended consequences and social dislocation, and **economic crises** reveal the irrationality of the system as a whole. In *Capital* 2 (1863–1878) he argues that 'social rationality' only becomes manifest after an economic crisis breaks out, when attempts are made to lessen the risks, but all to no avail. Naturally, he regarded his own **method** as 'rational', and in *Capital* 3 (1864–1865) he speculates on how the associated producers in communist society would rationally organize production and distribution. This form of reason involves taking into account the likely social consequences of decisions, in contrast to the individualistic instrumental reasoning prevalent in **capitalist** society.

reification   The way in which relations between people are transformed into relations between things. Reification (*Versachlichung*) is therefore closely associated with both **commodity fetishism** and **alienation**. In

Capital **1** (1867), chapter three, in his discussion of **money** or the circulation of commodities, Marx notes how the **exchange** of commodities in circulation differs both in **form** and **essence** compared to direct exchange. In direct exchange, a **commodity** exchanges for a commodity, one use **value** for another use value, so Marx gives the example of a weaver exchanging the linen he has created for a bible. However, in the process of circulation in **capital**, money is needed to buy commodities, so the weaver has to sell the linen for money with which to buy a bible. The process of direct exchange suddenly disappears from view through the intervention of money, and Marx refers to this as the original commodity, in this case linen, metamorphosing into money. A similar metamorphosis takes place for the bible seller who needs money to buy linen. So both the linen and the bible fall out of circulation as money takes their place, and money itself always implies the involvement of a third person. Circulation therefore breaks up the direct exchange of commodity for commodity, linen for bible, or bible for linen. An antithesis arises in the commodity between its use value and the private **labour** expended that needs to manifest itself as social labour and its value that has to manifest itself as **abstract labour**. This antithesis, Marx contends, is between the conversion of things into persons and of persons into things: the reification of persons. All the differences that made the labour expended on creating the linen and the labour expended on making a copy of the bible fall out of sight in the realm of circulation as money operates as a form of **appearance** of the measure of value that is imminent in commodities, namely labour time. Marx concludes that out of the natural origin of the exchange of commodities a network of social connections emerge that are beyond the control of human agents.

Later in the Appendix to this work Marx again refers to how reification occurs in relation to **production** when capital employs labour. He argues that the means of production confront the workers in this situation not as something for them to use for themselves, but as a way to subordinate them to these material conditions of labour. Again Marx says that this entails the personification of things and the reification of persons. As **capitalism** develops further this relationship becomes even more mysterious because the productive forces of social labour appear as the productive forces of capital, and the role of the workers and their labour falls even further from sight. **Machines**, for example, that are the products of labour, appear as the product of capital, and as a means to further increase the **exploitation** of the workers. Indeed, Marx says that **nature**, **science** and the products of the general development of history confront the workers as the powers of capital, rather than the powers of their creative selves. Things therefore appear as persons and persons appear as things in the reified world of capital. (See also **ideology**.)

religion   Marx was an atheist, and his early radicalism was heavily influenced by the criticisms of religion associated with theorists such as David Strauss, Bruno Bauer and Ludwig **Feuerbach**. In his *Doctoral Dissertation* of 1841 he praised Epicurus for rejecting notions of divine intervention, later calling him 'the atheistic philosopher *par excellence*'. In the appendix to the dissertation, on the relationship of humanity to God, he scorned the proofs of the existence of God, including the ontological proof, as 'hollow tautologies'. At that time the criticism of religion was the most controversial subject in German intellectual life and it played a vital role in the development of Marx's particular **form** of **materialism**. In the early 1840s he was an ardent admirer of Feuerbach, whose *Essence of Christianity* (1841) sought to demonstrate that religious ideas were human inventions reflecting material human **needs** in an alienated form.

   The criticism of religion was one of the most important themes in the work of the **Young Hegelians**, but Marx took the critique of religion much further than simply exposing it as an illusion. In his view it was not sufficient to replace the religious essence with a human essence if that human essence was considered only in a purely static way. What was needed was to resolve the material problems that gave rise to religious **consciousness**, and that, in Marx's view, was the task of **communism**. In the *Contribution to the Critique of Hegel's Philosophy of Right: Introduction* (1844) Marx opened by stating that 'criticism of religion is the premise of all criticism' and then moved on to offer his eloquent understanding of the strong psychological need for religion, conceived as 'the sigh of the oppressed creature, the heart of a heartless world … the spirit of a spiritless situation … the opium of the people'. While this has often been interpreted as a purely negative judgement, focusing on the addictive and debilitating **nature** of opium, in fact it recognizes the compelling material need for religious solace. He went on to argue that religious criticism has plucked the imaginary flowers from the chain that symbolizes oppression. However, the point is not to leave humans simply with a chain without fantasy, but rather to shake off the chain altogether and instead 'cull the living flower'. In other words, Marx wanted human **emancipation** not simply to resolve material oppression, but also to create a world that is full of human 'heart' and 'spirit'. Marx concluded that once the 'saintly' form of human self-alienation has been unmasked, the task is to unmask **alienation** in its 'unholy' forms. The criticism of theology is then transformed into the criticism of **politics**.

The move from articulating religion as alienation to interpreting **capitalism** as alienation had a lasting impact on Marx's theoretical development, as the passages on **commodity fetishism** early in *Capital* **1** (1867) show. In order to explain how real human relations in economic life appear in the 'fantastic' form of a relation between things, he invokes an analogy with 'the misty realm of religion'. Just as in religion 'the products of the human brain appear as autonomous figures endowed with a life of their own, which enter into relations both with each other and with the human **race**', so it is in the world of commodities produced by human hand.

Occasionally Marx inveighed against organized religion. In 1847 he responded to an article in a conservative journal, the *Rheinische Beobachter*, which invoked Christian social principles against the liberal demands of the German **bourgeoisie**. He commented that the social principles of Christianity had at various times justified **slavery**, serfdom and now the oppression of the **working class**, 'although they make a pitiful face over it'. He also asserted that Christian social principles taught the necessity of a **ruling class** and an oppressed **class**, and that the misfortunes of the latter are attributed to original sin or other sins. Marx denounces Christian principles for preaching 'cowardice, self-contempt, abasement, submission, dejection'. In 1855, in an article for the newspaper the *Neue Oder-Zeitung*, Marx criticized the heavy-handed scattering of a large anti-church demonstration in London, called to protest against church-inspired legislation restricting activities on Sundays. These measures were described by Marx as 'coercive' because Sunday was the only day when working people could enjoy themselves. He claimed they amounted to a desperate attempt by the church to retain its influence, despite being an 'obsolete social force' and the 'twin sister' of the English oligarchy. With regards to Judaism, Marx argued strongly in favour of Jews being granted political **rights** whilst writing his *On the Jewish Question* in 1843, emphasizing that 'the privilege of faith is a universal right of man'. Nevertheless, as he makes clear in that article and in a letter to Ruge also written that year, his rational support for equal rights did not prevent him from disliking the Jewish faith. Although his opposition to the social impact of organized religion is clear, Marx did not regard it as a significant political issue, in contrast to other revolutionary leaders such as Pierre-Joseph **Proudhon** and Mikhail **Bakunin**, who favoured aggressive opposition to religion. *The Communist Manifesto* (1848), for example, has little to say about religion, except that the demand for religious liberty had contributed to 'open **competition**' in the world of ideas.

revolution   There are two major conceptions of revolution in Marx's works: the social and the political. Social revolutions involve a cataclysmic change from one **mode of production** to another, as described in his 1859 **Preface to** *A Contribution to the Critique of Political Economy*. They occur when the relations of **production** come into **contradiction** with the forces of production. Political revolutions reflect the class struggles that develop within a mode of production in which the contending classes clash to establish political power. The political revolutions of Marx's day also included struggles for national independence, as, for example, in Poland, Hungary, Bohemia and Ireland.

The distinction between social and political revolution was made as early as 1843 in the *Critique of Hegel's Philosophy of Right*, in which he complained that the ambition of German radicals was limited 'merely' to political revolution, 'the revolution which leaves the pillars of the building standing'. It was at this point that Marx declared that full human **emancipation** could be achieved only through the revolutionary triumph of the ultimate exploited **class**, the **working class**, for this would abolish the source of its oppression, private **property**, abolishing class society itself and bringing about 'the total redemption of humanity'.

Marx summarizes the social revolution that gave rise to the **capitalist** mode of production in *The German Ideology* (1845–1846), in which he talks about the increased division of **labour** within feudal society and the rise of an independent **bourgeoisie** based on more intensive trade and manufacturing. This received 'an enormous impetus' from the discovery of America and the resultant influx of gold and silver, and also the opening up of the sea route to the East Indies. This mercantile era of **capitalism** goes on until the late eighteenth century, when large-scale industry developed. Marx points out that free **competition** inside the **nation** itself had to be won by political revolution, as in England in the seventeenth century and in France following the revolution of 1789.

The political revolutions to establish the political power of the bourgeoisie were still going on during Marx's lifetime and he played an active role in the German revolution of 1848. He supported the demand for a united democratic republic and also pressed for radical reforms to benefit the working class. In **The Communist Manifesto** (1848) he called for the 'forcible overthrow' of the class rule of the bourgeoisie, confidently predicting that the victory of the working class was 'inevitable'. In the aftermath of the 1848 revolutions, in **The Class Struggles in France** (1850) and in the *Address of the Central Committee to the Communist League* (1850), he used the term 'permanent revolution' to indicate incessant working-class revolutionary activity until the conquest of **state** power. However, following the wave of reaction after the defeats of 1848, Marx placed much greater emphasis on the development of the political strength of the working class in anticipation of a protracted **class struggle**.

Marx analyzed two working-class revolutions in France, in June 1848 and March 1871, but neither of them seriously threatened to achieve the social revolution that would put an end to the bourgeois mode of production. In both cases he was clear that they were premature. In **The Eighteenth Brumaire of Louis Bonaparte** (1852) he described the uprising of June 1848 as 'the most colossal event in the history of European civil wars'. However, although the working class had raised the demand for a social republic by its action in the February Revolution, at that stage in its development it could not possibly have turned that demand into a reality. Its achievement lay in exposing the naked class interests of the **bourgeoisie** and the hypocrisy of republican principles. Marx insisted that the workers were provoked into revolutionary action and that they would rise again in the future. He commented that workers' revolutions engaged in constant self-criticism and endured repeated interruptions of their own course, appearing to throw their opponent to the ground 'only to see him draw new strength from the earth and rise again before them, more colossal than ever'.

When writing about the **Paris Commune** (1871) in **The Civil War in France** (1871) Marx gave his full support to the Communards, defending the legitimacy of their action by rejecting the democratic credentials of the national government. He was tremendously enthusiastic about the participatory democratic processes adopted by the Commune, so much so that he hailed it as 'the glorious harbinger of a new society'. Despite his public endorsement of the Commune, it was clear to Marx that the proletarian revolution could only be advanced through **politics** rather than by following the insurrectionary model. In a speech in Amsterdam in 1872, Marx declared that it was entirely possible for the workers to achieve their goals through peaceful means in countries where political **democracy** was imminent. Five years later, when the 'bourgeois' French Third Republic was threatened by a military putsch, he wrote to his friend Sorge that he hoped it would survive so that France did not have to pass through another right-wing dictatorship. This was a totally different attitude from 1852, when he appeared indifferent to the fate of the Second Republic. Marx was opposed to setting down plans for how the working-class political revolution should develop. In an 1881 letter to Domela Nieuwenhuis he poses the rhetorical question as to whether any eighteenth-century Frenchman had the faintest idea in advance of the ways in which the demands of the French bourgeoisie would be accomplished. He concluded that 'the doctrinaire and necessarily fantastic anticipations of the programme of action for a revolution of the future only divert us from the struggle of the present'.

Ricardo, David (1772–1823)   Author of *On The Principles of Political Economy and Taxation* (1817) and seen by Marx, along with Adam **Smith**, as one of the great representatives of classical political economy. Indeed, Marx praises Ricardo for recognizing the presence of **class** antagonisms between **labour**, **capital** and landlords. He showed that labour and capital were in conflict with each other as an increase in **wages** implies a decrease in profits and an increase in profits implies a decrease in wages. Additionally, the interest of the **landlord** is opposed to the interests of all given the necessity of having to pay rent. However, just as with Smith, Marx challenges the theories of Ricardo in a number of areas. Although Ricardo recognized the presence of class struggles in society, he saw these only as conflicts over distribution. Moreover, he assumed that a society based on wage labour on one side and capital on the other was in some way natural rather than, as Marx points out, the consequence of denying the workers control over the means of **production** in a system based on private **property**. Such a lack of understanding of the real **nature** of production also led Ricardo to miss important distinctions that Marx was to discover, not least the difference between labour and **labour power** and thereby the source of **surplus value**.

In terms of **value** in general, Marx shows how Ricardo mistakenly subscribes to a value theory of embodied labour time, where the **commodity** produced is a simple representative of the labour time expended on it. For Marx, the value of a commodity is, on the contrary, the socially necessary labour time required to produce it, which can only be discovered once it has been put on the **market**. Indeed, in a letter to Kugelmann on 11 July 1868, where Marx is explaining the **law** of value, he points out that it was precisely Ricardo's error that in his first chapter on value he takes as given a variety of categories that have not yet been explained in order to prove how they conform to the law of value. Instead, as Marx indicates, the key to any **science** is to demonstrate how the law of value asserts itself, otherwise one would be presenting the science before the science. Marx clarified this further in his 'Notes on Adolph Wagner' of 1880 where he states quite clearly that his own **method** does not start out from concepts. Hence he does not start out from the concept of value. What he starts out from is the simplest social **form** in which the labour-product is presented in contemporary society, which is the commodity, and he analyses it right from the beginning in the form in which it appears. Ricardo, then, in Marx's view, was unable to grasp properly the real relations of society because his starting point was not rooted in the very reality of the phenomena he was trying to investigate.

rights Marx was consistently sceptical of appeals to human rights. His most interesting discussion of rights is contained in his early essay *On the Jewish Question* (1844) in which he rejected Bruno Bauer's argument that Jews should not be given equal political rights. Bauer argued that Jews should give up their **religion** before they could claim the universal rights of humanity, but Marx pointed to the example of the United States, where no single religion was privileged by the constitution and religious diversity and tolerance flourished. Marx then explored the distinction between the rights of the **citizen** and universal human rights. The rights of the citizen relate to the individual's role in political society, and include the civil liberties of political participation, **freedom** of speech and freedom of assembly. Human rights are broader and more abstract, relating to such things as **equality**, liberty, security and **property**. In different constitutions, religious freedom or freedom of conscience are regarded either as human rights or rights of the citizen. However, Marx points out that although the **language** of human rights appears to be communal in **nature**, the rights themselves reflect the real egoism of **civil society**, which is based on fierce **competition**. Rights, in other words, are protections against anticipated aggression in a fundamentally antagonistic society.

Whereas Bauer thought that Jewish **emancipation** would be harmful to the idea of a secular community, Marx argued that this community is illusory. He contends that the human right to freedom is not based on the association of fellow humans but rather on their separation. Marx therefore sees a **contradiction** between the **state** and civil society, between communality and egoism, a contradiction that will not be overcome until a social **revolution** abolishes private property and ushers in a classless society. Political **emancipation** is needed, and this means political rights for all faiths, but that should not be confused with **human** emancipation, which Marx associates with the classless society. Furthermore, as long as property is regarded as one of the rights of man and liberty is associated with it, the rights of man get in the way of achieving human emancipation.

Marx's negative attitude to constitutionally guaranteed rights was clearly expressed in *The Eighteenth Brumaire of Louis Bonaparte* (1852). He is sceptical of the nature of the guarantees of liberty provided by the constitution, which appear to bestow absolute rights to the citizens while qualifying them with provisos that the exercise of these rights must be compatible with 'the equal rights of others and the security of the public'. For Marx, the security of the public really meant the security of the **bourgeoisie**, and this get-out clause provided the state with the legal pretext to suppress any of these liberties should they threaten the interests of the dominant **class**. In *Capital* **1** (1867) Marx made it clear that he favoured concrete social reform, such as the legal limitation of the **working day**, to the 'pompous catalogue of the inalienable rights of man'.

ruling class   A term frequently used by Marx to refer to the elites who control economic and political power. Although it implies a homogeneous social class, Marx's political analyses reveal a complex array of rivalries between and within classes. Political power in most of the continental European states in his lifetime was in the hands of aristocrats, and most of the revolutions were aimed at achieving that power for the **bourgeoisie**.

Only rarely did all the propertied classes act in unison, as for example in Paris in June 1848, when they suppressed the workers' revolution that threatened their interests. At other times not only were there tensions between the aristocracy and the bourgeoisie, but also within the bourgeoisie, for example between industrialists and financiers. 'Ruling class' was therefore a catch-all term to indicate a network of power relations. In **The Communist Manifesto** (1848) Marx stipulated that the **working class** needed to raise itself to the position of ruling class by winning the battle for **democracy**. Once it had achieved this position its task would be to abolish private productive property, as a result of which a classless society would develop. The ruling class would then be a thing of the past.

The ruling class exerts control not simply through legal and coercive means, but also through dominance in the world of ideas. Marx had first argued that the 'ideas of the ruling class are always the ruling ideas' in **The German Ideology** (1845–1846), where it is specifically related to the class which has the means of material production at its disposal. The formula is repeated in the *Manifesto*, where he emphasizes the sweeping changes in ideas and outlooks that had taken place as a result of the bourgeois transformation of the economy. For the most part these changes developed while the bourgeoisie was still challenging the aristocracy for political supremacy, so it appears that ideological power precedes political power. The implication for the working class is that they will need to issue a radical challenge to the dominant ideas in the course of the **class struggle**, and Marx calls for 'the most radical rupture with traditional ideas'. His depiction of this class struggle was sometimes apocalyptic. In a speech delivered in London in 1856 on the occasion of the anniversary of the *People's Paper*, he told his listeners that in medieval Germany a secret society, the *Vehmgericht*, revenged the misdeeds of the ruling class by daubing a red cross on their doors so that the rulers knew that they were doomed by the '*Vehm*'. He commented that all the houses of the ruling classes of Europe were now marked with the mysterious red cross, concluding menacingly: 'History is the judge – its executioner is the proletarian'.

—S—

science   Marx operated with the nineteenth-century German conception of science (*Wissenschaft*), denoting rigorous analysis within any field of study. In **The German Ideology** (1845–1846) he announced his determination to move on from speculative philosophy to begin 'real, positive science, the expounding of the practical activity, of the practical process of the development of men'. He then goes on to describe the centrality of **production** in human development, manifesting itself in the emergence of social classes and **class struggle**. In order to better understand the basis for the class struggles of his day, therefore, Marx dedicated himself to studying the dynamics of the **capitalist mode of production**. In the Preface to **Capital 1** (1867) he described his own work as an example of 'free scientific inquiry', but he was always careful to state that no general laws could offer simple explanations of complex social phenomena.

His generalizations about historical development and the economic 'laws of motion' (*Bewegungsgesetz*) of capitalist production were intended to serve as an analytical framework within which further empirical study could take place or political strategies could be developed. Despite the appellation of 'scientific **socialism**' that came to be adopted after his death, Marx was dismissive of attempts to lend social analysis the certitude of natural science. In **The Poverty of Philosophy** (1847) he ridiculed Proudhon's attempts to invoke 'magic formula' to solve society's problems while displaying woeful ignorance of the real scientific insights of economists such as Sismondi, **Smith** and **Ricardo**. In **The Communist Manifesto** (1848) he derided the utopian socialist writers for trying to concoct 'a new social science', or new social laws that were supposed to create the material conditions for historical change. Later, he was dismissive of the efforts of the French sociologist Auguste Comte (1798–1857) to found a new science of society, speaking ironically of 'Comtist recipes for the cook-shops of the future'.

Marx's general conception of historical development (later termed **historical materialism**), first set down in The German Ideology and summarized in the 1859 **Preface to A Contribution to the Critique of Political Economy**, provided the theoretical framework for his scientific endeavour. However, the framework itself was not meant to be employed as a substitute for scientific analysis of social and economic developments.

Marx warned against using it as 'a recipe for neatly trimming the epochs of history' and said that it had no value if it was divorced from real history. Many years later, in 1877, in a letter to a Russian journal he emphasized that his generalizations served only as a guide to empirical and comparative work that alone will establish the truth, and 'one will never arrive there by using as one's master key a general historical–philosophical theory, the supreme virtue of which consists in being supra-historical'. Marx was consistently wary of 'eternal' or universal laws, but at the same time quite confident that the generalizations that he made about historical development and the operation of the **law** of **value** would stand the test of time.

The Prefaces and Postfaces to the various editions of *Capital* 1 speak openly about his scientific **method**. In the Preface to the first French volume he excused the difficulty of the opening chapters of the book by commenting that 'there is no royal road to science, and only those who do not dread the fatiguing climb of its steep paths have a chance of gaining its luminous summits'. His scientific intention was to penetrate the surface **appearance** of phenomena to reveal the essential causal relations behind them, a procedure initially developed by **Aristotle**. In the Preface to the first edition of *Capital* 1 he stated that in the study of economic forms, neither microscopes nor chemical reagents can be used, and that 'the power of **abstraction** must replace both'. His object of study, the capitalist mode of production, is regarded as a totality involving production, distribution, **exchange** and **consumption**, but production itself is the predominant or determining sphere. Marx proceeds by abstracting from the totality the basic categories of production, beginning with the **commodity** and moving on to exchange and the production of **surplus value**. The analysis eventually builds up to an exposition of the system as a whole in ***Capital 3*** (1864–1865), thus completing his move from the abstract to the concrete. However, the abstractions themselves originated from his own observations of the mode of production. At every stage of his analysis he provided evidence from British government sources and elsewhere of how the system was experienced by the workers. He also engaged in relentless critique of the other theorists who had sought to explain how **capitalism** worked, and ***Theories of Surplus Value*** (1861–1863), initially intended as the fourth volume of *Capital*, consists of three volumes of detailed analysis of the work of political economists such as Smith, Ricardo and Malthus. As to the findings of his science, across a range of writings Marx predicted the global spread of the system, the ever-increasing importance of technology, the domination of sectors of the economy by large firms, and recurring industrial and financial **economic crises** of greater intensity.

Although not as immersed in natural science as his friend **Engels**, Marx kept abreast of the latest developments and related them to wider social issues. He paid particular attention to scientists such as Justus von Liebig and Karl Nikolas Fraas, who separately analyzed the destructive side of modern agricultural methods and the disastrous unintended consequences of deforestation on cultivation. In a speech celebrating the anniversary of the *People's Paper* in London in 1856, Marx summarized the negative **dialectic** of science and technology under capitalism, arguing that the 'new fangled' sources of **wealth** are turned by some 'weird spell' into sources of want. **Machines** could make life more fruitful and shorten work-time, but instead they are accompanied by starvation and overwork. As fast as we use science to master **nature**, we become enslaved to it. He comments that 'even the pure light of science seems unable to shine but on the dark background of industry'.

Marx developed an array of skills in order to assist his scientific endeavours. He mastered a wide range of scholarly sources in several languages and also taught himself advanced mathematical techniques. A glimpse of this can be found in a letter to Engels towards the end of 1865, in which he provides his friend with an impressive demonstration of differential calculus.

Shakespeare, William (1564–1616)   English playwright and poet. Marx was introduced to Shakespeare's works as a schoolboy by his future father-in-law Ludwig von Westphalen and was one of his most favoured authors throughout his lifetime. Indeed, Marx's daughter Eleanor commented that Shakespeare was the bible of the Marx household. Marx's interest in Shakespeare, as in all **art**, is not simply aesthetic, but also as a way to understand society critically. For example, in his first work, ***Critique of Hegel's Philosophy of Right*** (1843), Marx considers Hegel's discussion of the legislature and criticizes Hegel's use of **mediation** in relation to the sovereign's role as a middle term between the executive and the estates. The fact that the executive also mediates between the sovereign and the estates, and that the estates mediate between the sovereign and **civil society** results in the sovereign mediating between things that should be made distinct from each other as real extremes. To illustrate his point, and show Hegel's error here, Marx refers to the claim of the lion from *A Midsummer Night's Dream* that he is both a lion and not a lion but 'Snug'. Marx uses this proclamation to show how the lion is at one moment an extreme lion of opposition and at another moment the 'Snug' of mediation. Instead, real extremes cannot be mediated, according to Marx.

The fusion of the aesthetic with a critical appreciation of society also figures in a critical letter Marx wrote to his friend Ferdinand Lassalle about his play *Franz von Sickengen* in 1859. Marx suggests that Lassalle should have 'Shakespearized' more by expressing modern ideas in their purest **form** instead of falling into the trap of Friedrich Schiller's approach in using characters as mere mouthpieces for the spirit of the times. Marx proposes that one way Lassalle could have done this was by focusing on the **peasantry** and the revolutionary elements in the cities as an active background to the play, rather than the overemphasis on the more radical elements of the nobility.

Marx also utilizes Shakespeare quite explicitly in his critique of **capitalism** both in his early and later writings. In his ***Economic and Philosophical Manuscripts*** (1844) Marx quotes approvingly from *Timon of Athens* to show how Shakespeare brilliantly grasps the insidious **nature** of **money** by showing how it is an alienated form of our human **essence**. In ***Capital 1*** (1867) Marx finishes the important opening chapter on the **commodity** with his discussion of **commodity fetishism** by quoting the character Dogberry from *Much Ado About Nothing* to show how political economists wrongly invert categories and denude them of their social origin. As Dogberry says to the night-watchman Seacoal, 'To be a well-favoured man is the gift of fortune; but reading and writing comes by nature.' Political economists make the same mistake by seeing **exchange value**, for example, as being part of the commodity rather than a social relation imparted onto an object by human beings.

slavery   The total ownership and control of other human beings for use as forced **labour** was an important issue for Marx. It was the defining aspect of the ancient **mode of production**, identified by Marx in ***The German Ideology*** (1845–1846) and the 1859 **Preface to *A Contribution to the Critique of Political Economy***. For Marx, slavery was not simply an important historical stage in human history, but was 'an economic category of the greatest importance' even in the modern era. In ***The Poverty of***

Philosophy (1847) he explained that slavery in the United States was at that time producing cotton, one of the first major commodities of modern industry. Slavery had given the **colonies** their **value** and the colonies were central in the development of world trade, a precondition for large-scale industry.

When the American Civil War broke out in 1861, Marx and **Engels** wrote thirty-seven articles on the **war** to the liberal Viennese newspaper *Die Presse*. Marx summarized the war of the Southern Confederacy as 'a war of conquest for the extension and perpetuation of slavery', driven by an 'oligarchy' of 300,000 slave-holders. He was a passionate advocate of turning the war into revolutionary struggle to free the slaves, noting in an article in August 1862 that pressure was growing to do that. Lincoln issued the proclamation to end slavery the following month, prompting Marx to write to Engels that events in America 'are such as to transform the world'. Towards the end of the conflict, on behalf of the General Council of the **First International** (1864–1872), he wrote a letter to President Lincoln thanking him for leading his country through 'the matchless struggle for the rescue of an enslaved **race** and the reconstruction of a social world'. Marx was impressed by the solidarity shown by the Lancashire cotton workers, who despite facing redundancy because of the blockade that halted the cotton trade showed their solidarity with the slaves and pressured the government not to assist the Confederacy. In the Inaugural Address of the First International, Marx praised the heroic resistance of these workers to the criminal folly of the ruling classes, who would have plunged headlong into an 'infamous crusade' for the perpetuation of slavery in America. Marx also noted, in chapter ten of *Capital* **1** (1867), how independent workers' movements failed to develop in the United States as long as slavery 'disfigured' a part of the republic. He commented that 'labour in a white skin cannot emancipate itself where it is branded in a black skin'.

Marx discussed the importance of slavery in the genesis of industrial **capitalism** in chapter thirty-one of *Capital* 1. He explains how Liverpool 'grew fat' on the basis of the slave trade, the port having 15 slave ships in 1730 but 132 by 1792. The cotton industry of Lancashire, which benefited from the work of the African slaves in the USA, employed its workers at minimal **wages**, using children in a way he described as 'child-slavery'. Marx comments that 'the veiled slavery of the wage-labourers in Europe needed the unqualified slavery of the new world as its pedestal'. He ends the chapter by commenting that 'capital comes dripping from head to foot, from every pore, with blood and dirt'. Marx often spoke of 'wage slavery' in order to draw attention to the unpaid hours of labour in an apparently 'free' labour process.

Smith, Adam (1723–1790)   Scottish philosopher and founding father of classical **political economy**, of which *An Inquiry into the Nature and Causes of the **Wealth** of Nations* (1776) was the pivotal text. Marx saw Smith as one of the great representatives of political economy due to his analysis of the real relations of society such as the **commodity**, division of **labour**, **value** and **capital**. However, he disagreed with Smith in a number of areas. He first discusses Smith in his ***Comments on James Mill's Elements of Political Economy*** (1844) and criticizes him, amongst others, for seeing society simply in commercial terms and so reducing human beings to nothing more than merchants who engage in **exchange** and trade as owners of private **property**. For Marx, this was a clear case of how economics depicts humans in an estranged **form**. In the ***Economic and Philosophical Manuscripts*** (1844) Marx discusses Smith in relation to **wages** and argues that they are determined through the fierce struggle between **capitalist** and worker. He berates Smith for arguing that the normal wage is the lowest that is compatible with common humanity, which, given the way capitalists can drive down wages, leaves workers with a bestial existence. Smith, therefore, even though he says that the whole produce of labour belongs to the worker, also says at the same time that what the worker actually receives is the absolute minimum necessary for him to exist, not as a human being, but as a worker. Similarly, the division of labour process, which is lauded by Smith for increasing the productivity and wealth of society, is seen by Marx as impoverishing workers and reducing them to mere **machines**. As Marx observes later in ***Capital*** 1 (1867), Smith knew the negative consequences of the division of labour process, but he saw this as being an unfortunate necessity for a civilized society, a necessity that inevitably fell to the great body of people to endure, that is, the labouring poor. As Marx developed his value theory, he also showed the inadequacies in Smith's approach by developing his own **labour theory of value**, which achieved its pinnacle through a critique of David **Ricardo**.

socialism   One of a number of terms developed in the 1830s and 1840s to denote the ideas and movements that protested against the oppressive

nature of the **market** economy. Marx, following the lead of Moses Hess and Friedrich **Engels**, preferred to declare himself a communist, with a clear commitment to revolutionary opposition to the existing economic and political system. In *The Communist Manifesto* (1848) Marx gave critical accounts of a number of forms of socialism, applying the word in a very broad way to indicate opposition to the **capitalist** economic system. Even the romantic conservatism of Thomas Carlyle was characterized as 'feudal socialism' simply because of its opposition to the radical individualism that accompanied the rise of **capitalism**. Other sub-species of 'reactionary socialism' were described as 'petty bourgeois' socialism and 'true socialism', both of which were condemned because they offered no viable alternatives to capitalism. The *Manifesto* also rejected 'bourgeois socialism', associated with the work of **Proudhon**, and 'critical-utopian socialism and communism', associated with the followers of Fourier and Saint-Simon in France and Robert **Owen** in Britain. Although there is some praise for the way the utopians offered radical alternatives to capitalism, ultimately they too are dismissed because of their failure to support the political struggles of the **working class**.

Marx aggressively opposed reformist socialism that sought concessions from the **state**, as is evident in his discussion of the socialists in France during the Second Republic (1848–1851), as well as his interventions in Germany during the formative years of the Social Democratic Party in the 1860s and 1870s. In France he was highly critical of the *Montagne*, the alliance of representatives of the **petty bourgeoisie** and workers set up in early 1849 to re-establish socialist **politics** following the suppression of the workers' uprising in June 1848. Marx dubbed this 'social **democracy**' and likened its parliamentary efforts to Joshua blowing down the walls of Jericho with the sound of trumpets. Some of his criticisms focused on tactical errors, but there is undisguised hostility to the principle of the **class** alliance, which, according to Marx, infected the working class with petty bourgeois weakness. In general the pursuit of compromise was regarded as insipid, cowardly and pathetic. He accuses the representatives of being consoled by picking up their attendance fee and engaging in outbursts of 'moral indignation and tub-thumping oratory'. He was appalled at the failure of the *Montagne* to fight the withdrawal of universal male franchise in May 1850. When the remaining revolutionary newspapers were banned, Marx comments that 'they deserved their fate'.

In the German case, his opposition to the weakly reformist elements in the newly united Social Democratic Workers' Party is clearly expressed in a circular letter sent to party leaders in 1879. It denounced those bourgeois groups within the party that wanted it to moderate its programme and its rhetoric in order to avoid provoking the hatred of the bourgeoisie. In general Marx considered that these elements were trying to dilute the revolutionary **essence** of the Party and were contributing nothing of educational **value** to the members. He reiterated the battle-cry of the **First International** (1864–1872) that 'the **emancipation** of the working class must be the work of the working class itself'.

Marx is often associated with views on socialism that he did not express. For example, he used the phrase 'scientific socialism' on only one occasion, in his 'Conspectus of Bakunin's *Statism and Anarchy*' (1874), and then he dismisses its significance as no more than a contrast to **utopian socialism**. Similarly, although he distinguished between a newly emerged phase of communist society and a more advanced phase in the *Critique of the Gotha Programme* (1875), he never referred to the first stage as 'socialist'.

species-being   A term (*Gattungswesen*) used by Marx in his early writings to refer to human **essence**. Although he adopted it from the philosophy of Ludwig **Feuerbach**, Marx placed far greater emphasis on the centrality of **production** in defining human distinctiveness. In the *Economic and Philosophical Manuscripts* (1844) Marx argued that humans were essentially creative and social beings, but their existence as workers was so desperate that it amounted to **dehumanization**. He considered **alienation** from species-being to be one of the features of life in the **capitalist mode of production**. In the sixth of his *Theses on Feuerbach* (1845), Marx rejected Feuerbach's notion of species-being as a 'mute' conception of the human essence, abstracted from the historical process. (See also **human nature**.)

state   The political expression of **class** rule, conditioned by the economic structure prevailing in **civil society**. Although it varied in its specific **form**, Marx considered that the state was bound to serve the interests of the class which dominated the **mode of production**. The origins of this view are to be found in his 1843 *Critique of Hegel's Philosophy of Right*, in which he rejects Hegel's contention that the differences between the various interests in society could be successfully mediated by an administrative class of economically self-sufficient landowners who had no interest of their own to advance, but only the interests of society as a whole at heart. Marx refutes the idea of such a 'universal' class, insisting that the state was an expression of class interest, precisely the class interests of the large landowners, and the laws passed by this state were designed to protect these interests. This rejection of the state as a neutral force was critical in the development of Marx's **communism**. Until 1843 he thought that securing a representative democratic state would resolve social antagonism, but by the time he writes **On the Jewish Question** in September 1843 it is clear that he regards a democratic state as only a means through which the **class struggle** could be openly fought. He asserts that political **emancipation** should not be confused with human emancipation, which can be achieved only through the development of a classless society.

Perhaps the best-known characterization of the state by Marx appears in **The Communist Manifesto** (1848), when he argues that the executive of the modern state is only 'a committee for managing the common affairs of the whole **bourgeoisie**'. Although this is taken to imply an instrumental relationship in which the state merely carries out the instructions of the **ruling class**, it is more nuanced than that. Committees normally have a great deal of autonomous power *vis-à-vis* the members they formally represent, and in the case of the state this is to be expected, since it is not always evident that the ruling class is a homogenous body with clearly defined common interests. This is illustrated in Marx's detailed analysis of the French Second Republic (1848–1851) in **The Eighteenth Brumaire of Louis Bonaparte** (1852), which dispels any simple deterministic reading of the relationship between class and state.

Marx identified the various political groups and associated them with a class interest. No fewer than three different factions of the bourgeoisie contended for state power, but the state apparatus was controlled by a fourth party, the directly elected President, Louis Bonaparte. His electoral support came from the **peasantry**, by far the most numerous class in France. Bonaparte exploited the divisions within the bourgeoisie to usurp power in December 1851 and crown himself Emperor. In this situation, Marx comments that the state power appears to be 'completely independent'. However, he argues that this was an illusion. State power is not suspended in mid-air because Bonaparte represents the smallholding peasantry. The peasants, though, hardly formed a class at all, for despite their shared conditions of existence, their lack of community, national bond or political organization meant that they lacked the resources to represent themselves. They therefore had to be represented, and their representative 'must at the same time appear as their master'. This gave tremendous autonomy to Bonaparte and his state apparatus, but it was circumscribed in one important respect. For Bonaparte to succeed he needed to placate the various competing interests in France and make the economy prosper, and in particular he needed to reconcile differences between the sections of the bourgeoisie. Theoretically, the significance of this analysis of the Bonapartist state is that the state can operate with some independence from any particular social class, and even impose solutions to intractable problems on rival factions of the ruling class. Despite the subtleties of the analysis of the *Brumaire*, Marx reverted to an instrumental characterization of the state as the 'engine of class despotism' in **The Civil War in France** (1871). For Marx, although the state can exercise some independence at times of political crisis, especially when it can achieve popular support, ultimately it will be obliged to operate in favour of the ruling class by optimizing the conditions for the **accumulation** of **capital**.

The issue of what Marx thought the **working class** should do with the state once it had conquered political power is not so clear. The practical measures suggested in the *Manifesto*, and also in *The Demands of the Communist Party in Germany* (1848), involve a major role for the state, yet Marx was consistently hostile to state power. In a review written in April 1850 with **Engels**, Marx argued that for communists 'abolition of the state makes sense only as the necessary result of the abolition of classes'. This implied an agreement with the anarchist goal of a stateless society, but a rejection of the idea that it could be done immediately after a **revolution**. As long as there were still social forces working towards the preservation or restoration of class-based society, there would have to be a coercive apparatus to protect the new order, and Marx consistently termed this the **dictatorship of the proletariat** in which 'dictatorship' was conceived as a combination of radical democratic forms and the means to defend majority power from external or internal threats. He enthused over the participatory **democracy** adopted by the **Paris Commune** (1871), particularly the measures to limit the power of unelected state officials. In the *Civil War in France* he concluded that the working class cannot lay hold of the ready-made machinery of the state and wield it for its own purposes. The post-revolutionary state would still have a 'few but important' centralized functions, and it would be run by 'strictly responsible' agents. For Marx, having defined the state as an instrument of class rule, it logically followed that the state should dissolve with the abolition of classes. Clearly, however, there would need to be a significant role for democratic public governance of some sort to oversee socially controlled **production** and distribution.

surplus value   Defined by Marx in **Capital** 1 (1867) as the addition to an initial sum of **money** that has been invested in a process of **production**. A **capitalist** invests money (M) by buying **labour power** (LP) – the capacity to **labour** – and means of production – raw material, machinery etc. – which are **commodity** inputs (C). Through productive capital (P) these commodity inputs produce commodities (C'). C' is greater than C because it contains surplus value in the commodity-form. However, the capitalist has to realize this surplus in the **form** of money through **market exchange** to receive M', which is greater than the original money (M) that was invested. Marx explains this production of surplus value occurs within the circuit of **capital** denoted as M-C (LP, MP)...P...-C'-M' where M' and C' are greater than M and C respectively. In the realm of exchange, the total social surplus value across the economy takes the form of **profit**, rent and interest. Indeed, Marx sees his understanding of surplus value in this way as being independent of these forms as one of the best points of his book, alongside his twofold characterization of labour.

Marx argues that labour power, the capacity to work, is the source of surplus value. In contrast to those political economists who suggest that the surplus arises from inequalities in exchange, such as **Ricardo**, Marx shows how a seemingly fair exchange could result in the creation and extraction of surplus value. This allows him to locate the creation of the surplus in production rather than circulation and leads him to develop his notion of the rate of surplus value or rate of **exploitation**.

The rate of surplus value refers to the ratio between the surplus labour (S) expended by a worker that is in excess of the necessary labour or variable capital (V) required to satisfy basic subsistence requirements. For example, suppose a worker has to perform five hours of necessary labour (V) in order to reproduce herself and her **family**. A capitalist sets the **working day** at ten hours, which means that the worker labours five hours for herself and five hours for the capitalist. The worker has performed five hours' surplus labour and the capitalist has accrued a surplus value equal to five hours of labour time. The rate of surplus value or exploitation is, in this instance, (5/5 x 100 =) 100 per cent.

Marx denotes two ways in which this surplus value is extracted. Absolute surplus value refers to the way capitalists attempt to lengthen the working day and thereby increase surplus value. Relative surplus value involves reducing necessary labour whilst still making the worker labour the full working day. This can be accomplished through productivity increases by making people work harder or expelling some labour and introducing machinery into the production process. Marx uses this increase in dead labour over living labour for his theory of the **tendency of the rate of profit to fall**. The working day, therefore, is an arena of **class struggle** between capitalist and worker over the pumping out of surplus value.

The concept of surplus value is rejected by neo-classical economists who locate the origin of the surplus in abstinence and the marginal productivity of capital. However, even within Marxist discourse, surplus value and the **labour theory of value** upon which it is based has come under sustained attack. Problems are particularly identified with the quantitative relationship between surplus value measured in **value** terms and profits that are measured in terms of prices. Some critics indicate how prices and profits can be determined without any reference to values and surplus values. However, in a famous letter to his friend and fellow communist Ludwig Kugelmann, written in 1868, Marx states clearly that there are bound to be disparities between values and prices or surplus value and profit. The reason is because of the anarchic nature of capitalist production, where no social regulation of what should be produced to ensure the continuation of society takes place. As producers cannot know whether the labour they have expended on making commodities was socially necessary or not until they have entered market exchange, there are bound to be such discrepancies, and consequently not a direct relation to the private labour time that has been expended. Moreover, it is through such discrepancies that capital is such a volatile system and prone to **economic crises**. (See also **Transformation Problem**.)

—**T**—

teleology The philosophical idea of 'final ends' operates in two different ways in Marx's work. First, Marx flatly condemns teleology in accounts of **nature**. He praises Epicurus for rejecting teleological influences on the natural world, and he also praises Darwin's *Origin of Species* for discrediting teleological accounts of natural history. In both cases he clearly opposes the idea that nature is somehow predetermined by divine forces. However, Marx's account of historical development has a strong teleological element in the sense that he portrays certain historical developments as the necessary outcome of existing tendencies. In *The Communist Manifesto* (1848) Marx argued that the fall of the **bourgeoisie** and the victory of the **working class** 'are equally inevitable', and in an 1852 letter to Weydemeyer he claims that the **class struggle** necessarily leads to the **dictatorship of the proletariat.** In the 1859 **Preface to *A Contribution to the Critique of Political Economy*** he asserts that the fall of bourgeois society constitutes the close of the prehistory of society, and only after its demise will humanity begin to plan our social development. In the Preface to *Capital* **1** (1867) Marx talks about the natural laws of **capitalist production** working themselves out 'with iron necessity', while in the Postface to the second edition he refers to his rational **dialectic** as revealing the 'inevitable destruction' of the existing system. In *The Civil War in France* (1871) he makes a teleological reference to the 'higher **form** to which present society is irresistibly tending by its own economical agencies'. This notion of the 'higher form' makes a number of appearances in his work and is consistent with an underlying conviction in human progress.

tendency of the rate of profit to fall This important theoretical argument, first outlined in the *Grundrisse* (1857–1858) and then set down in part three of *Capital* **3** (1864–1865), exposes the chronic instability of **capitalism**. Marx presents the underlying reasons for the recurrence of systemic breakdowns in the **form** of **economic crises**. Assuming a fixed rate of **exploitation**, he argues that the rate of profit depends on the relationship of the amount of **money** expended as **wages** on living **labour** (variable **capital**) and the amount expended on raw materials and the means of **production** (constant capital). The smaller the portion expended on labour, the smaller becomes the rate of profit. As **competition** constantly drives capitalists to spend proportionately more on constant capital in order to increase productivity, the tendency is for the rate of profit to fall over time. Marx describes this as 'in every respect the most important **law** of **political economy**', and he links it to the contradictions which reveal themselves in 'crises, spasms, explosions, cataclysms'.

There is a much more careful analysis of the tendency in part three of *Capital* 3, in which Marx supplies mathematical illustrations to show the rate of profit falling when constant capital increases in relation to variable capital, which he terms an increase in the organic composition of capital. Although he argues that this was the actual tendency of **capitalist** production, he points out that it could be delayed by counteracting factors, which he examines in a separate chapter. These include an increase in the rate of exploitation, depression of wages, cheapening of constant capital and foreign trade. Nevertheless, these factors are not sufficient to resist the long-term tendency, which is carried along by the expansionist dynamic of the system, leading to risky investments and business failures. Although the theory does not constitute a direct explanation of why crises occur, Marx certainly considers that it explains the pressures on the system that makes crises inevitable. In general, capitalism has to set its course on the unlimited expansion of production, but this goal comes into **contradiction** with its basis in the exploitation of the great mass of producers, for capitalists are constantly struggling to find effective demand for their products. Marx concludes that 'the true barrier to capitalist production is capital itself'. He comments that this internal contradiction seeks resolution by extending the external scope of production, but this simply heightens the contradiction between the conditions in which exploitation takes place and the conditions in which profit is realized. The desperate struggle to retain profitability leads to risky investments, business failures, takeovers and mergers. Marx predicts the necessity of **state** intervention and even the emergence of monopolies in certain sectors, posing the threat that 'the animating fire of production would be totally extinguished'.

Theories of Surplus Value* (1861–1863, posthumously published 1905–1910)** The intended fourth volume of ***Capital that was unfinished and first published in three parts after Marx's death under the editorship of Karl Kautsky, a leading theorist of German social **democracy**. Marx intended them to be his critical assessment of the main theorists of **political economy**. Part one begins with a brief consideration of the mercantilism of Sir James Steuart on the issue of **profit** being explained simply from the realm of **exchange** through the sale of a **commodity** to another person. Marx rejects this interpretation and emphasizes that the real **value** of the commodity is contained in the socially necessary **labour** time required to produce it. He then examines the physiocratic emphasis on the sphere of **production**, which they mistakenly reduce simply to land and agricultural production. Marx then examines the theories of Adam **Smith**, particularly in relation to the issue of productive and unproductive labour, and finishes by offering a very brief sketch of Hobbes on labour, Locke on rent and Hume on interest and profit. Part two begins with a consideration of rent and explores this further along with the theory of profit and **surplus value** in the work of **Ricardo**. Marx sees Ricardo as inheriting weaknesses from Smith that made Ricardo confuse these two categories. Part three begins with an attack on Malthus for being a mere apologist for the interests of the **bourgeoisie**. He outlines the disintegration of the Ricardian school of political economy and the emergence of 'vulgar' political economy that was nothing more than an unscientific mouthpiece for **capital**.

theory and practice   Refers to Marx's contention that theory and practice must always relate to each other and not be kept distinct. For example, in his *Contribution to the Critique of Hegel's Philosophy of Right: Introduction* (1844) Marx argues that theory becomes a material force only when it grips the masses and in this way it also becomes radical. Similarly, in the *Theses on Feuerbach* (1845) he criticizes **Feuerbach** for privileging theory over practice instead of uniting the two in revolutionary, practical and critical activity. Consequently, when theory is apt to descend into mysticism, as it so often does for Feuerbach, it can only be made rational through human practice and the contemplation of that practice. (See also **praxis**.)

Theses on Feuerbach **(1845, posthumously published 1888)**   A series of eleven short aphorisms within which Marx outlines his disagreements with **Feuerbach**, particularly over the **nature** of his **materialism**. These important philosophical principles were developed more extensively in *The German Ideology* (1845–1846). In the Preface to his own work,

Ludwig Feuerbach and the End of Classical German Philosophy (1886), **Engels** informs us that these notes were written down in haste, but remain invaluable as they constitute the germ of Marx's own new world-view. In the first thesis, Marx states bluntly that the main defect in all previous types of materialism, even including the more enlightened materialism of Feuerbach, relates to understanding things contemplatively or in the **form** or **appearance** of the object. Even though Feuerbach tried to overcome **idealism** by distinguishing sensuous objects from thought objects, he still failed to see human activity objectively. He therefore wrongly privileges theory over practice instead of seeing them in a unity with each other. In contrast, Marx argues that his own superior form of materialism understands things subjectively through human activity and practice. Marx reiterates this point in the fifth thesis.

In the second thesis, Marx considers the issue of objective truth, and argues that it can be proved, not simply in thinking, but by putting thinking into actual practice. In the third thesis, Marx rejects those inferior materialists who simply believe that circumstances determine the way people are, rather than realizing that circumstances themselves are determined by people. He says that these materialists therefore purport to be educators, but the need is to educate these educators themselves, otherwise they claim superiority over other people, resulting in elitism. Instead, people are not passive, and they can change through their own practical activity. In thesis four, Marx again takes Feuerbach to task, but this time in relation to his attitude towards **religion**. Whilst Feuerbach correctly sees religion as a form of self-**alienation**, he attempts to overcome this through secularizing the religious. However, in doing so, he detaches the secular from itself and turns it into an **abstraction**, instead of understanding it in **contradiction** and revolutionized in practice. So for example, the holy **family** of religion is an alienated form of the earthily family of the secular, but to avoid treating the earthly family as an abstraction itself, it needs to be destroyed in **theory and practice**.

In thesis six, Marx persists with this theme and accuses Feuerbach of resolving the religious **essence** into human essence again in an abstract manner. Marx contends that the human essence is not an abstraction inherent in each **individual**, but is in reality the ensemble of the social relations. Feuerbach's failure to realize this means that he abstracts from historical processes and so misses their materialist basis. Additionally, he sees the human essence only in its generality when it should be grasped socially, because by changing our social relations in practice we can change ourselves. This leads into the seventh thesis, where Marx chides Feuerbach for not seeing that the abstract individual he analyzes is in fact part of a particular society. In the eighth thesis, Marx makes the general point that all social life is essentially practical and that all theory finds its solution in human practice and comprehension of this practice. In thesis nine, Marx shows the limits of inferior or what he terms here contemplative materialism, in that its failure to understand sensuousness in practice means it is left to analyze only single individuals and **civil society**. Such old materialism, as he says in thesis ten, is in contrast to his new materialism, which embraces human society or social humanity. Finally, in the eleventh and perhaps the most famous thesis, Marx concludes by declaring that 'the philosophers have only *interpreted* the world, in various ways; the point is to *change* it'. Hence, Marx's materialist outlook has at its basis the unity of theory and practice and acts as a clarion call to revolutionary activity.

trade unions   Marx was an enthusiastic supporter of trade unions as associations of workers dedicated to furthering the **rights** and interests of their members, although he had important reservations concerning the limited nature of their ambitions. In *The Poverty of Philosophy* (1847), in opposition to Proudhon's rejection of trade union action, Marx supported the actions of workers combining together to defend their **wages** against the employers in a 'veritable civil **war**'. He insists that this is a decisive stage in the formation of a '**class** for itself', conscious of its own interests. In *The Communist Manifesto* (1848) Marx writes about the formation of trade unions as a progressive stage in the evolution of the struggle of the **working class** against the **bourgeoisie**, repeating the observation from *The Poverty of Philosophy* that 'every **class struggle** is a political struggle'. Unions worked for improvements in wages and legislation to restrict working hours, and Marx made allies with the British trade unionists in forming and sustaining the **First International** (1864–1872). In the Inaugural Address he argued that securing the passing of the Ten Hours Act in Britain in 1847 was not just a great practical success but represented the victory of a principle, because for the first time '.he **political economy** of the middle class succumbed to the political economy of the working class'. In practice the trade unions of Marx's day were craft-based unions led by people who were not socialists, and this limited vision of class representation drew criticism from Marx in **Value, Price and Profit** (1865). In the Instructions for Delegates to the Geneva Congress of the International he argued that the trade unions had been too focused on local and immediate struggles with **capital**, having 'not yet fully understood their power of acting against the system of wage **slavery** itself'. He urged the unions to act as organizing centres for the 'complete **emancipation**' of the working class, to organize among the worst paid trades, and to convince the world that their efforts are not 'narrow and selfish', but rather aim for the emancipation of the 'downtrodden millions'.

Transformation Problem   Refers to the issues surrounding how **value** is transformed into a '**price** of **production**' and how **surplus value** is transformed into **profit**. Marx considers these transformations as occurring amongst many capitalists within a dynamic process of **competition**, as discussed in **Capital** 3 (1864–1865). For Marx, the real relations of the operations of **capitalism** must be understood through his **labour theory of value** in order to expose the process of **exploitation** and the tendency towards **economic crises** that reverberate throughout the system. In **Capital 1** (1867) Marx shows how surplus value originates from the exploitation of the worker's **labour power** and how value, the socially necessary **labour** time required to produce a **commodity**, regulates the exchange of commodities. He does this by assuming that commodities **exchange** at their values in order to highlight the specific way unpaid surplus labour is extracted from the workers. In _Capital_ 3 he no longer assumes that commodities exchange at their values and moves from the example of **individual** capitalists to include many capitalists engaging with each other in a process of competition. Marx is therefore deepening and enriching his analysis of capitalism set out in volumes one and two, and he contends that in a process of many capitalists in competition with each other, the origin of surplus value becomes even more mystified. As Marx indicates, these real relations where value is determined by labour time appear in a reverse form in the process of competition. More and more it appears that capital is the creator of surplus value because the presence of labour power becomes hidden from sight. Marx contends therefore that we have to penetrate 'behind the semblance, the inner **essence** and the inner form of this process' to understand correctly the real operations of capitalism.

The transformation problem has caused much controversy amongst commentators both within and without the Marxist tradition. Such criticisms have normally focused on the technicality of transforming values into prices of production and surplus value into profit resulting in many mathematical models trying to prove either that this can or cannot be done. This is then used to either affirm Marx's analysis or condemn it outright. However, for Marx, the technical transformation of values into prices was not his chief concern; rather, he was more preoccupied with offering a theory of distribution to expose the real social processes that regulate capitalism. This is why he saw surplus value as the 'invisible essence' to be investigated, while treating profit as the surface phenomenon that mystifies the real social relations of production.

—U—

utopian socialism   The dominant **form** of socialist thought in the early nineteenth century, inspired in France by the writings of Charles Fourier (1772–1837) and Henri-de Saint Simon (1760–1825) and in Britain by Robert **Owen** (1771–1858). Marx was anxious to distinguish his own theory from utopian socialism and he was highly critical of its abstract nature, its 'fantastic standing apart' from the **class struggle**. In a letter to Arnold Ruge in 1843 he declared that he was not in the business of 'constructing the future and settling everything for all times', committing himself instead to the 'ruthless criticism of all that exists'. In the section on utopian socialism in **The Communist Manifesto** (1848) Marx derides the utopian socialists for failing to recognize the **class** basis of social antagonism and for making cross-class appeals to social harmony. As the class struggle developed, he thought, utopian socialism became increasingly out of touch with reality. Nevertheless, it is clear from these passages that Marx respected the historical contribution of utopian socialism in providing 'valuable materials for the enlightenment of the **working class**' and by depicting egalitarian alternatives to **capitalist** society. In particular he was attracted by Robert

Owen's practical focus on transforming factory life and by Charles Fourier's emphasis on the need for the **emancipation** of **women**. Marx also found the economic literature of the utopian socialists to be useful in developing his own critique of **capitalism**. While criticizing Proudhon's ignorance of economics in *The Poverty of Philosophy* (1847) he praised the 'remarkable' work of John Francis Bray in his *Labour's Wrongs and Labour's Remedy* (1839). In *Capital* **1** (1867) he favourably cites Thomas Hodgskin's *Political Economy and Labour* Defended Against the Claims of Capital (1825) as well as William Thompson's *The Distribution of Wealth* (1824), the work in which the concept of **surplus value** found its first expression. Politically, however, Marx was anxious to dissuade workers from following the 'castles in the air' promoted by utopians such as Étienne Cabet, whose *Voyage en Icarie* had inspired many to try to set up alternative communities. In the *Manifesto* he accused them of having to appeal to the feelings and purses of the **bourgeoisie** and of violently opposing all political action on the part of the working class, claims laced with polemical exaggeration. In an 1877 letter to Sorge he condemned utopian socialism for 'playing with fantastic pictures of the future structure of society', concluding that it was 'silly, stale and basically reactionary'.

—V—

value   A social relation referring to the fact that as products of **labour**, commodities embody a certain amount of socially necessary labour time that is part of the labour of society as a whole. Value is therefore *not* the private labour of a particular **individual**. In *Capital* **1** (1867) Marx states that the substance of value is **abstract labour**, which is human labour abstracted from its particular concrete **form**. In the making of a coat, for example, the value of that **commodity** is not represented by the actual amount of labour expended by a certain individual in its creation. Instead, the value of the coat is the portion of the social labour of society that has been assigned to that commodity. The magnitude or size of this value is determined by the amount of socially necessary labour time to produce a commodity. The socially necessary labour time itself is the time it takes to produce any use value under the conditions of **production** and average degree of skill and intensity of labour that prevail in a society at a given time. So if the average time it takes to make a coat is, say, six hours, then that is the socially necessary labour time for making a coat.

The only way we can tell if the labour expended on the coat is socially necessary is by offering the commodity up for **exchange** on the **market**. In exchange the coat confronts other coats that are similar or different and which have been created by other producers. Exchange therefore shows whether the **labour power** expended on the production of the coat was socially necessary or not. The concrete, specific labours expended on the coat therefore take the form of abstract labour in the realm of exchange. Abstract labour becomes the measure of value in a society where human labour as wage labour becomes general, and that society is **capitalism**.

Marx's value theory, unlike conventional labour theories of value, is therefore specific for understanding **capitalist** relations of production. This is why Marx criticizes all previous political economists for not asking the crucial question of why labour is expressed in value, and why the measurement of labour by its duration is expressed in the magnitude of the value of the product. They have therefore been unable to discover the form of value, which they treat with indifference and external to the **nature** of the commodity itself, that turns value into exchange value. They fail to see that the value-form of the product of labour is the most universal form of the bourgeois **mode of production**, and as such it gives this mode of production a transitory and not, as vulgar political economists assume, a permanent character. They are therefore in thrall to **commodity fetishism** and cannot penetrate through the appearances generated in a system of commodity exchange. Indeed, commodity fetishism itself is what really distinguishes Marx's theory of value from that of classical political economists, particularly **Ricardo**, and many misinterpretations of Marx's value theory have arisen by ignoring this part of his argument.

Value, Price and Profit **(1865, posthumously published 1898)**   Also known as *Wages, Price and Profit*, this was a speech given by Marx to the **First International** in 1865 and was first published in 1898 by his daughter, Eleanor. Marx stated his theory of **surplus value** in public for the first time in this speech, and the work itself is generally seen as one of the best introductions to his **labour theory of value** and a useful starting point before embarking on *Capital* **1** (1867).

Marx presents a critique of a trade unionist, John Weston, who was a socialist and follower of Robert **Owen**. Weston argued that the social and material prospects of the **working class** could not in general be improved by wage increases, and deduced from this that the efforts of the **trade unions** to secure wage increases have a harmful effect on other branches of industry. Such arguments were based on what was known at the time as the 'iron **law** of wages' or 'theory of wages fund', which contends that due to **population** pressures wages cannot rise above minimum levels of subsistence. The argument is that the expenditure of **capital** from profits accrued in any given period for the payment of wages is a rigid and definite sum that cannot be added to. So the wage of each worker is calculated by dividing up this wages fund in relation to the total number of workers in society. Consequently, any attempt by trade unions to increase wages can only have a negative outcome for society as a whole. Weston therefore concluded that the standard of living of the workers could only be achieved through the creation of producers' cooperatives.

Marx rejects these arguments through his **value** theory by showing that these quantities are not fixed at all, and that the division between wages and the expenditure of capital can vary. He argued that wages themselves were determined by the social conditions and standards that prevail in different societies, and hence were variable. Similarly, the expenditure of capital accrued from profits was also not fixed, as the maximum rate of **profit** depends on the physical minimum of wages and the physical maximum of the **working day**. Profits are therefore the outcome of the continuous struggle between capital and **labour**, and as such can be high or low depending on the respective powers of these opposing forces.

Additionally, Marx showed that increases in wages did not affect the prices of commodities, and that as capitalists were always attempting to lower the average level of wages, trade unions were crucial in protecting workers' living standards. However, Marx also maintained that increases in wages were not enough to challenge capital, as the ultimate goal for the **emancipation** of the working class was to abolish the wages system rather than preserve it.

—W—

***Wage Labour and Capital* (1849)**   Originally delivered as lectures to the working men's club in Brussels in December 1847, they were first published in the **form** of articles in the *Neue Rheinische Zeitung* during April 1849. They appeared as a pamphlet in 1891, modified by **Engels** to reflect the development of Marx's thought since the 1840s by, for example, substituting **labour power** for **labour** because of the importance of the concept for Marx's analysis of capital. It is as an excellent introduction to Marx's economic ideas.

In the original work, Marx states that he wants to deal more closely with economic relations upon which the existence of the **bourgeoisie** and its **class** rule and the **slavery** of the workers are founded. He says that in doing so he will present his arguments as simply and as popularly as possible in order to be understood by the workers. One of his main considerations is to define what **wages** are and deduce how they are determined. Marx's answer is that wages are a special name for the **price** of labour, which itself is a **commodity** that workers sell to capitalists in order to live. Wages are therefore determined by the same laws that determine the price of any other commodity, that is, they are determined by **competition**. So wages rise and fall in relation to supply and demand through the competition between capitalists as the buyers of labour, and workers as the sellers of labour. However, the cost of **production** of labour is also determined, as for any other commodity, by the labour time necessary to produce it, which is labour power. Consequently, the cost of production of labour is the cost of existence and reproduction of the worker. Wages are the price of this cost of existence and reproduction. For simple labour, wages will be low and so constitute a wage minimum, which applies across all those who perform that labour, and around which the wages of the whole of the **working class** oscillate. Such are the general laws that regulate wages.

When Marx then considers what occurs in the **exchange** between capitalists and wage-workers, he deduces that whereas the workers receive their means of subsistence in exchange for their labour, capitalists receive labour for their means of subsistence. As productive activity, this labour not only replaces what the workers consume, but also gives a greater **value** to the accumulated labour than it previously possessed, that is, it serves as a means of new production, which is capital. So workers are not simply producing commodities for capitalists, they are also producing capital, that is, values that can be used anew, which both commands their labour and creates new values. As such, the workers are therefore increasing capital and so increasing their own slavery to the system through which capitalists exploit them, and enrich themselves by accruing **profit**. Moreover, the antagonistic relations between capitalists and workers centre on the desire for workers to increase their wages and the desire of capitalists to increase their profits. Marx realizes that if capital grows rapidly then wages may rise along with profits, but the latter will do so more rapidly. Although workers may have improved their position in material terms, their social position has deteriorated relative to the social position of capitalists, which has increased far greater with far greater **wealth**. The antagonism between the interests of the workers and the interests of capitalists remains even where the workers improve their material existence. Marx therefore mocks those economists who say that the interests of the workers and the capitalists are the same.

wages The **market price** of **labour power** that workers sell to capitalists to receive an income with which to satisfy their **needs**. Marx argues that wages are determined through the antagonistic struggle between capitalists and workers, and wages themselves hide the fact that workers are exploited.

In *Capital* **1** (1867) Marx suggests that when the capitalist pays a wage, he or she ignores the unpaid surplus **labour** that has been performed throughout the **working day**. If a worker has, for example, received £40 for a day's work, this hides the fact that through the expenditure of labour power the worker will have had to work longer or more intensely to create a surplus for the capitalist. The £40 is therefore only the paid portion of the working day. So the wage-form hides the fact that working day is split into necessary labour that is paid for and surplus labour that is unpaid. In wage-labour even surplus or unpaid labour appears as paid and so hides the hidden reality of **exploitation** in **capitalism**.

To illustrate this further, Marx considers how people were exploited in slave societies. Here the slave must also work in order to reproduce him or herself, and create a surplus that will be taken by the master for his or her own **consumption**. However, because of the total control that the master has over the slave, there is some **form** of mystification here because the necessary labour the slave performs for him or herself actually appears as though it is labour for the master. All the slave's labour therefore appears as unpaid labour, in contrast to **capital**, where all the worker's labour appears as being paid. In **feudalism**, the exploitation that takes place is far more open and less mystified. The lord owns the means of **production**, which is the land, and while he allows the serfs to work on that land, the labour done by the serfs to reproduce themselves is clearly demarcated from the compulsory labour that they must do for the lord.

Consequently, for Marx, the transformation of labour power into the form of wages shows capital to be a system where in **appearance** the relation between the worker and the capitalist seems fair and just. The capitalist is buying labour power at the market rate, and the worker is selling his or her labour power for what the market deems it to be worth. However, once the worker puts this labour power into action as concrete labour, he or she is creating over and above the necessary labour needed for reproduction, which is **surplus value** that is pocketed as unpaid labour by the capitalist. In this way, Marx solves the mystery of wages that operates in the appearances of capital. (See also *Wage Labour and Capital*.)

Wages, Price and Profit   (See *Value, Price and Profit*)

war   Conflicts between nations were judged by Marx according to their strategic value in advancing the political cause of the **working class**. For example, he considered that the Franco-Prussian war would be the prelude to a war between Germany and Russia, commenting in a letter to Friedrich Sorge in 1870 that this would be a 'midwife to the inevitable social **revolution** in Russia'. Although he did not provide an analysis of the causes of war, his comments in *The Communist Manifesto* (1848) make it clear that he related it to **exploitation**. He argued that when **class** antagonisms within a country decline, so too will hostilities between nations. Marx gave his total support to the north in the American Civil War because it was fighting to free the slaves. Towards the end of 1864 he wrote a letter to President Abraham Lincoln on behalf of the General Council of the **First International** (1864–1872), congratulating him on his re-election and optimistically predicting that, just as the American War of Independence had led to a new era of ascendancy for the middle class, so too would the successful Antislavery War lead to the ascendancy of the working class. He was sceptical of the distinction between defensive and aggressive wars, commenting that the Prussian war against France lost all claims to be defensive when the French Emperor was captured, and instead became a war of conquest. Marx anticipated major wars in Europe and was convinced that the experience of such conflicts would cause the working classes to reject the chauvinistic patriotism stoked by the **ruling class.**

wealth   In the opening sentence of **_Capital_ 1** (1867) Marx states that the wealth of societies in which the **capitalist mode of production** prevails appears as an immense collection of commodities and that the **individual commodity** appears as its elementary **form**. Consequently, he begins his investigation into **capital** with the analysis of the commodity. Marx sees capital as a commodity-producing society within which wealth is accrued through the buying and selling of commodities. Therefore wealth is the necessary outcome of capitalist **accumulation** and the extraction of **surplus value**. Within this process, he argues that increases in productivity and the development of the productive forces undergo a dialectical inversion so that instead of freeing the workers they exploit and dominate them. They distort the workers to a fragment of what it is to be human, degrade them to the appendage of a machine, turn their work into a torment, alienate them from the intellectual potentialities of the **labour** process, transform their life-time into working-time and drag their wives and children under the 'juggernaut of capital'. As capital accumulates the situation of the workers, whether their **wages** are high or low, grows worse. The outcome is 'accumulation of wealth at one pole' and 'at the same time accumulation of misery, the torment of **labour**, **slavery**, ignorance, brutalisation and moral degradation at the opposite pole'. So wealth in this sense is not simply a matter of some people having more **money** than others, because, as Marx says, even if the workers get an increase in wages they are still in a situation of **exploitation** and will always be relatively worse off than those who are appropriating their unpaid surplus labour. It is interesting, therefore, that to support his argument here Marx approvingly cites a Venetian Monk named Ortes, whom Marx regards as one of the greatest economic writers of the eighteenth century. He praises Ortes for understanding the antagonism of capitalist **production** as a universal natural **law** of social wealth, as Marx has argued, even if his solution of religious devotion left something to be desired to say the least. Additionally, Marx cites those writers such as Storch and Destutt de Tracy who also recognize that wealth and **poverty** must go together, but accommodate themselves to the fact as though it is some natural fate that cannot be overcome.

women Marx first talked about women's position in society in the *Economic and Philosophical Manuscripts* (1844). After denouncing the 'brutish' treatment of women in 'crude' communist movements in early sixteenth-century Germany, he concludes that the predatory attitude of men towards women is the 'infinite degradation in which man exists for himself'. He goes on to state that only when the relationship between men and women is experienced as the most natural relationship of human being to human being can we claim to have developed our **essence** as social beings. He argues that from the relationship between the sexes it is possible to judge humanity's 'whole level of development'. In *The Holy Family* (1845) he describes the general position of women in modern society as simply 'inhuman'.

In *The German Ideology* (1845–1846) Marx argues that the natural division of **labour** within the **family** led to an unequal distribution of power, leading to the 'latent **slavery**' of mothers and children. This latent slavery was identified as the first **form** of private **property**, but Marx does not speculate on how this domination developed. He argues that there are three 'premises' for human life: the **production** of material life itself, the creation of new **needs** and the creation of new people through family relations. These three factors are regarded as three 'moments' that have co-existed from the dawn of history, but, as modern feminist critics have pointed out, Marx's social theory emphasizes the first two points but neglects the importance of the role of the family.

The position of **working-class** women is discussed in various places in *Capital* **1** (1867), but the descriptions based on official reports in the chapters on 'The Working Day' and 'Machinery and Large Scale Industry' are particularly revealing, not only in terms of the appalling conditions faced by working women, but in Marx's reaction to them. He recounts the death of Mary Anne Walkley, aged 20, who had worked for over 26 hours continually in a high-class dressmaking establishment along with 30 other young women in a small room without sufficient air in between sleeping in a small, badly ventilated dormitory. The attending doctor ascribed the death directly to the working and sleeping conditions. Marx also described the dreadful conditions in bleaching factories, where women and girls worked long hours in temperatures up to 100° Fahrenheit. In the chapter on large-scale industry he noted that the introduction of machinery had encouraged capitalists to increase the employment of women and children. He cited harrowing evidence implying a close relationship between shockingly high mortality rates and the employment of mothers for long hours, with opiates being 'pushed' on men, women and children to dull their pain. He talked about the 'moral degradation' that arose out of the **exploitation** of women and children, and later in the chapter he denounced their treatment as 'sheer abuse', 'sheer robbery' and 'sheer brutality'. Marx supplied graphic accounts of the hideous working conditions of sewing machinists as well as the even more horrendous experiences of women surface workers at collieries who had to drag tubs of coal to the canals and railway wagons.

Despite this appalling reality, towards the end of chapter fifteen of *Capital* 1 Marx argues that bringing women into employment created a 'new economic foundation for a higher form of the family and relations between the sexes'. In other words, the tribulations faced under private property could give way to genuine **equality** once the social relations of production were transformed. In his preamble to the programme of the French Workers' Party in 1880, he proclaims that 'the **emancipation** of the producing **class** is that of all human beings without distinction of sex or **race**'.

working class   Marx defined the working class in *Capital* **3** (1864–1865) as 'the owners of mere **labour power**'. He frequently referred to the working class by the Ancient Roman word **proletariat**. In the *Grundrisse* (1857–1858) Marx accepts that groups of workers depending on the sale of their labour power had existed in many pre-capitalist societies, but only with **capitalism** does the wage relation become the dominant **form**. However, Marx notes that in all social classes there are middle and transitional levels that blur the boundaries between them, making the question 'What makes a **class**?' more complex than it first appears. Unfortunately, the manuscript that begins this discussion, comprising chapter fifty-two of *Capital* 3, then comes to an abrupt halt, leaving scholars to argue about precisely who counts in and out of each social class.

Marx's early formulations of the working class in modern society assume an emerging class of manual workers owning nothing and depending entirely on selling their **labour** (he arrived at the concept of labour power only in 1857 in the *Grundrisse*). For Marx, they hold a transformative significance in human history. In the **Contribution to the Critique of Hegel's Philosophy of Right: Introduction** (1844) he identified the working class as the class destined to win not only its own **freedom** but to emancipate humanity as a whole. The oppression of the proletariat is regarded as the complete loss of humanity, and its **emancipation** will lead to the complete 'rewinning' of humanity. In the **Economic and Philosophical Manuscripts** (1844) Marx describes the dire **poverty** of the working class. In times of prosperity the workers live in 'static misery', while in times of distress no one suffers more than them. They work like 'slaves in the service of avarice', shortening their life expectancy and being 'reduced' to the level of **machines** by the introduction of mechanization in the modern factory. He again specified the 'world-historic role' of the working class in **The Holy Family** (1845), arguing that because its condition represented extreme inhumanity, only by winning its freedom will it be able to abolish all the inhuman conditions of social life. He considered that this struggle for human freedom would arise because the class would be 'historically compelled' to conduct it, due to its pivotal role in the economic structure. In **The Poverty of Philosophy** (1847) Marx predicts that the working class, in a 'total **revolution**' against the **bourgeoisie**, will replace the old **civil society** based on private **property** with an association that will exclude social classes.

Marx outlined the historical development of the working class in **The Communist Manifesto** (1848). As the bourgeoisie develops, so too does the working class, as workers can find work only so long as their labour increases **capital**. The workers sell themselves piecemeal like any **commodity** and are subject to all the fluctuations of the **world market**. As modern industry develops, the small workshop gives way to the huge factory, and the workers are subjected to a despotic military discipline. The workers struggle against this despotism, first as individuals or small groups, and later within specific branches of industry. Eventually the working class organizes itself into a national body, developing a **class consciousness** to challenge the economic and political dominance of the bourgeoisie. Its struggles are hampered by **competition** among the workers themselves, but the working class movement recovers from these setbacks and rises again, more resolute and powerful. Marx consistently argued in favour of workers' movements that could go beyond local and purely economic struggles to organize nationally on both economic and political issues. After the eclipse of the Chartist movement in England in the 1850s there were very few national working-class movements in Marx's lifetime, but he was confident that they would develop, and charged them with winning the battle for **democracy** and assuming the mantle of the new **ruling class**. In the *Manifesto* it is suggested that the practical measures of a working-class government would include nationalization of major industries and land as well as other measures such as a progressive system of taxation, the creation of a national bank and free **education** for all children.

Although these class struggles are conducted within each nation-state, Marx considered them to be part of a wider international struggle to abolish the **capitalist mode of production**. He therefore greeted the formation of the **First International** in 1864 with great enthusiasm and threw himself energetically into work on its General Council. He had particularly good relations with the British leaders of **trade unions**, but was opposed in his support for the development of legal national working-class parties and unions by the anarchists. Following the 1872 Hague Congress of the International, he made a speech in Amsterdam in which he declared that it was possible for the workers to achieve power through peaceful means in countries that were moving towards political democracy. The leadership role played by Marx in the First International reflected his conviction that the struggle for social revolution had to be an international one, and in the **Critique of the Gotha Programme** (1875) he expressed his anger at the neglect of an international dimension in the first draft programme of the German Socialist Workers' Party. Both here and in an 1879 circular letter to German socialist leaders he warned against any dilution of the idea of **class struggle**.

In **Capital 1** (1867) Marx analyzed the **exploitation** of the workers, revealing how **surplus value** is extracted from them despite the apparent fairness of the purchase and sale of labour power. There are also graphic illustrations of the appalling working conditions and social life of workers in England, at that time the only country in which the workers were in a majority. Marx's interest in the differentiation of functions within the class is evident in his discussion of productive and unproductive labour in manuscripts now added as an appendix to *Capital* 1, 'The Results of the Immediate Process of **Production**'. Although he defined productive labour as that which creates surplus value directly, he added that increasingly the 'real lever' of the overall labour process was not the **individual** worker but the 'aggregate worker', including those who performed services that helped to sell the product. He specifies that the labour of clerks, while not directly producing surplus value, enabled the capitalist to extract surplus value, and was therefore a source of **profit**. This suggests a broad view of who is to be counted as members of the working class.

working day In *Capital* **1** (1867) Marx argues that in the history of **capitalist production** what constitutes the norm for the hours of a working day is a process of **class struggle** between the capitalist **class** and the **working class**. In chapter ten of that work he gives an extensive and detailed historical account of this process to expose the often quite brutal struggles that took place over the length of the working day. He argues that if the working day is a site of class struggle then that struggle is over the extraction of **surplus value** in a process of **exploitation**. The working day is therefore split into two parts: the necessary **labour** that the worker **needs** to perform to reproduce him or herself and the extra that the capitalist makes him or her perform to extract surplus value in the pursuit of **profit**.

In the nineteenth century there were tremendous arguments by political economists and politicians and reformers over the length of the working day. But as Marx makes clear, these arguments were only taking place, and were only officially recognized by the **state** as a result of a long class struggle. These struggles resulted in the Factory Acts that led to reductions in the working day by the state, and Marx used the reports of the factory inspectors to show the appalling way workers – men, **women** and very young children – were treated in the 'werewolf-like hunger for surplus value' by capitalists.

The majority of capitalists tried to resist this legislation under the assumption that the longer they made workers work, the more absolute surplus value they would obtain. Additionally, capitalists introduced night work to prolong the working day to twenty-four hours, often by making workers do a week on days and then a week on nights. As the working day increased in this way, even the legal system became so confused that one judge needed the help to discern legally what was day and what was night. As Marx colourfully comments, '**capital** was celebrating its orgies'.

However, extending the working day in these ways had negative effects on the capacity of workers to replenish themselves both physically and mentally. Through working-class resistance and the intervention of the state as the regulator of the social relations of production, shorter working days were imposed, from initially twelve to ten hours in the mid-nineteenth century. Capitalists tried to get around such legislation in a number of ways, but many of them did not realize that shortening the working day could actually increase the amount of relative surplus value by making the workers work harder and thereby more efficiently over a shorter period of time. This takes place through a process of class struggle where workers attempt to resist this extraction of their labour and capitalists attempt to enforce it, a process that continues into the present day. However, Marx argues in **Capital 3** (1864–1865) that once this struggle has been overcome by the working class, a communist society would see the shortening of the working day as a pre-requisite for reaching the 'true realm of freedom'.

world market   The establishment of a world market was regarded by Marx in **Capital 3** (1864–1865) as one of the 'cardinal facts' about **capitalist production**. In **The German Ideology** (1845–1846) the existence of a mass, totally dependent **working class** is said to presuppose a world market, lending the **class struggle** a 'world historical significance'. Marx explained the decisive role played by the importation of gold and silver from the Americas in stimulating capitalist relations of production in Europe. In **The Communist Manifesto** (1848) he argued that the **bourgeoisie**, through its **exploitation** of the world market, gave a 'cosmopolitan character' to production and **consumption** in every country. Old national industries are replaced by new ones that draw their raw materials from all over the world and sell their products 'in every quarter of the globe'. No place is immune from this new 'civilization' as the cheap prices of commodities **form** the 'heavy artillery' which 'batters down all Chinese Walls' and compels all countries to conform to the bourgeois **mode of production**. In chapter thirty-one of **Capital 1** (1867) Marx described vividly the importance of extracting bullion from the Americas and slaves from Africa in order to develop production in Europe. He also emphasizes the development of an international banking system to extend credit for world trading. The world dimension of the bourgeois mode of production, present from its outset, meant for Marx that the working class would have to act as a 'world historical' **class** ready to extend its national struggles into the global arena in order to create a new mode of production no longer based on private **property**.

—Y—

Young Hegelians   Marx became an ardent admirer of this German philosophical movement during his years as a student at the University of Berlin.
The movement developed after the death of **Hegel** in 1832 and focused
on the radical critique of **religion**. Marx was deeply impressed by the
contributions of David Strauss, Ludwig **Feuerbach** and Bruno Bauer to the
de-mystification of religious thought, and by Arnold Ruge for his rejection
of the Christian **state**. He was also introduced to the idea of **communism**
by Moses Hess and Eduard Gans, who foresaw the coming **class struggle**
between the **bourgeoisie** and the **proletariat**. However, Marx became
impatient with the unwillingness of the Young Hegelians to move from
abstract philosophizing to revolutionary **politics** based on the analysis of
social and political issues. The first indication of this can be found in his
argument against Bruno Bauer in *On the Jewish Question* (1844) and
further criticisms of his erstwhile philosophical allies fills the pages of *The
Holy Family* (1845) and *The German Ideology* (1845–1846). Even those
Young Hegelians who advocated **socialism** were mocked by Marx as 'True
Socialists' who remained entirely aloof from real political struggles.

—Z—

Zasulich, Vera (1849–1919)   One of the first translators of Marx's work
into Russian, Zasulich prompted an important theoretical contribution from
Marx on the issue of stages of historical development. In 1881 she asked
about the possibility that the ancient **form** of communal land ownership
in Russia, the *Obshchina*, could serve as the basis for a socialist system
of land management, thereby missing out the **capitalist** form of development. Marx intended to publish a full reply on the subject and produced
three lengthy drafts before settling for a short letter. He stressed that in
Capital **1** (1867) he had said that the expropriation of the agricultural

production that had occurred in Britain was already in process elsewhere in Western Europe, but the 'historical inevitability' of this process related only to that part of the world. It was a change of one form of private **property**, smallholding, to another form, the large agricultural business. In Russia the commune would have to move from communal ownership to private ownership, and it was entirely possible that it could instead skip that stage and develop into a modern, efficient form of collective ownership compatible with a communist society. The issue prompted Marx to teach himself to read Russian, and in the final years of his life he made copious notes from an array of sources on the social and political situation in Russia.

Bibliography

Works by Marx

Marx, Karl and Engels, Frederick, *Collected Works* in 50 Volumes (London: Lawrence & Wishart, 1975–2000).

The main collection of Marx's writings in translation.

Marxists Internet Archive available at http://www.marxists.org/. An excellent resource in relation to Marx's thought and Marxism in general containing the collected works in English and in many other languages.

Marx, Karl, *Selected Writings*, David McLellan (ed.) (Oxford: Oxford University Press, 2000).

The best selection of Marx's writings in one volume covering extracts from all his major works, the complete texts of many of his shorter writings and some of his most important correspondences.

Cambridge Texts in the History of Political Thought have two useful volumes covering a selection of Marx's texts as follows:

Marx, Karl, *Marx: Early Political Writings*, Joseph J. O'Malley (ed.) (Cambridge: Cambridge University Press, 1994).

Marx, Karl, *Marx: Later Political Writings*, Terrell Carver (ed.) (Cambridge: Cambridge University Press, 1996).

Verso have produced a boxed set entitled *Marx's Political Writings* containing the following three volumes that were previously available from Penguin:

Marx, Karl, *Revolutions of 1848*, David Fernbach (ed.) (London: Verso, 2010).

Marx, Karl, *Surveys from Exile*, David Fernbach (ed.) (London: Verso, 2010).

Marx, Karl, *First International and After*, David Fernbach (ed.) (London: Verso, 2010).

Penguin publish the following core texts of Marx as follows:

Marx, Karl, *Early Writings*, Lucio Colletti (ed.) (Harmondsworth: Penguin, 2000).

Marx, Karl, *Grundrisse*, (Harmondsworth: Penguin, 2005).

Marx, Karl, *Capital: Volume 1* (Harmondsworth: Penguin, 2008).

Marx, Karl, *Capital: Volume 2* (Harmondsworth: Penguin, 2006).

Marx, Karl, *Capital: Volume 3* (Harmondsworth: Penguin, 2006).

Selected Works on Marx

Biographies

McLellan, David, *Karl Marx, A Biography* (Basingstoke: Palgrave, 2006).

Wheen, Francis, *Karl Marx* (London: Fourth Estate, 1999).

General

Althusser, Louis, *For Marx* (London: Verso, 2005).

Anderson, Kevin B., *Marx at the Margins: On Nationalism, Ethnicity, and Non-Western Societies* (Chicago and London: Chicago University Press, 2010).

Arthur, Chris, *New Dialectic and Marx's Capital* (Leiden: Brill, 2002).

Avineri, Shlomo, *The Social and Political Thought of Karl Marx* (Cambridge: Cambridge University Press, 1971).

Balibar, Etienne, *The Philosophy of Marx* (London: Verso, 2007).

Benner, Erica, *Really Existing Nationalisms: A Post-Communist View from Marx and Engels* (Oxford: Clarendon Press, 1995).

Bottomore, Tom (ed.) *A Dictionary of Marxist Thought*, 2nd ed. (Oxford: Blackwell, 2006).

Breckman, Warren, *Marx, The Young Hegelians, and the Origins of Radical Social Theory* (Cambridge: Cambridge University Press, 2001).

Brudney, Daniel, *Marx's Attempt to Leave Philosophy* (Cambridge, MA: Harvard University Press, 1998).

Burns, Tony and Fraser, Ian (eds), *The Hegel–Marx Connection* (Basingstoke: Macmillan, 2000).

Callinicos, Alex, *Marxism and Philosophy* (Oxford: Oxford University Press, 1989).

——, *The Revolutionary Ideas of Karl Marx* (London: Bookmarks, 1993).

Carver, Terrell, *Marx and Engels: The Intellectual Relationship* (Brighton: Harvester, 1983).

——, *A Marx Dictionary* (Cambridge: Polity, 1987).

—— (ed.), *The Cambridge Companion to Marx* (Cambridge: Cambridge University Press, 1991).

——, *The Postmodern Marx* (Manchester: Manchester University Press, 1998).

Cleaver, Harry, *Reading Capital Politically* (London: AK Press, 2000).

Cohen, G. A., *Karl Marx's Theory of History: A Defence* (Oxford: Clarendon Press, 2000).

Collier, Andrew, *Marx: A Beginner's Guide* (Oxford: Oneworld, 2008).

Cowling, Mark (ed.), *The Communist Manifesto: New Interpretations* (Edinburgh: Edinburgh University Press, 1998).

Fine, Ben and Saad-Filho, Alfredo, *Marx's Capital*, 5th ed. (London: Pluto, 2010).

Foster, John Bellamy (2000), *Marx's Ecology: Materialism and Nature* (New York: Monthly Review Press, 2000).

Fraser, Ian, *Hegel and Marx: The Concept of Need* (Edinburgh: Edinburgh University Press, 1998).

Fromm, Erich, *Marx's Concept of Man* (New York: Continuum, 1992).

Gilbert, Alan, *Marx's Politics: Communists and Citizens* (Oxford: Martin Robertson, 1981).

Harman, Chris, *Zombie Capitalism. Global Crisis and the Relevance of Marx*, (London: Bookmarks, 2009).

Harvey, David, *The Limits to Capital* (London and New York: Verso, 2006).

——, *A Companion to Marx's Capital* (London and New York: Verso, 2010).

Hoffman, John, *Marxism and the Theory of Praxis* (London: Lawrence and Wishart, 1975).

Hook, Sidney, *From Hegel to Marx. Studies in the Intellectual Development of Karl Marx* (New York: Humanities Press, 1958).

Kain, Philip J., *Marx and Ethics* (Oxford: Clarendon Press, 1991).

Kliman, Andrew, *Reclaiming Marx's 'Capital': A Refutation of the Myth of Inconsistency* (Lanham: Lexington, 2006).

Larrain, Jorge, *Marxism and Ideology* (Basingstoke: Macmillan, 1983).

Lebowitz, Michael A., *Beyond Capital. Marx's Political Economy of the Working Class* (London: Macmillan, 1992).

Lenin, V. I., *The State and Revolution* (Harmondsworth: Penguin, 2009).

Mandel, Ernest, *The Formation of the Economic Thought of Karl Marx: 1843 to Capital* (London: New Left Books, 1971).

———, *Marxist Economic Theory* (London: Merlin, 1971).

Marcuse, Herbert, *Reason and Revolution* (London: Routledge, 1986).

McCarney, Joseph, *Social Theory and the Crisis of Marxism* (London: Verso, 1990).

Meikle, Scott, *Essentialism in the Thought of Karl Marx* (London: Duckworth, 1985).

Ollman, Bertell, *Alienation: Marx's Conception of Man in Capitalist Society* (Cambridge: Cambridge University Press, 1976).

———, *Dance of the Dialectic* (Urbana and Chicago: University of Illinois Press, 2003).

Peffer, Rodney G., *Marxism, Morality, and Social Justice* (Princeton: Princeton University Press, 1990).

Prower, S. S., *Karl Marx and World Literature* (Oxford University Press: Oxford, 1976).

Rosdolsky, Roman, *The Making of Marx's 'Capital', Volumes 1 & 2* (London: Pluto, 1977).

Rose, Margaret, *Marx's Lost Aesthetic: Karl Marx and the Visual Arts* (Cambridge: Cambridge University Press, 1989).

Rubel, Maximilien, *Marx: Life and Works* (Basingstoke: Macmillan, 1980).

Rubin, I. I., *Essays on Marx's Theory of Value* (Delhi: Aakar, 2008).

Smith, Tony, *The Logic of Marx's Capital* (Albany, NY: State University of New York, 1990).

Sowell, Thomas, *Marxism: Philosophy and Economics* (London: Allen & Unwin, 1986).

Thomas, Paul, *Karl Marx and the Anarchists* (London: Routledge, 2009).

Wheen, Francis, *Marx's Das Kapital: A Biography* (London: Atlantic, 2006).

Wilde, Lawrence, *Marx and Contradiction* (Aldershot: Gower Press, 1989).

———, *Ethical Marxism and its Radical Critics* (Basingstoke: Macmillan, 1998).

Wolff, Jonathan, *Why Read Marx Today?* (Oxford: Oxford University Press, 2003).

Wood, Allen W., *Karl Marx*, 2nd ed. (London: Routledge, 2004).